TURNI
THE THI
AROUND

TURNING

THE THING

AROUND

PULLING AMERICA'S TEAM OUT OF THE DUMPS—AND MYSELF OUT OF THE DOGHOUSE

by Jimmy Johnson
as told to Ed Hinton

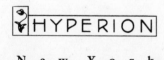

New York

Johnson, Jimmy [date]

Turning the thing around: pulling America's Team out of the doldrums—and myself out of the doghouse / Jimmy Johnson as told to Ed Hinton.

p. cm.

ISBN 1-56282-725-1

1. Johnson, Jimmy. 2. Football—United States—Coaches—Biography. 3. Dallas Cowboys (Football team) I. Hinton, Ed. II. Title.

GV939.J613A3 1993

796.332'07'7092—dc20

[B]   93-24918

CIP

First Edition

10 9 8 7 6 5 4 3 2 1

To Brent and Chad, the most loving sons and best friends a man could hope for. You have understood so much. Maybe this will help you understand more about the times I wasn't there. What you have always known, and what I want you to know now, is that I love you very much.

ACKNOWLEDGMENTS

T
hanks first to three guys with the same name: to Rich Dalrymple, former sports information director at the University of Miami, for keeping us on the straight and narrow with the details of the Miami years; to Rich Dalrymple, current public relations director of the Dallas Cowboys, for keeping us similarly straight on the Dallas years, as well as helping sort through hundreds of photographs; and to Rich Dalrymple, the friend and confidant who read this manuscript day by day with an untiring combination of enthusiasm and constructive criticism.

Thanks to Bill Parcells, former head coach of the New York Giants and now of the New England Patriots, not only for the kind Foreword to this book, but for his advice and encouragement back before the Cowboys were quite so successful. Also thanks to Brian DeFiore, our editor at Hyperion, for believing in the worth of this project from the outset, for a sound but gentle editing hand, and for letting us be ourselves. The original believer in this project was Sterling Lord, the gentleman giant of New York literary agents, who guided us not only with his superb business savvy but his own fine eye for words and stories.

Most of all, to all whom I have coached, and coached with: Thank you for making this a story worth telling.

How could a guy come in and take shotgun blasts in the face at two different programs, and win the national championship with one and the Super Bowl with the other? Now wouldn't that be a pisser?
—Joe Brodsky, Dallas Cowboys' (and former Miami Hurricanes')
running-backs coach during April minicamp, 1992

CONTENTS

CONTENTS

FOREWORD

J immy Johnson came into the National Football League with extraordinary pressure on him, because he had achieved so much in college coaching, and a tremendous number of people in professional football were very skeptical about what he would be able to do, playing with the big boys. I was not among those skeptics. Early in 1989, Jimmy's first year in the league, I began to view him as a very dangerous adversary.

As a direct competitor with him—I was then head coach of the New York Giants, in the NFC East division with the Dallas Cowboys—I think I recognized more quickly than some that he was a guy to be reckoned with. As it turned out, he certainly proved to be that.

I felt that he was a guy who had an idea. I watched him and talked to him, and I could see what he was trying to do, that he had a plan, a philosophy. Here was a guy working his butt off, trying to get it done. Even in that first year, when the Cowboys went 1–15, I could see that they were better each time we played them.

Bringing the Cowboys from the bottom of the league to a Super Bowl victory in only four years was a tremendous job. I know how much it took for him to get that done. I just know. I can relate it back to my own situation, when we won only three games my first year with the Giants, and our team really wasn't very good—I mean, it was bad, like Dallas was when Jimmy took the job. Then the next year we made the playoffs, and we got better, and the fourth year, we were able to win the Super Bowl.

A lot of people would say Jimmy inherited a worse team in Dallas than we did in New York. And he probably did. At least I had Phil Simms and Lawrence Taylor and a few other guys in place.

In the draft, he was able to make some moves, and certainly he was aggressive. I'm sure he'd like to have a few of those picks back, but overall, he did a helluva job. That's not open to opinion. It's a fact. I could see them improving, piece by piece. I could see it when Troy Aikman was in place at quarterback. I remember the first day Emmitt Smith started to play. He played against us a little bit, not much, because he wasn't quite ready, but I would look at him in warmups and I could tell he was going to get better.

Jimmy made a few adjustments along the way, but I didn't ever see a big change in his philosophy. He knew what he wanted to do, and how he wanted to build things. He has a philosophy, he has put it in place, and he has acquired the people to implement that philosophy. I think that's the only way—the *only* way—to be successful in professional football. The people who constantly change plans, change people, change philosophies, are the ones who end up being the also-rans. The ones who can stick to what they believe in are the ones who emerge at the top.

I left the Giants in the spring of 1991, just after our second Super Bowl victory, and spent a couple of seasons in television, as a color commentator with NBC. While I was out of coaching, I had opportunities to visit with Jimmy from the broadcasting side. I could see what he was doing. I could see how much he was putting into it. I had been there myself. I knew how bad he wanted to prove that he could do it.

In October 1992, I was in Dallas to do the color commentary on the Cowboys–Seattle Seahawks game. The Friday night before the game, Jimmy and I went to dinner, had a couple of beers, and talked for about four hours. Most of the conversation involved his asking me questions about how we had prepared for the two Super Bowls we had won with the Giants. He was researching, planning. When I was preparing for the Super Bowl, coaches who had won it were kind enough to advise me, and I gave Jimmy every bit of information I could. I didn't know he was going to the Super Bowl. He didn't know he was going to the Super Bowl. But I definitely saw that he had a team that was ready to contend. I felt, even in October, that the Cowboys were at least going right down to the end of the playoffs.

And when the Cowboys won Super Bowl XXVII on January 31, 1993, and Jimmy was standing there on the sidelines at the end of the game, and he was smiling, I knew exactly how he felt. *Exactly.* I just knew the euphoria that he was feeling. I had been in the same place myself a few years back—the same sideline in the same stadium, the Rose Bowl, in Pasadena—in 1987, when our team was able to win our first Super Bowl. As I watched Jimmy, I had a vivid recollection.

Now he's got a whole new deal to contend with. After you win, you pick lower in the draft and it's much harder to add to your team. He's going to have to fight that battle. But he knows what he has to do. After he won the Super Bowl, I'm sure he would have liked to have had at least two or three weeks off. He took three days. Then he went straight to the scouting-combine workouts in Indianapolis, to evaluate college players. He had to concentrate extra hard, to spot talent the other teams, picking higher in the draft, might miss and pass over. He knows.

Now that I'm back in coaching, it's easy to smile about Jimmy, from the distance of a different division, the AFC East, where I won't have to face this dangerous adversary twice a year.

BILL PARCELLS
Head Coach
New England Patriots

TURNING

THE THING

AROUND

INTRODUCTION: HAIR

L et's deal immediately with, and try to eliminate, one distraction from our larger discussion of life and games. There isn't much I can, or intend to, change about my hair. It is the way it has to be.

Sure, I've heard and read all the one-liners in the media. Some are pretty good. Like when comedian Dennis Miller said at the 1993 American Sports Awards in New York, "Ease up on the fluorocarbons, Jimmy. Remember: without ozone, there is no end zone." (Hey: As long as they let me take home the trophy as Coach/Manager of the Year in 1992 in all sports, amateur and professional, they could say anything they wanted.) Some of the one-liners are stretching, sort of silly. Take, "a defensive front as immovable as Jimmy Johnson's hair." Please.

I take them all in stride. Hair jokes, in fact, provide good metaphors for one major theme of this book: misconception.

Sprayed hair has become associated with what society perceives as mental and ethical lightweights—"talking head" TV anchormen, car salesmen, success-course hustlers, politicians—just bright enough to hoodwink the even less intelligent. If I'm taken lightly going in, so be it. To any general, CEO, coach, or author, the element of surprise is a fundamental advantage.

Yet the image that has sprung up from my scalp was an uncalculated bonus—a byproduct of necessity. I have several ugly scars in my scalp, from playing street football without a helmet as a child in Port Arthur, Texas. The hardest hitters then were two black kids we called Baby Joe and I.E. And when they knocked you out of bounds—off the grassy median of a boulevard where we played—your head was likely to hit the curb or the pavement. Thus, my best friend in high school, Jim Maxfield, called me "Scar Head."

I suppose I could go back to a short haircut and have those scars shine through under the stadium and TV lights, for everyone to see. You have to figure a coach called Scar Head Johnson would be a shoo-in for the All-Madden Team. I can hear John up in the broadcast booth saying, "See, he's got the scars, he's got the headset, he's yelling, he's jumping up and down, he's got the whole deal." And John and all the other color commentators could keep rehashing the stories about Baby Joe and I.E., which in a way would be a plus, for it would give Baby Joe and I.E. some recognition for what they were: catalysts in my life and career.

While acquiring my scars on DeQueen Boulevard—where my family lived in Port Arthur while I was growing up—I not only learned the toughness that is vital in football, I was granted freedom: I was never shackled by the ethnic hangups and prejudices which so many people my age and older have had to work to shed. I never thought there was any difference between the black kids and me, except that I knew—and didn't like—that we went to separate schools in the segregated Port Arthur of the early 1950s. Of all the breaks I've had in life, ethnic freedom is one of the best and most basic. But it's something I don't wear on my sleeve—or on my head.

I kept a short burr haircut through my college years at the University of Arkansas. Then in the late sixties and early seventies, as I worked—and I mean worked—through the ranks of assistant coaching, I let my hair grow fairly long and free, somewhere short of a hippie look, but freer than what was called "mod" in those days. Nobody said anything about it then. It was just hair, and a lot of it, and everybody had it. There was of course a Broadway musical of the time titled *Hair*, and much of young America was in a frenzy to the beat of bands like Big Brother and the Holding Company, whose featured singer was a girl I went to high school with, Janis Joplin.

While Janis was knocking 'em—and ultimately, tragically, herself—dead, I was slugging it out in the trenches of coaching, in outposts such as Picayune, Mississippi, and Ames, Iowa. The old school weirdo with the flying hair—we called Janis "Beat Weeds" back in Port Arthur—had become somebody, a titan at her passion and profession. In my career, I was a nobody apprentice. My hair didn't matter enough for even smalltown sportswriters to mention. But I was no less passionate about my profession, and there were times when I was so excited, so animated, that my hair was flying almost as wildly on the football field as Janis's was on stage.

Then came the late seventies and early eighties and more understated hairstyles. As assistant head coach under Jackie Sherrill at the University of Pittsburgh in 1977 and 1978, I took on a large share of the public-speaking and appearance responsibilities normally associated with the head coach. I got my hair trimmed so that it no longer fell over my ears. The style seemed fairly middle-of-the-road to me, and it was certainly the only compromise for me. My hair is very fine, but I've got a lot of it, and it's very straight. Believe it or not, this is just the way it grows—except that if I didn't spray it a little on the front, it would be down in my eyes all the time, and would blow every which way in the wind. I want to be neat.

My first head coaching job was at Oklahoma State in 1979. The football program was on NCAA probation due to recruiting violations under my predecessor. Yet another investigation was ongoing, into further allegations of violations under the previous coaching staff. I took what I knew would be an uphill job all the way, because I wanted a chance to prove myself in a very visible football conference, the Big Eight. After we stabilized the OSU program and got off probation, we were allowed to play on television, mainly regional, and in a couple of postseason bowl games. There, my hair began to gain some visibility.

I suppose my hair first gained national notoriety on November 30, 1985, my second year at the University of Miami, when we beat Notre Dame 58–7 in Miami. The nationally beloved and pitied Gerry Faust was coaching his last game for Notre Dame before resigning under pressure. Irish team morale was a shambles, and, as I wouldn't learn until years later, it wasn't so much out of players' love and pity for Faust as the opposite. Miami's morale was sky-high. We had recovered completely from the troubles of 1984, the transition year after Howard Schnellenberger's regime ended and mine began at Miami. We went in ready to romp, and Notre Dame went in ripe to be routed.

In the fourth quarter, Ara Parseghian, a former Notre Dame coach who was by then a CBS color commentator, said, "It's time for Jimmy Johnson to show some compassion . . ." Not that Ara hadn't hung some lopsided scores on troubled opponents in his time, mind you. And not that I could have eased what happened, short of ordering my third stringers to lie down and go to sleep on the line of scrimmage. But this was Notre Dame, the team America loves to love. And with Miami's role in the rout, spiced by Ara's words, the Hurricanes suddenly became the team America loved to hate. Notre Dame–Miami would be, for years to come, the most notorious, bitter, exciting rivalry in college football. And my hair would become something of a black hat.

The public perception of Miami as a renegade team in the mid-and-late eighties was, I deeply believe—I know in my heart—a misconception. I'll go into that later, thoroughly.

While we were working to turn the thing around in Dallas, to bring the Cowboys back from being the worst team in the NFL when my staff and I arrived there in 1989, to the 1993 Super Bowl championship after the 1992 season, my hair seems to have found its way back into the limelight.

So maybe it's time to show you the scars in my scalp, and a lot of what goes on beneath them: how I think, what I think, why I think it.

One question I've been asked a lot since we won the Super Bowl is, simply, "How did you do that? How have the Cowboys come so far, so fast?" In fact, I started hearing that question before we even got to the Super Bowl. In January 1993, the week before we played San Francisco in the NFC Championship game, the *New York Times* sent a business writer to Dallas to interview me about how we'd turned the thing around so fast, from a business perspective.

Well, a legion of national sports media people were in town, and we were practicing for a crucial game. We just didn't have time to give the *Times* business writer the long, one-on-one interview he wanted. So he began to try to gather his story piecemeal, by working in questions at the daily press conferences. He kept asking how we'd done this, or how we'd done that, and I kept putting him off with cute, sometimes curt answers.

He persisted for a while, and finally I said, "Listen: I don't mean to be short with my answers. But I can't outline to you what it has taken forty-nine years of life to develop. There is no easy, one-two-three-four-five outline. I know you can find a stack of books at any bookstore on everybody's opinion of how to be successful. It's not that easy for me. It has to do with dealing with people, and how we structure our organization. There is not enough time to explain that, because there is not enough time in the day for me to explain what has transpired over the last forty-nine years."

I have just turned fifty as we have taken the proper time and forum—this book—to discuss what I have seen of life and games and turning things around.

I am now known as "the only coach ever to win both the NCAA national championship and the Super Bowl." A lot of people have memories of me being carried off the field after winning the national college championship in the 1988 Orange Bowl, pumping my arms in ecstasy over the success there, and they have memories of me holding up the Super Bowl trophy after we beat Buffalo in 1993. But there were many times when things weren't quite so joyous. Without the lows, the highs might never have happened, and certainly I wouldn't have felt them as fully.

Through the worst and the best of times in my adulthood, for thirty-two years, I have known and respected Jerry Jones, who bought the Cowboys in 1989 and hired me to help him turn the thing around. A lot of people have tried to figure out the relationship between Jerry and me, and there's a tremendous amount of misconception. On one hand you've got a group thinking we're buddy-buddy and that we've done a lot of things socially, from the time we graduated from college at Arkansas to the time we came to the Cowboys. On the other extreme, there are those who think Jerry's and my egos are destined to clash. The truth is somewhere in between. But there again lies a long-running story, covering not just our years in Dallas but the nature of our relationship since 1961 in Fayetteville, Arkansas.

Because of the responsibility and freedom Jerry has given me in choosing and coaching people, I am often questioned about the Cowboy turnaround in the manner a magician would be asked after a trick: "How'd you do that?" Indeed, my girlfriend and buddy, Rhonda Rookmaaker, has for years called me "The Trickster." And what we've accomplished in Dallas was, in a manner of speaking, wizardry. No, I am not giving you the kind of cute, curt answer I gave the *New York Times* guy. I am actually beginning to explain how we did it.

One of the most telling, if odd-sounding, conversations I've ever had about myself and the way I coach came during happy hour at a pub near the Cowboys' training complex a year or so ago. Ed Hinton, now my collaborator on this book, was at that time doing a story on me for *Sports Illustrated*. Ed, Rhonda, and I had had a few pops (I enjoy a beer or two or three and make no bones about it). There was no small talk that evening. Cheerful, happy-hour talk, sure. But efficient. I despise small talk. We weren't on our way to dinner. I don't like going out to dinner because dinner drastically increases the risk of small talk. But you can get a lot done over beer and nachos, and every word was leading us somewhere. We were talking about public perceptions of me, from Miami to Dallas, and at one point I turned to Ed, and I said:

"I am not a bad man."

He said, "You sound sort of like in *The Wizard of Oz* when Dorothy—or, in your case, the public—threw back the curtain, saw that the wizard was just a man standing back there, and said, 'You're a bad, bad man!' And the wizard said, 'No, I'm a very good man. I'm just not a very good wizard.' "

I thought for a moment. "I won't even go so far as to tell you I'm a good man," I said. "But I am a pretty good wizard."

Tin Man had a heart, Scarecrow had a brain, and Lion had courage. They just needed to be told. That's my job. Everybody needs to be—and can be—motivated, no matter how much money he or she makes. Different personalities require different catalysts. Lion had to be yelled at. Tin Man had to be touched. Scarecrow had to be challenged. After that, they were a helluva team.

Wizardry is by no means magic. Wizardry is a thorough understanding and application and projection of reality. Wizardry is seeing a person as the very best that he can be, treating him on that level, and waiting for him to rise to it. He always will, given time. But neither the NFL's nature, nor mine, will let me wait on him for long.

Wizardry is quite logical, but it is at times emotional, because it is entirely human. Nowhere in this book will I attempt to convince you that I am a good man. I will try to show you that I am not a bad man. I am a very selfish man and a very generous man—the two are not incompatible. I care about others, keeping in mind that I couldn't possibly care about them the way they do, and that they couldn't care about me the way I do. The hardest misconception for me to swallow is that I am an unfeeling man. Somehow that seems to go with the hair.

Perhaps the most misunderstood I've ever been was on the morning of January 3, 1987. Miami had lost the national championship to Penn State, 14–10, in the Fiesta Bowl in Tempe, Arizona, the night before. Penn State, coached by Joe Paterno, had been billed as the good guys in this "Shootout in the Desert," and my Miami players and I had been billed as the bad guys.

That particular Miami team was not only the most maligned, but was, beyond any doubt, the best college football team I've ever seen—both as players and, as we shall see later, as human beings. Our Heisman

Trophy quarterback, Vinny Testaverde, had missed a lot of practice because of minor injuries suffered in a motor scooter accident, and because of the travel involved in accepting the Heisman and the other awards that were pouring in on him. In the game, Vinny was intercepted five times, and we lost.

All that night, I was heartsick. Devastated. To lose a national championship was one thing. But for *this* team to lose it! Then the next morning came the followup press conference. Absolutely miserable, I showered, shampooed, dressed in a suit and tie—and yes, combed and sprayed my hair—and went downstairs to face the media. I don't recall many, if any, questions regarding how crushed and disappointed our players were. And there weren't a lot of questions about how and why we'd lost. There were lots of questions about our image. Under the circumstances, it was awfully tough to listen to that stuff, let alone try to answer. But I tried to be calm and composed.

Much later, I was told that some of the sports writers were sitting in the back, whispering cracks: "Look at Johnson's hair. He's just lost the biggest game of his life, but that hair's still perfect. He's not even fazed." I guess they thought I had to look like a wreck to prove I felt like one.

They confused my hairstyle with what was going on beneath it—with how I really felt. Which was as bad as I've felt in my life—before I got to Dallas, that is . . .

I

MIA'S NIGHT

L inda Kay and I were lying in bed, in hiding, registered under an assumed name at an Embassy Suites hotel in Dallas.

"Jimmy," she said, "is this what you really want to do?"

"It's not a matter of what I want to do," I said. "It's what I *have* to do."

That was good enough for her. After twenty-six years, my wife knew me very well. She lay there silently with her own thoughts, which I'm sure were anxious ones. This would be an enormous upheaval in her life. Neither of us knew just *how* enormous at that moment—or maybe we did; maybe we both sensed it all. But Linda Kay didn't say anything further. After she drifted off to sleep, I lay there with my eyes open.

In the past ten and a half days—from lunchtime on Valentine's Day through this, Friday night, February 24, 1989—I had learned more about Jerry Jones than I had in the previous twenty-eight years I'd known him. Certainly I'd spent more time with him in these days than I had in all the twenty-four years combined since we'd left on our separate paths from the University of Arkansas.

As football teammates at Arkansas, we had roomed together in hotels on Friday nights before Razorback games. Even though we'd both gotten married as undergraduates, and had lived with our wives in off-campus apartments, our head coach, Frank Broyles, had believed in isolating the team from the hoopla building up to both road and home games, so he had required the team to stay in a hotel on Friday nights even in Fayetteville. Two linemen with alphabetically adjacent names, Johnson and Jones, had been paired.

How well do you get to know a guy on a few Friday nights in the Holiday Inns of Waco or Fort Worth or Austin? Not very. You get off the plane, board the bus, ride to the hotel, pick up your room key, throw your things in the room, go to the team dinner, then into team meetings, then to the room to make curfew. Maybe you lie there on your beds talking about the opponents for a few minutes, or bitch a little about how hard practice has gone all week, but that's about it. Lights out. Jerry and I had spent a grand total of about thirty such nights together in our lives. Then we'd gone out into the world, rarely to see each other over the next twenty-four years.

Neither Jerry nor I had planned to pursue football after playing in college. We had both intended to enter business. Jerry had done so, and had made himself a fortune in insurance, oil, and gas. I had detoured off the road to becoming an industrial psychologist, and had never found my way back. One interim coaching job, three months at Louisiana Tech, to make some quick money to support a young family until I could finish graduate school, had left me addicted. I had been a coach ever since.

You don't exactly hang out with your rich former college teammates when you're dragging a family and a U-Haul trailer all over the country, trying to establish yourself as a coach. In the early years, Linda Kay and our sons, Brent and Chad, had sacrificed terribly but cheerfully, packing up and moving on a week's—sometimes a day's—notice from me. Brent was born in Fayetteville, Arkansas, but his first memories were of Picayune, Mississippi. Chad was born in Picayune but took his first steps in Wichita, Kansas, and toddled right on into Ames, Iowa. Brent began anticipating first grade in Clemson, South Carolina, but actually attended first grade in Norman, Oklahoma. And so on. And on. And on. By Pittsburgh in the late seventies, it dawned on me that Brent and Chad were not only brothers but best friends. Which was both understandable and vital, in that each was the only kid the other had known for any real length of time. If it was a hard road for me, it was harder for my wife and boys.

Jerry Jones's business centered mainly in Arkansas, Texas, and Oklahoma. Of course, you don't do business in that area of the country without keeping at least informally in touch with football. Socially, Jerry knew lots of coaches and lots of high-rolling alumni from the Big Eight and Southwest Conference schools. Jerry's path didn't cross with mine anymore than it crossed with those of many other coaches. He probably saw, for example, Barry Switzer of Oklahoma and Fred Akers of Texas at least as often as he saw me.

Once, with his social and business connections, Jerry had put me in touch with the right people to get my first head-coaching job, at Oklahoma State in 1979. It was a tough decision to take that job, because Oklahoma State was on NCAA probation, with yet another investigation ongoing, before they offered me the position.

Then, after we'd built something from rock bottom at Oklahoma State, Jerry had asked Frank Broyles, by then athletic director at Arkansas, to interview me for the head-coaching job at my alma mater after the 1983 season. We'd just won eight games that year at Oklahoma State and had just signed a magnificent running back, Thurman Thomas. I hadn't even thought about applying for the Arkansas job after Lou Holtz was fired—or quit, depending on which reports you believed. I had it fine in Stillwater, Oklahoma. But when Frank Broyles, my old coach, called and invited me to Fayetteville to talk about coaching at my alma mater, I felt bound by honor and sentiment to listen. That turned out to be a phony, token interview all the way—Broyles had already offered the job to Ken Hatfield. Frank lied to me and embarrassed me—made me look like a reject when in fact I was never in the picture and had never asked to be. That left me with a bitter taste for that whole bunch at Arkansas, specifically Broyles. He became the first of three men I have written off in my life, all for failing to be men of their word. (I did feel somewhat better in 1987 after sending one of my University of Miami teams out to kick my nationally ranked alma mater's ass, 51–7, in Little Rock. We led them 38–0 at halftime.)

Other than the Oklahoma State and Arkansas occasions, I had been thoroughly on my own. Jerry had been a friend from a distance, but hardly what you could call a patron of my career. In retrospect, I can see that Jerry had been keeping an eye on my career from afar, much as a big investor—which he is—would keep an eye on a small business which he thinks has growth potential.

We'd had a casual, friendly, distant acquaintance and each had respected the other's endeavors. We'd never made any sort of pact. The nearest we'd come to that had been a very tacit, brief conversation in 1982. Jerry's eldest son, Stephen, was then a high school football player who wanted to polish his techniques. Jerry was in Oklahoma City a lot anyway, so he would send Stephen out to our Oklahoma State summer football camps in Stillwater. One afternoon, Jerry had flown Stephen out from Little Rock, and stopped by my house.

I'd been a head coach for only a few years and was just starting to make a little money. I had a big entertainment area in the den of the house at Stillwater Country Club, right on the first green. With both of us leaning against the bar, having a beer, I said, "Jerry, I really admire the way you go about making money. It's something I'd like to do."

"Jimmy," he said, "you go to bed every night thinking about football and wake up every morning thinking about football, and that's all you think, all day long. That's exactly what I do in making money."

And now on the night of February 24, 1989, as I lay awake, I realized that if Jerry Jones and I had ever come to an understanding, it had been that afternoon at my bar in 1982. He was throwing virtually everything he owned onto the table, into the pot. On this night, he'd pretty well wrapped up his purchase of the Dallas Cowboys for more than $140 million. And now that it was time to see if he could win this bet, he was turning over a hole card he'd been holding all these years. Even I, the hole card, hadn't taken him seriously until February 14, Valentine's Day.

And now here I was, about to back his bet with all I owned, all I loved, all I'd worked for, all I'd have to leave behind. I'd finished my fifth season as head coach of the best, most visible, most colorful—and, yes, the most controversial—college football program in America, the Miami Hurricanes. We'd won the national championship in 1987 and had barely missed two more, in 1986 and 1988, by a grand total of five points in two games. In fact, we'd been a serious contender right into bowl season for the national titles for four of my five years there—all except the troubled first year. There was no reason why we shouldn't win several more national championships—rather, a *lot* more national championships.

Brent had finished law school at the University of Texas, and Chad was graduating from—of all places, and he got a big kick out of this— Florida State, one of Miami's twin-tower archrivals in football. (Notre Dame being the other.) Linda Kay and I had bought a new, wonderful house for just the two of us outside Coral Gables, at Riviera Country Club, and had planned to move in within weeks. We also had an apartment right on Miami Beach. I was near white sand and blue water, and that geographical condition alone had always been enough to make me happy. And the ethnic diversity which bothered some people about Miami was cultural heaven to me. I enjoyed being in the Jewish community, the black community, the Latin community, and the plain old Florida cracker community. Moving to Dallas was not going to be the problem. Leaving Miami was going to be the *big* problem. But the notion of leaving had come in stages, the first of which had sounded to me like a virtually moot point.

The first indication I'd had of Jerry's interest in buying the Cowboys came in midseason of 1988. He called and asked if I would act as an intermediary with Tex Schramm, the Cowboys' president who'd been put in charge of selling the franchise for then-owner H.R. "Bum" Bright. Jerry wanted me to call Tex just to give him, Jerry, some credibility—so that at least Tex would know something about Jerry, and take him seriously as a prospective buyer, before they held their initial meeting.

I knew Tex, and Coach Tom Landry, and the whole Cowboys group. In fact, the previous Super Bowl had been played in Miami in January 1988, and I'd gone as a guest of the Cowboys organization. The game was between San Francisco and Cincinnati, but the grand old Dallas franchise of course had a luxury skybox. I had sat with Tex and his wife Marty, Tom and his wife Alicia, and Gil Brandt, chief of the Cowboys scouting operation. The very sight of that group—Schramm, Landry, Brandt—had long been as synonymous with the Cowboys as the blue star on the silver helmet. If there was royalty in the NFL, this was the court. The franchise had been somewhat unique in the league, in that the ownership—first the founding Murchison family and then Bright—had remained in the background and let Texas E. Schramm run the show.

So Jerry called me to be a bit of a go-between. He said at the time that it was just an interest, and that it was probably a longshot that the purchase would actually happen. I pretty well dismissed it as just one of those things. I really didn't put a whole lot of stock in it.

Not then, and not through February 1989, and not to this day, has Jerry Jones ever asked me, "Will you be the coach of the Cowboys?" And not to this day have I ever said, "Yes, I'll do it." From that moment by my bar in Stillwater in 1982, in any conversation we ever had, it was almost a mutual assumption that if he ever went into professional football, he'd love for me to be the coach. His words would always be something like "The two of us, with the energy we have, back to back, can accomplish some great things." But it was just conversation. I really hadn't thought much about it.

Besides, when you're head coach of a very visible and successful program, more days than not you find yourself named in all sorts of coaching-change rumors and speculation. Already that winter of 1988–1989, I'd heard rumors that I was going to San Francisco to replace Bill

Walsh, who was retiring as the 49ers' coach. Word was that Eddie DeBartolo, the 49ers' owner, wanted me, but that Walsh wanted to consider his existing staff and was pushing George Seifert for the job. I'd met Eddie and liked him, and we'd talked occasionally, but never about the possibility of my coaching for him. The story now goes that Walsh didn't sway DeBartolo until Seifert was boarding a plane for Cincinnati to interview for that job, and that they got him off the plane and gave him the 49ers job. I don't know. I read it in some California newspapers.

Also in 1988, Gil Brandt had phoned and asked if I'd be interested in coming to Dallas as Landry's defensive coordinator, with the understanding that Landry would set in motion a plan for his retirement and my promotion to head coach. I wasn't interested. There would have been too many complications, including the matter of who would and wouldn't be retained from his old staff. I'd already been through one nightmare trying to keep together someone else's staff, and I wasn't about to try it again.

Then, as the Philadelphia Eagles had started their 1988 season poorly with Buddy Ryan's firing imminent, Eagles owner Norman Braman, a resident of Miami and an acquaintance of mine, had begun asking around about me. That had set Tex Schramm to thinking. So Tex had phoned and asked if I'd be interested in the Dallas job if Landry were gone. The insurmountable obstacle was that Tex absolutely did not want to be the one to tell Landry it was over. Tex wanted to do something, but he didn't know how to get it done. So the issue was closed.

Just after Christmas of 1988 had come the one coaching-change rumor I could, and would, snuff in seconds. I'd just finished my radio talk show on WIOD in Miami, the week of our Orange Bowl game against Nebraska. As soon as we went off the air I was handed a message: "Call Jerry Jones." I called him from the radio station.

Jerry said, "Jimmy, I'm kind of acting as a go-between just to check what interest you might have if the Arkansas job comes open." Word was that Hatfield might be leaving. His program had never quite shaken the cobwebs from the punch my Miami guys had landed in 1987. I did not even hesitate. I said, "Jerry, absolutely no interest."

He said, "What if something along the lines of head coach/

assistant athletic director, or someday even head coach/athletic director, could be worked out?"

I said, "Jerry. Emphatically no. The only way I'd ever leave Miami would be for professional football."

Jerry said, "Well, you know, I'm still working on this other thing."

I said, "Yeah, well, that's fine, if that develops." Again I sloughed it off.

Then, on February 13, 1989, I attended the Davey O'Brien Awards—a huge deal, named for the legendary 140-pound quarterback from TCU—in Fort Worth. I got in late, just in time to put on my tuxedo and go the the awards. As I checked into the hotel, the lady at the desk handed me a stack of messages. I didn't even look at them. I stuck them in my pocket and hurried up to the room to change clothes, then hurried to the dinner. Tex Schramm and Tom Landry were at that dinner.

The next morning, while getting dressed to go to the airport, I started looking through the stack of messages. One said: "Call Jerry Jones." I went to the airport, checked in, and was waiting to board the flight when I called Jerry from a pay phone. He said, "Hey, this thing with the Dallas Cowboys may be happening. And I would like for you to drive out to their complex and see what you think of it." There had been a large loan on the complex, and Jerry had to decide whether he was going to let it go back to the bank or pay the money to stay in it. That was part of the negotiations with Bum Bright.

For the first time, I thought the purchase might actually happen. I still have the watershed minute recorded in an old pocket appointments book: American Airlines Flight 154 left for Miami at 11:55 a.m. Without me.

The Cowboys' complex in Valley Ranch is about a fifteen-minute drive from Dallas/Fort Worth International Airport. I got off the flight, got my bags, rented a car, and drove out to inspect the complex. I stuck my head into Tom Landry's office—the office I would soon occupy—just to say hello. Then I saw Tex, who said, "Hey, you ought to get your friend to buy this club." He said it in a joking way. Little did he know it was about to happen.

Jerry sent his Lear jet to pick me up at Dallas's older, smaller airport, Love Field, after I'd toured the complex. His pilots flew me to Little Rock, where I spent a few hours with him talking about his plans. He wanted me to sit in with him and Bum Bright during the negotiations for the club. But first, he wanted me to fly back to Miami, to put in motion a tentative plan for getting together a new coaching staff for the Cowboys. Most of the assistant coaches I wanted to bring to Dallas were in Miami, either at the university or with the NFL Dolphins. There is a March 1 deadline after which you're not allowed to talk to NFL assistant coaches about changing jobs from one franchise to another. That didn't affect the assistants I wanted to hire from the University of Miami. But Dave Wannstedt, my right-arm of a defensive coach and my best friend, had recently gone to work for the Dolphins. I also wanted to hire David Shula, who was also working as an assistant to his dad at the Dolphins.

I drove out to the Dolphin complex to talk to head coach Don Shula. I told him there was a possibility Jerry might be buying the Cowboys, and that I would be replacing Tom Landry as head coach. Don was shocked. His first response was, "What's going to happen to Tex?" Don wasn't as close to Tom as he was to Tex. Don and Tex were really close friends. They were both on the NFL Competition Committee, an elite group that decides on any rules adjustments from season to season.

I said, "Well, I guess everything's going to be fine. I really don't know. Jerry and I haven't talked about that."

Tex, being charged with the sale of the franchise, would of course have structured the deal so that he would have stayed, and kept control. But Jerry didn't want Tex in control. Jerry wanted control. Jerry operates somewhat like another, even richer, Arkansan, the late Sam Walton of Walmart: no middle men. Cut straight to the top. Jerry went straight to Bum Bright.

The next eight days I spent shuttling rapidly, secretly, between Florida and Texas and Arkansas. That was mainly to keep speaking engagements, one in Miami on February 17 and one in St. Petersburg on February 22. I kept them for two reasons: first, it kept up the appearance of normalcy in public; second, and most important, I keep my commitments. I absolutely expect others to be as good as their word, and I am as good as mine.

I flew back to Dallas on February 23 and sat in with Bum and Jerry on the twenty-fourth, as they worked out the final details. I wasn't active in the negotiations. I think my role was more symbolic, just to remind Bright constantly, with my presence, of how serious Jerry was—so serious his new head coach was sitting right beside him. I know now why Jerry is such a great salesman. I don't think "if" is in his vocabulary. He always talks as though the deal is already done. He doesn't say, "Here's what we could do," he says, "Here's what we're going to do."

Now all my life, I've loved doing a deal. But even for me, these recent days had been a dizzying swirl of Lear jets and closed doors and assumed names and millions upon millions of dollars. I, and certainly Linda Kay, needed some time to digest some of this. And I thought maybe even the ever charged Jerry needed it too. Jerry came up to my hotel suite and I said, "Why don't we order up some nachos and some beer, and just kinda talk for a while?" I meant room service, behind closed doors.

And this was the moment, the borderline, where Jerry's expertise ended and mine began. For days I'd been learning from Jerry. Now he was going to start learning from me—more precisely, he was going to learn from a mistake he made against my judgment and advice. At this moment, Jerry unwittingly detonated what the Dallas public, and many NFL fans around the nation, will remember as the notorious "Mia's Incident" or "Mia's Night," of February 24.

Jerry said, "Oh, I know this little Mexican restaurant near here where we can go." Jerry had never dealt with the media. He'd been in the oil and gas business and been a pretty private person. I knew the media very well indeed. I knew better than to stick my hairsprayed head out in public for one unnecessary moment in a situation like this.

I said, "Jerry, people are going to recognize me." He didn't realize the visibility that the University of Miami coach had. We'd been in the national spotlight for a long time.

He said, "No, this is just an out-of-the-way place. We can slip in and out of there and nobody will even notice."

Mia's turned out to be a nice, small place. But it was very crowded. And little did we know that it was one of Tom Landry's favorite restaurants. At least Landry wasn't there that night. He was the only element missing from a complete fiasco. The moment I walked in, everybody started saying, "Hey, Coach! Hi, Coach! How you doin', Coach!" Jerry was kind of taken aback, but we got a table.

Ivan Maisel, the national college football writer for the Dallas *Morning News,* had been staking out The Mansion, the hotel where Jerry was registered, all day and half the night. Ivan and I knew each other from various national championship bowl games and such, so he had been assigned to wait for Jerry and/or me to show up at The Mansion. Ivan finally got tired of waiting, and he and his girlfriend went out to dinner. At Mia's.

When Ivan spotted us he just walked over, wearing that tiny, amused, knowing smile of his. Neither Ivan nor I was particularly surprised at the encounter. Instead of saying, "Checkmate," Ivan just said, "Hey, Coach, how you doin'?" There was no need whatsoever for me to tell Jerry, "I told you so." I simply introduced Ivan Maisel of the Dallas *Morning News.*

Ivan slipped over to a pay phone, called the *Morning News,* and told them to get a photographer out there. Then he came back and asked if we would comment. We declined, but did allow them to take a picture. I mean, by that point, what the hell?

I doubt there's a major paper in the country, or any paper at all in Texas, that hasn't run that picture at some point. *Sports Illustrated* has run it: Jerry and I grinning at each other over empty beer mugs, with Linda Kay barely visible in the background, holding a nacho. Mia's Night.

It was late on Mia's Night, after we'd returned to the Embassy Suites, that I lay awake. Even then, the presses at the *Morning News* were rolling off hundreds of thousands of copies of the picture that would detonate the uproar.

For the moment, the restaurant incident was the only element of the entire matter that I could smile to myself about. And I smiled only fleetingly. The Cowboys, the previous season, were dead last in the NFL. Not just the NFC East division. Not just the NFC. The league. America's team had plummeted to rock bottom. I wasn't yet sure why, and when I found out, it would be a shock. All I knew then was that we faced a monumental rebuilding task, and that we would have to work under the microscopes of the vast Texas media and the national, indeed international, following of the Cowboys. (If a Londoner in Regent Street or a Tokyo commuter in Shinjuku Station can name you one NFL team, it's the Dallas Cowboys.)

I was 100 percent certain I would take the job. But I was not 100 percent enthusiastic about it. Linda Kay knew that, and that's why she'd asked. But if I hadn't taken it, I would have always second-guessed myself. That's why I told her I had to. I just had reservations about taking a team that was so far behind the rest of the league. About starting all over at the bottom after working so hard, accomplishing so much, at Miami.

I had a flashback of my ultimate high. The rush. The incredible, enormous high that I can't put into words. All I can do is refer you to a widely published picture of me being carried off the field by my good Miami guys after the 1988 Orange Bowl, in which we beat Barry Switzer's Oklahoma Sooners 20–14 (it wasn't nearly that close) to clinch the 1987 national championship. In that picture, my hair is a mess, my face is ecstatic, and my arms are thrust toward high heaven. Somehow I knew, even at the moment that picture was snapped, that I could never experience such a high again, at that level of football. Another NCAA Division I championship, or another, or another, would never be quite like that. To get that high again, I would have to win it all at a higher level. The highest. The NFL.

My thoughts ebbed and flowed. I am a Texan by birth. But I come from an atypical corner of Texas, Port Arthur, on the Gulf of Mexico. I grew up loving the sea. I don't fish much; I don't sail; I do scuba dive; mostly, I just love to lie on the beach, looking at the water. It's an almost mystical peace. I still, and always will, have my cabin at Crystal Beach, between Port Arthur and Galveston. So in many ways Miami, by the sea, seemed closer to home than landlocked Dallas.

And so I would be leaving home, both geographically and, though it wasn't a conscious thought with me there in the dark, spiritually. I didn't quite realize it then, but I would soon be leaving Linda Kay. It was very difficult to sort out in my mind, and it remains very difficult to discuss. But I will try, as we go on. For now, I'll tell you that it was the hardest and saddest thing I've ever done, but that I did what I had to do.

If our final words of Mia's Night sounded as if they had something of a double meaning, perhaps they did. Linda Kay knows me awfully well. And so when she asked, "Jimmy, is this what you really want to do?" maybe she sensed what it meant for us.

But here is the very last thought that could have come to my mind, Linda Kay's, or Jerry's that night in the Embassy Suites: That the almost forgotten technicality of rooming together on Friday nights before games was about to be blown into an issue that would become the most demeaning description of our new partnership: "old college room-mates." That would deteriorate into "the old roomies," and then "the bobos." At least I could appreciate the fine Texas vernacular, if not the mythmaking, one columnist indulged in as he skewered our partnership, writing that Jerry had bought his old roomie "a play pretty." That's the old folks' term for a toy.

II

MASSACRE AT VALLEY RANCH

O n the morning of February 25, as the Mia's picture hit the streets of Dallas, Linda Kay and I flew back to Miami—or, frankly, I got the hell out of Dodge. As one columnist put it, "As soon as he realized he was discovered, he scurried for cover like a cockroach when the kitchen lights go on." Jerry's Lear headed out of Dallas too, but toward Austin, in search of Tom Landry. I knew what was coming down, and simply didn't think it would be proper for me to attend the press conference Jerry would conduct that evening.

Landry, Schramm, and Brandt had built the Cowboys from the ground up, since the franchise's beginnings in 1960. Landry had for years been referred to on the streets and ranches and oil rigs as "the only coach the Cowboys ever had." And listen: Nobody idolized Tom Landry more than one little old Southeast Texas boy who'd been a high school player in Port Arthur at the Dallas franchise's outset, and played college ball in the Southwest Conference as the Cowboys gathered might. Landry had taken the Cowboys to five Super Bowls and won two.

But now the Cowboys were in deep decay and would have to be rebuilt from the ground up. They hadn't had a winning season since 1985, and in 1988 they'd gone 3–13. I daresay that not since the early sixties, when they were an expansion franchise, had they been so far behind the rest of the league in player personnel. This I could see from mere preliminary examination, and I hadn't even done any real exploratory surgery yet. At first I told myself they must be better than the 3–13 record indicated. I would discover they were worse.

The grand old triumvirate of the Cowboys was done. All that remained was to tell them, as decently as possible, that it was over.

Schramm was told first. It couldn't have been a shock to him, in that he knew he'd been completely bypassed in the negotiations. Then Tex went with Jerry to help break the news to Landry. Jerry would face Landry. Jerry would have it no other way. When he learned that Landry wasn't in Dallas, he flew to Austin, where Landry was relaxing at his resort home on a golf course. Tex and Jerry waited until Landry had finished his Saturday afternoon golf game. It was reported that Tex wept as he spoke.

Sports Illustrated led its account of the firing with Landry's initial response: "You've taken my team away from me." A state and a nation concurred, at least sentimentally. The Cowboys were America's Team and Texas's Team and Dallas's Team, but at the very marrow they were perceived as Landry's Team. Landry had in recent years come under criticism, both locally and nationally, as the Cowboys dropped in the standings. There had been public opinion polls showing that a majority of people thought Landry should retire. But now, in the last week of February 1989, many of those same sports columnists and commentators who'd been urging Landry to go, now expressed shock and outrage that he was gone.

Landry's martyrdom was automatic and mostly unavoidable—although Jerry, bless his heart, went into his initial press conference at Valley Ranch and walked right into his second media buzzsaw.

Here he'd just stepped off his private jet from firing the legendary Landry that very afternoon. The news had flashed out of Austin. The assembled media people in Valley Ranch were like a family who'd known that a loved one couldn't last but were no less shocked and heartsick when the end had come. The media people reflected the sentiments of the Texas public. Jerry, still very much the media virgin, was just a happy guy who'd just completed the biggest deal of his life, and saw neither a way nor a reason to conceal his joy. Jerry came in and faced the microphones and lights and said, "It's like Christmas."

Oh, I guess the Dallas media could conceivably have been more offended and dumbfounded. But I'm not sure how. Unless maybe Lyndon Johnson had come bouncing off Air Force One after his emergency swearing-in ceremony on November 22, 1963, and said, "It's like Christmas."

Jerry, who'd meant to be sensitive and decent, was rocketed into the public eye as insensitive and indecent—a rich hick from Arkansas. If there is a species of primate that Texans hold lower than Oklahomans, "Okies," it is Arkansans, migrating across the line into God's own Republic with their Ozark Mountain and Mississippi Delta dialects, looking to make a buck. Jerry would use expressions such as "we would gee and hah" for his and Bright's reaching of accords in the negotiations. "Gee and hah" began as a farmer's commands to his mules in plow harness to turn left or right. If two people gee and hah, or gee-hah, they cooperate, or get along. Arkansas people love to use many such expressions. The Texas satire machine pounced on Jerry's well-intended Arkansas colloquialisms.

Even one of the Cowboys' active players of the time, linebacker Jeff Rohrer, was quoted as being so openly blasphemous of his new boss as to say, "Jed Clampett is the only other oilman I know, and he would have given a better interview than Jerry Jones."

Wildfire word in the streets had it that the "hostile takeover" of the stately Dallas Cowboys—roughly tantamount to the invasion of holy

Texas—was at hand. Worse than barbarians at the gate, these vile Arkansas Hawgs had crossed the boundary line—there's a helluva lot more than a state line between Arkansas and Texas—and were rooting up the hallowed ground at Valley Ranch. It was a little like Aunt Pittypat's panicky cry in *Gone With the Wind:* "Yankees in Georgia! How did they ever get in?"

Jerry Jones and Jimmy Johnson were just about the least welcome s.o.b.'s in Texas since Antonio López de Santa Anna deployed his army around the Alamo, interestingly enough, during the last week of February 1836. If Santa Anna's deeds were more heinous than ours, you couldn't have told it by the Texas media precisely 153 years later. Santa Anna, moving slower, didn't commit the Alamo massacre until March 6. Jerry, in what would become known as "The Massacre of the 25th," or "The Saturday Night Massacre" or "The Massacre at Valley Ranch," announced the dismissal of Tom Landry, and the fall from power of Tex Schramm and Gil Brandt (both of whom would depart later), on the evening of February 25. And you'd have thought Bill Travis, Davey Crockett, and Jim Bowie had been done-in all over again.

Jerry gave them another item to tee off on. He vowed to commit what, to the Texans, was an unnatural act. Where the Murchisons and Brights had owned from a distance, Jerry promised to be a hands-on owner, in direct control, down to "the socks and jocks" as he put it. Direct control meant to the media that Schramm's and Brandt's days with the Cowboys were numbered, though Jerry didn't fire them that night. Well, the pundits convicted Jerry on the spot of being one of those meddling owners. George Steinbrenner and Jed Clampett rolled into one. Now Jerry and I might not have been "bobos" all these years, but I knew him to be anything but the rube they called "Jethro Jones." Here was a truly shrewd and efficient and incredibly energetic business-man who'd not only gotten off on the wrong foot with the public, but stepped in cow flop with that wrong foot.

Even with my experience at dealing with the media, I don't think I could have helped the situation had I been at Valley Ranch that Saturday night. I still believe I did the right thing by staying away from the announcement of Landry's dismissal—the right thing out of personal respect to Landry and his achievements, and the right thing regarding protocol and appearance to the public. And for all my media experience, I was in a way as naive as Jerry. I knew there would be some shock and sadness over Landry's departure, but I didn't expect nearly as much hoopla as there was.

And besides, I absolutely had to go back to Miami for a few more days. Not just to resign, and not just to settle various business affairs with my attorney, my buddy, my best friend outside football, Nick Christin. The main thing was, I had to say goodbye to about one hundred good citizens, wonderful human beings, fine football players— the Miami Hurricanes.

In Miami that final weekend, I met with our football team and I wouldn't do any interviews of any sort. I was slipping in and out of the Hurricane football complex because I didn't want to make any public statements until I got back to Dallas and had a press conference there.

It was a very emotional time with the players. We'd been through so much together at Miami (which I will address at considerable length later). The last words I said to them, referring to what was then the biggest, hottest rivalry in college football, were "Beat Notre Dame." I just about broke down as I left the podium, because I could not finish my little speech with the line—a traditional inside joke on our team— that I had always used to conclude remarks to them about Notre Dame. I could no longer promise to hold up my end of the bargain: "You kick Notre Dame's ass, and if that leprechaun messes with me, I'll kick *his* ass."

I left the room in tears with Rich Dalrymple, Miami's sports information director and my jogging buddy. We jogged across the practice field as we'd often done, only this time we were in coats and ties. I was going out that way, rather than through the office and out the front door where a squadron of reporters and camera crews was camped out.

We jogged straight to Rich's car without being seen, and he drove me to the airport, where Jerry's plane was waiting to take me back to Dallas. If Jerry's "Saturday Night Massacre" press conference had given the Texans a modern-day Alamo cry, they were preparing their own little version of a modern-day San Jacinto for me. San Jacinto was where the Texans got their revenge on Santa Anna.

In the initial shock wave, when I was generally viewed as an Arkansas Hawg myself, one acknowledgment that I was at least a native-born Texan came in the form of an anonymous phone call to my mother down in Port Arthur. It was long distance from Dallas. The voice was a woman's.

"Are y'all the parents of Jimmy Johnson?" the voice said.

"Yes, ma'am," Mother said. Mother was pretty proud, pretty happy at that moment. Mother loves football—gets terribly hoarse from screaming at the television screen. And now her youngest son was going to live closer to home than he had in decades.

"Well," said the voice, "you can just have him back down there in Port Arthur, because we don't want him in Dallas. They're saying up here that this is going to put Port Arthur on the map. But I want you to know it's going to wipe Port Arthur clear *off* the map!"

Mother just listened. Didn't respond. After the woman in Dallas hung up, Mother went into the den and told Daddy about it. Port Arthur is a town that knows storms. The night they drove me up to enroll in college at Fayetteville in 1961, the 50,000-watt radio stations kept blaring out stories that Hurricane Carla was about to wipe Port Arthur "off the map." Port Arthur was still there when they got back. But this time, this night in 1989, my parents knew a different kind of storm was brewing in the flatlands up north.

Growing up in Southeast Texas, you couldn't ask for better parents, right down to their absolutely perfect Southeast Texas names, C.W. and Allene. C.W. stands for nothing but C.W.—that's his name. He is, as we shall see, a master seat-of-the-pants psychologist. My ways of getting people to do what I think is best, in such a low-key fashion they hardly realize I'm persuading them, are probably founded in my Daddy's ways. Mother has never been the chatty type. She says what she has to say, and that's it. But I'll tell you what: If you tease her, be prepared to catch a verbal zinger right back. So frankly, she showed a lot of mercy on that woman on the phone from Dallas. Careful restraint of verbal firepower, I get from Mother.

Daddy mostly keeps his own counsel as he thinks things through. But once he's ready to act, he acts. Just like that. So it went, on the morning of Tuesday, February 28, the day of my first press conference in Dallas. By 6 a.m., Daddy had a cup of coffee in one hand and the Port Arthur *News* in the other. He turned straight to the sports section. Yes, that storm up north was going to hit Dallas full force later in the day. His youngest son was walking right into it.

A retired dairy supervisor, Daddy now keeps busy driving—ferrying new cars from distant dealers to customers who are looking for a specific, perhaps hard-to-find, model. On an hour's notice, he might board a plane to, say, Baton Rouge or Abilene, pick up a car, and drive for hours back to Port Arthur or Houston. So hopping a plane in a hurry is no big deal to Daddy at all.

He looked up from the paper, thought for a moment, and told Mother, "I think I'll go catch a plane." She understood.

Frankly, I couldn't have told you that morning, or any other morning, even how old my Daddy was. (He was seventy at the time.) I almost never remember his or Mother's birthdays, or their anniversary. I might call to wish them a Merry Christmas on, oh, December 27 or 28. I am generous, and I give gifts, but not when the plastic commercialists tell me to. I am simply not a traditionalist with holidays and cards and flowers and gifts and the "proper" things at the "proper" times. Somehow I've gotten the rap, for example, of not respecting Christmas. I respect the religious holiday as much if not more than those who let the department-store ads and commercials tell them how to observe it. I don't let convention tell me what I want to do, or when I want to do it.

My family gets together about once a year, usually down at Crystal Beach, and we let our hair down—really cut up. Otherwise, we don't even talk much on the phone. We say what we need to say, and that's about it. No chitchat, no small talk.

I arrived at the Cowboys' complex that Tuesday morning in a daze. Everything had happened, and was still happening, so fast. As I jumped out of the car that had whisked me to Valley Ranch, there were only a few minicam crews outside to tape my arrival. The real media army was waiting inside in the conference room. I got out of the car, looked around, and there, on the steps, off by himself, away from the camera crews, stood my Daddy.

I was so confused and stressed that for a moment I almost wondered whether I was hallucinating. But it was indeed my Daddy.

We didn't need to say anything. I hugged him and we walked into the Cowboys' building with my arm around him.

The Los Angeles *Times* estimated that there were more than two hundred media people waiting for me in the news conference room. I would call that a very conservative estimate. The big room was packed. Crammed. I had participated in mass press conferences leading up to four bowl games that were either direct showdowns for the national championship of college football or had direct effect on the titles.

But never . . . ever . . . had I walked into anything . . . like . . . this. In fact, I would not see anything remotely resembling it again until the week of Super Bowl XXVII in Pasadena, California.

But this was not just coverage. The tension in the room was tangible. This was not a press conference so much as a massive interrogation. It even seemed as if they'd turned the camera lights up a couple of notches.

At a national championship game, you talk to the media in a more relaxed setting. Most of the stories and questions are positive: "Hey, you've had an eleven-and-oh season, and what about this game?" Even though you might be a little uptight about the game itself, it's still a relaxed setting.

This was as if I were about to declare war on another country. Clearly I was seen as the invader. I can't say this enough: It was tense. Tense. Tense. And, knowing the reaction Jerry had had three days earlier, it really was almost devastating.

I'm a big boxing fan and sometimes think in boxing analogies. After shaking the cobwebs from the initial blow, I gathered my senses. And I decided to rope-a-dope.

Likely, each one of them had come in that morning with his or her own shock that Landry and Schramm were out. Just as likely, they'd stood around talking, waiting for me to arrive, and worked one another up even more.

There wasn't going to be any of this, "Well, tell us about winning the national championship" business. Every question was going to be a zinger. And you knew as soon as you got through answering that one, they were going to throw another zinger right at you.

What about the use of steroids? What about the conduct of your players? What about the attitudes of your players? What about a [some vague allegation of some minor] recruiting violation fifteen years ago when you were an assistant coach? Oh? It turned out none of it was ever tied to you, and it wasn't anything major in the first place? Yeah, yeah, well, what about it anyway?

On and on and on. Anything negative they could think of, they brought up. Really, it was such a grind that it's hard for me to recall what they were talking about. I do remember one guy who kept asking me asinine questions with such frequency and regularity that it was almost like a drum cadence for the others.

But my strategy was rope-a-dope. I was just lying on the ropes, letting them take their swings, knowing that eventually they would punch themselves out. Occasionally I'd peek-a-boo between my gloves, dropping in a mention of Port Arthur anytime I got a chance, trying to get the point across that I was a native-born Texan. I knew better than to be any more aggressive than that, because I didn't yet have the credibility with them on which to take an aggressive stance, and I knew I wasn't going to earn credibility quickly. (That is, I knew I was going to get my ass kicked sixteen times that fall. Lucky me, though: As it turned out, I only got my ass kicked fifteen times.)

Eventually the neo–San Jacinto fighters filed out in exhaustion, but I don't even recall when or how the press conference ended. I do recall that when I came down out of the ring—ah, off the podium—I asked

Doug Todd, who was then the Cowboys' public relations director, "Who was that guy who kept badgering me?"

"Oh," Doug said. "That's Dale Hansen. He does the color commentary for the Cowboys' radio network."

Oh, great.

It also turned out that Dale Hansen was a sportscaster for one of the local TV stations, Channel 8. Believe it or not, I like him now and we get along fine. But one night while the news of the purchase was breaking, he went on television and said, "We're getting reports that some guy by the name of Jerry Jones is going to buy the Cowboys and make Jimmy Johnson the coach. I will say this: The day that some guy by the name of Jerry Jones buys the Cowboys and makes Jimmy Johnson the coach is the day they need to peel the star off the helmet."

Four years later, after we'd won the Super Bowl, the Dallas *Morning News* would look back in perspective, reprinting a sampler of the pundits' remarks to the public immediately following the press conference of February 28, 1989. Here are some.

Bill Lyon, Philadelphia *Inquirer:* "To coach the Cowboys, Jones has replaced Landry with Jimmy Johnson. Right off the top, that's a bad trade-off. The Cowboys have taken a precipitous plunge in class. . . . Presumably, Jones thinks Johnson can run up the score in the NFL like he has at Miami. The suspicion is that they are both in for a comeuppance." Referring to Miami's rout of Notre Dame in 1985, Lyon continued, "You don't see many 58–7 finals in the NFL." (But as it turned out, you *did* see a 52–17 Super Bowl, didn't you?)

Jim Murray, Los Angeles *Times:* "Jimmy Johnson, by all accounts, isn't a humble man. He can't be. He just stood there while they fired America's Coach and gave him his team. It's as if the rustlers just shot John Wayne. I guess we'll all just have to get another team."

Frank Luksa, Dallas *Times-Herald:* "[Johnson's] first trophy is the Bad Taste Award. What was Johnson doing in Dallas the last few days? Why didn't he stay out of sight until the last minute?

"Johnson's local presence confirmed the worst. He had acted the proverbial vulture perched on a high wire, waiting for the body to quit twitching. Johnson flew back to Miami prior to the Saturday Night Massacre at Valley Ranch. Jones said he and Johnson decided it would be 'inappropriate' for the latter to appear at the news briefing.

"You wonder why. Johnson already had danced around the edges of Landry's wake. Why miss the funeral?"

Blackie Sherrod, Dallas *Morning News* (And this was as near to nice as anybody got): "It ain't gonna be easy, Jimmy Johnson. . . . In comparison, the University of Miami was a nap in a hammock. Just one skinny point kept you from three consecutive 11–0 seasons with the college kids. That's like yacht time.

"No more. Welcome to U-boat duty. It may be several years before the Dallas Cowboy periscope breaks surface. You're accustomed to being the cock of the walk. In Dallas, you could be the pavement."

Blackie forever dubbed Jerry and me the Arkansas Jaybirds, JJ and JJ. And even that nickname conjured images of a pair of blue jays, bothersome birds, swooping in, screeching, pestering, pecking. Yet Blackie was about the least harsh critic we had.

I try not to ever seem sullen or defensive around the media. I don't refuse to talk to them over what they've said or written, and I don't cut them off from the players. If you refuse to talk to a writer, he's going to unload on you twice as hard, and it's your fault, because you haven't even given yourself a chance to explain your side.

So I never lock them out. Rope-a-dope them occasionally, yes.

In the transition months I would alternate between rope-a-dope and peeking out to try to explain my side. Jerry kept walking into punches, though.

People were looking for any kind of flaw. Anything they could throw a rock at: my sprayed hair; Jerry being from Arkansas; Jerry's "gee-and-hah" colloquialisms. Every time you turned around it was something: Jerry saying things he didn't mean in the way that they sounded: "Troy [Aikman] looked good coming out of the shower"; Jerry announcing that he was considering changing the famous, to the point of being an institution, Cowboy Cheerleaders' costumes to bicycle stretch shorts.

Jerry had been a wheeler-dealer who believed in brainstorming, just tossing any idea that had possibilities right out in the open, and then if it didn't seem feasible, he just discarded it. But he was used to doing that in his office, in the oil-and-gas business, where if you decided to cancel some big drilling operation up in western Canada it didn't lead the six o'clock news or the morning sports section.

He didn't realize that now, in his new position, every word of every sentence was going to be scrutinized and that people were looking for something negative, and that if he left the door cracked open just a hair, they were going to kick it wide open.

But I didn't try to advise him. Jerry didn't need that. He was a very big boy who'd made many millions of dollars and developed a good thick skin along the way. To Jerry's credit, whenever somebody would have a horribly negative reaction to something he might have said, he'd come in the next day and laugh about it and keep right on going.

I kind of got a kick out of it all. It was something that put a little humor in days that would get more and more and more miserable before we started to turn the thing around.

III

REALITY

F or all the resistance we met at the outset, the real slap in the face didn't come until April. I had taken this job knowing that the Cowboys were last in the league the year before. They had lost thirteen games in 1988, but as I looked over the scores I tried to see that they had played some teams close. I didn't know enough about professional football back then to see that that's the way most scores are in the NFL. Most of them are tight games. You live and die by the won-lost column.

When I held my first minicamp in April, I found out how far back in last place the Cowboys were, and why. And it truly was a slap in the face. I didn't realize just how poor we were until we got all the veterans in and started timing them in the 40-yard dash, which of course is a key indicator of a football player's speed. I had always been around quick, fast players. I may have been just a lil' ol' college coach coming into the exalted NFL, but it doesn't take some savvy genius to read stopwatches, and to know that speed and quickness are absolutely vital to the way this game is played nowadays, whatever the level, from peewee to professional.

I found myself comparing the Cowboys not to the other NFL teams—that was out of the question—but to the team I'd just left at Miami. I wouldn't say it publicly at the time—wouldn't dare—but I had just left a better football team at Miami than what I was inheriting, and yet I had moved up to the professional level. The Hurricanes could have beaten the Cowboys, and beaten them bad, simply firing off the line of scrimmage, putting moves on them in the line, darting past them, juking around them, generally running up and down the field on them. No offense to the individuals we had with the Cowboys that spring. Some had been truly great players, but were long past their prime.

When we put the watches on the veterans that day, I walked off the field astonished. I held a meeting. After I talked about how slow they were, I got to thinking about it, and I wanted to cushion it a bit, because I didn't want the team to rebel against the new college coach who'd come over. So I said, "Well, we may not be very fast, but we'll be in such great condition that if we run a 4.7 forty, we'll still be running a 4.7 in the fourth quarter." (To give you some gauge, a "burner" receiver is down in the 4.35 range in the forty. I can live with a defensive lineman who runs a 4.7 forty, but not with 4.7 as a team average.)

The thought that we were going to have not just problems, but big problems, set in. I called my staff into a meeting. I had retained a couple of guys from Landry's staff (Neill Armstrong remains with me parttime today) and brought in David Shula from the Dolphins. I wanted some guys with NFL experience on both sides of the ball, but the bulk of my staff came from the University of Miami.

Dave Wannstedt, my good right arm, would be my defensive coordinator. He'd been with the Dolphins very briefly, but had been with me most of the time since my Oklahoma State years. Butch Davis, also with me since Oklahoma State, would coach the defensive line. Tony Wise had been with me at Oklahoma State, then gone home to upstate New York to coach at Syracuse for a while, before rejoining me at Miami, and then at Dallas to coach the offensive line. Hubbard Alexander, "Ax," had remained from Howard Schnellenberger's Miami staff to work with me there, and came with me to the Cowboys as receivers coach. Dave Campo came from Miami to coach defensive backs, and Steve Hoffman to coach kickers (I believe in leaving absolutely no element of the game to chance; yes, kickers need careful coaching).

And then there was Joe Brodsky. In 1989, Joe was fifty-five years old and had lived every one of those years in Miami. For thirteen years he had been one of Florida's most successful high school coaches, then moved to the University of Miami in 1978 under Lou Saban, and had stayed with Schnellenberger and then me. After fifty-five years in Miami, Brodsky probably had never even tried on a pair of cowboy boots in his life, but when I asked him to come with me to Dallas to coach running backs for me, he started packing. That's the kind of bonding and loyalty we build on my staff.

Formally, as in press conferences, I refer to them as "my staff." To people who know us and the way we operate, I always refer to my coaches and their wives as "my crew." Because you will soon know how we work, you might as well start thinking in terms of my crew. We don't have to waste a lot of time communicating. We do it very efficiently. They know exactly what I want in a player. They know exactly what I expect on the field. And vice versa. We just know what to expect from one another. We've known one another too well for too long. When I bring in a new guy, I bring in more the person than the coach—someone I'm certain will click with our chemistry right away.

I had no concern whatsoever about the Miami guys making the transition from college to professional football. I wanted to have the right kind of people that I could work with, who could learn and develop, and have the right kind of chemistry for a group that was going to be with each other night and day, year round.

Anyway, that day in April when the hard, hard reality set in, I told the crew, "I'm not going to meet with the players as often this year as I have in the past or I will in the future, for the simple reason that I can't lie to them. I can't go in one day and tell them about being a close-knit group and having unity, having feeling for one another, when I'm going to cut three or four of them the next day."

So, rather than even talk to the players, it was as if I blocked myself out and treated the situation a little more coldheartedly than I would otherwise. I suppose that chill filtered through the team and out into the media by osmosis, and so the image problems kept getting worse. I couldn't let that matter. This was an absolutely necessary part of the massive radical surgery needed to begin getting this thing turned.

There was a very delicate step to this initial surgery: dealing with some veterans whose careers had been so great and their reputations so enormous that they were walking icons, not far removed from the status of Landry himself in the lore of Texas and the NFL.

Ed "Too Tall" Jones and Randy White had been two of the best defensive linemen ever to play this game. Danny White had been a Cowboys quarterback since so far back in the glory days that he had started out as an understudy to Roger Staubach and then become Roger's successor. I would tread lightly and carefully with these guys— not for PR purposes, but out of sheer respect and admiration for what they had done in the past. Not as far past prime, but getting there, were stars such as defensive back Everson Walls and linebacker Eugene Lockhart.

Randy White is a helluva guy. I really like him. (And, since he retired in 1989, he has come out to our practices and talked to our defensive linemen about pass rush, and he has talked to our defense as a group. He has really been a positive influence.) But in the spring of 1989, watching Randy White trying to get into a stance was about like watching *me* trying to get into a stance. Guys who are making a million dollars a year are never going to retire. The saying goes that when the time comes, you have to tear the jerseys off their backs. I wouldn't say goodbye, either, if I were a player making that kind of money. I would wait until somebody told me it was time.

And so I had my session, my one-on-one, man-to-man talk with Randy. I didn't want to cut him. I told him, as I would tell others, that they had been too great for too long to go out that way, and that they owed it to themselves to retire with honor. I finished that first conversation with enormous respect for Randy. He took it like the man he is, and he took it gracefully, and he went out with honor.

Danny White was really persistent in trying to continue to play. And in fact, we redid his contract. But once we got into work on the field, I knew it was just a matter of time. In our first draft as a coaching staff, we made quarterback Troy Aikman of UCLA the top pick in the league. Still Danny wanted to play. That summer we took Steve Walsh, the quarterback who'd won the national championship for me at Miami, in the supplemental draft, and I said, "Danny, you're not going to be in the picture." Still he wanted to go to preseason training camp, and I took him. But not long into camp, Danny finally faced the facts, and he too retired with honor.

Ed Jones had had a good year in 1988, and played his final year with us in 1989. We were going at a fast pace all season, because we were trying to evaluate players. And poor old Ed . . . for instance, we have a 12-minute conditioning run that we do. It's a great conditioning drill, but it tends to be hard on guys who are in their late thirties. But Ed never complained. He would fight through it every time, and I would look over there at him and I would hurt.

Ed Jones, of all the players I have ever worked with, is the one who truly said "professional." He approached it in that manner. He truly approached it as a job. And he truly approached you as his employer. I really enjoyed working with him, even at the end of his career. I would have loved to have coached Ed Jones when he was in his prime.

But there was another parting far harder for me and for the one I had to tell than the sum total of those conversations with the great players of yore, and all those journeymen and younger players who had to be told that it was over for them. That April an even harder rain set in than the professional reality—the personal reality.

I had been married to Linda Kay since before I turned twenty. We had a great life for twenty-six years. We never had arguments. I don't even recall any negative conversations of any kind. We had a great deal of feeling for each other. She was and is a very intelligent, sophisticated, dignified woman. By 1989 our boys were grown, well-educated, and on their own. Linda Kay has always loved to travel, and we had plenty of money, and so we were at a stage in our lives when many couples would be off to Paris and Rome, just the two of them, on long vacations.

But here we were in temporary housing, an apartment the Cowboys had provided for us in Valley Ranch, and I was getting into another round-the-clock, 365-day-a-year struggle up from the bottom with a football team. Plus, and foremost, I was and am Jimmy Johnson, not the guy of the couple in the leisurely midlife bliss described above. I don't like to travel and I grow very tired, very rapidly, of formal social functions.

One day in April I was out on a jog. I am not a fanatic runner, but I am a faithful jogger. Two or three miles a day, followed by a walk back of equal or greater distance. The jog unclutters my mind, and the walk back lets me think clearly. If I'm jogging with somebody—I usually jog with my assistant coaches—I often have some really productive conversations on the walk back. If I'm jogging alone, it's a great time for me to meditate.

I jogged from the apartment out through a very posh development. We were planning to buy a big house, so I was looking at all the nice houses as I went. I thought of living in another big house. I thought about the social scene. And then I thought, "No. No. This is not what I want to do."

I came back to the apartment, and I said, "I want a divorce." I left that day, and I did not see Linda Kay again until Brent's wedding in June of 1992.

To this day, I care for her a lot. But I did what I had to do. You get to the point where you've had children that you love, had your family, and they grow up. They can take care of themselves and you say to yourself, "Hey, I've done my deal and now I'm going to do what I want to do. Yes. I'm at the age where I ought to be able to do what the hell I want to do." But not many people are bold enough to actually take that step. Not many have the opportunity.

I wanted to live alone. I live alone now. And I will always live alone.

There has been so much speculation that I left Linda Kay as part of the process of clearing the decks of my life, to focus totally on rebuilding the Cowboys. That may have been part of it, but it was certainly not all of it, nor even the primary reason. Dallas provided an opportunity to change our lifestyles. And getting a divorce had been in the back of my mind for some time.

Even if we'd sensed it in February, on Mia's Night ("Jimmy, is this what you really want to do?" and "It's what I *have* to do"), our final afternoon together was very emotional for both of us, but I think especially for Linda Kay. It is not easy, remembering her crying that afternoon. But, classy lady that she is, she gathered herself and looked at me, and said, meaning the Cowboys, "You'll make this work. I know you. You have blinders on."

That first year, besides the football, besides evaluating all those players, I had to help out in an enormous housecleaning of the business side of a franchise which turned out to be astonishingly fat, wasteful, outdated and in some areas abusive. Jerry was doing most of it and was teaching me on the fly. But he couldn't do it all, and besides, I had some expertise to offer in some business areas.

One typical day, I called in Steve Orsini, our ticket manager, and we went through the entire complimentary tickets list. Just plain old friends of individuals who might or might not still work at the complex were getting comp tickets. I started making phone calls, eliminating people getting comp tickets.

Then I went through the list of everyone who was getting a courtesy car. For instance, I phoned one woman who had been furnished a courtesy car from the Cowboys for a long time, and she hadn't even worked for the Cowboys for more than two years. When I phoned her, she kind of laughed and said, "Well, Coach, I knew this call would come someday."

Those were just some of the abuses that had been going on. I was beginning to understand some of the reasons why they'd lost something like three or four million dollars the year before Jerry and I got there. (I think Jerry, even the first year, made some money. He would say he lost a little bit that first year. But I don't think I'd be out of line telling you that he's made a bunch of money in the time that we've been here. But they were losing money every year, just because of the way the franchise was run.)

A big deal was made out of the fact that, during our first season, Mother and Daddy asked for some extra tickets (we'd given them their comps) and I sent them the extras along with a bill. Well, there is a right way to do things, and if I'm to demand that everyone in this organization do things the right way, it must start with me.

Then I had a look at all the figures for our TV show. The payment to the Cowboys in 1988 from Lee Martin Productions, for the Tom Landry Show and the special edition of the Tex Schramm Show, was $40,000. One of them made $50,000, and one of them lost $10,000. I said, "Forty thousand dollars for two TV shows? Somebody's making a bunch of money around here, and it isn't the Cowboys."

I phoned the head of the production company, Lee Martin himself, and said, "I'd like to have a meeting. These figures—something's wrong here. I've had TV shows for the last ten years, and something's up here."

It was kind of a funny meeting, because he was almost like the little kid with the expression on his face when he's caught with his hand in the cookie jar. He walked in, and, without even trying to negotiate, he said, "Well, evidently, y'all don't want to do it in a first-class manner. So if that's the case, good luck to you." And he walked out the door without even discussing it.

After Martin's people had left the room, Jerry looked at me and the expression on his face said, "You were smart enough to figure out that somebody was making money and it wasn't the Cowboys. But now we don't even have a TV production company! What do we do now?"

I said, "There's a woman who handled the shows for me in Miami—Brenda Bushell. I can bring her in to do some consulting work if you want to, and let her set up the shows."

Jerry said, "Bring her in and let's visit. I don't know anything about doing radio and TV."

So Brenda flew in from Florida and got it going, and that first year, the profit for the Cowboys from our TV shows was three-quarters of a million dollars.

I even did some player contracts at first, but told Jerry pretty quickly that he'd better handle them all. If I ever tried to handle contracts again, we'd have a revolt from the players around here. I've got a real problem about money: If it's mine, I'll give it away; if it's the company's, I'm too tight-fisted. Jerry not only is more liberal than I am, but doesn't get nearly as flustered during negotiations. (Here's a perfect example: In the summer of 1992, on my crew's annual vacation together, which I pay for, I gave Mike Woicik, our strength and conditioning coach, a $5,000 chip at a casino in Nassau. Five thousand dollars in cash out of my pocket, for the hell of it, because Mike is one of my guys and we were having a *good* time. Then in March of 1993, after we'd won the Super Bowl, Mike came into my office and said, "Coach, you once took care of me out of your own pocket. And I want you to know I appreciate that. But, Coach, I've been looking around the league at what other strength and conditioning coaches are making, and I just think I ought to be making more money." Well, before I got all worked up as I usually do over company money, I just said, "Mike, I think what you're making is fair. But if you don't, I suggest you go see Jerry.")

Obviously I was wearing too many hats that first spring. But we got things set up organizationally like we wanted it, and then went on with our business. One item of business, which for some reason had escaped me, was brought to our attention by the league office. I'd been on the job nearly two months when the NFL notified us that if I was going to work for the Dallas Cowboys, I had to be under contract. And why wasn't I under contract? Well, I, uh, I'd forgotten to sign one. Forgotten to negotiate one. Jerry was in my office one day and mentioned that the league office wanted it done.

When he got up to leave, he said, "How long do you want to make it for?"

I said, "I don't care."

He said, "What? Five years? Ten years?"

I said, "I don't care."

He said, "Let's make it ten years."

I said, "Okay."

As the worst team in the league in 1988, we got the first pick in the draft of 1989. How was a lil' ol' rookie staff out of college ball going to handle the swirling, wheeling, dealing, high-pressure one-day stock market that is the NFL draft? Well, for openers . . .

I'd been aware of Troy Aikman since he was a tenth grader in high school in Henryetta, Oklahoma, and I was head coach at Oklahoma State. We had made a major effort to recruit Troy at Oklahoma State, and actually felt I had a pretty good chance. I'd been in his home and knew his family. But in the last week of recruiting, Troy visited Oklahoma, and Barry Switzer told him they were going to throw the football all over the field with him. Oklahoma had for years been a run-oriented wishbone offense. But Switzer had recruited Marcus Dupree, the incredibly big, fast and agile running back that the entire football world had coveted out of high school in Philadelphia, Mississippi. Switzer planned to make Dupree the tailback in an I-formation offense, and with Marcus as his only featured runner, Switzer could look at throwing the ball more from the I.

Well, as it turned out, Switzer and Dupree didn't exactly hit it off. Dupree didn't develop and headed home to Mississippi, and there sat Troy Aikman, running a wishbone offense.

Meanwhile, I'd gone to the University of Miami. We played Oklahoma there, in Norman, in 1985. In the second quarter, two of our defensive linemen, Jerome Brown and John McVeigh, rushed Troy. Oklahoma had horrible pass protection, because they were a wishbone team trying to throw the ball, which was of course out of character. Our guys tackled Troy in the backfield and broke his leg. That was the last Troy ever saw of Owen Field.

And it changed his career, very likely for the better. Troy realized the situation with the Sooner wishbone and wanted to transfer. I called Troy and urged him to transfer to Miami. But his father was living in California, and I think with a nudge from Switzer, Troy transferred to UCLA. Barry knew that if Troy went to Miami then Barry was going to have to face him, and face him with a great team, because we'd beaten Oklahoma soundly that year, and did in our next two outings against them.

A key to our success at Miami was strong quarterbacks—Bernie

Kosar, Vinny Testaverde, Steve Walsh. Troy had more physical talent than any of the three. And I knew the type person he was from my Oklahoma State days of trying to recruit him. He's a tremendous competitor, intelligent, with a strong arm.

In April 1989, I got Troy Aikman at last. I flew to Los Angeles and worked him out (I believe in evaluating a player in person before I draft him; that's an important procedure I'll address later) and made him the number one pick in the draft. I knew he could be one of the cornerstones in building an outstanding football team.

In the weeks prior to that draft, although I was going to choose Troy, I kept it to myself. I wanted to see what kind of trade offers we could get from around the league for the number one pick. Also, by not tipping our hand, we were better able to negotiate a contract with Troy's agent, Leigh Steinberg—that is, Leigh didn't have quite as much leverage if he wasn't certain we were going to take Troy, though I never had any intention of drafting anyone else.

In the second, third, and fourth rounds that year, we picked up some guys you might have heard of since (they all were destined to start for us in Super Bowl XXVII): running back Daryl Johnston out of Syracuse, center Mark Stepnoski out of Pitt, and defensive end Tony Tolbert out of Texas-El Paso. Not bad for a bunch of college coaches playing the big bad NFL market for the first time, eh? Like I say: if you go out and work your ass off evaluating players firsthand, and you have a good enough eye for talent, more times than not you'll make your picks count.

In the early drafts of our regime, we also had the benefit of having seen or coached virtually every blue chip player in America ever since he was recruited out of high school. In 1989, we knew Daryl Johnston well, because Tony Wise had coached at Syracuse when Daryl first got there. And later, while we were all at Miami, we had played Syracuse. We had kept in close touch with Pitt over the years, and knew Mark Stepnoski had the intelligence to be an outstanding player. And I had coached Mark in the East-West Shrine Game. Tony Tolbert was an NFL projection of what we'd done in the defensive line at Miami—take a big, quick linebacker and make him a lineman. Tony was a 230-pound linebacker who'd been captain of his team at Texas–El Paso. By Super Bowl XXVII, he would be a 270-pound defensive end, destined for the Pro Bowl.

In the second round of 1989, I made my first NFL draft trade. I did a deal with the dean of NFL wheeler-dealers, Los Angeles Raiders' owner Al Davis. We traded places with the Raiders in the second round, and Al gave us a sixth-round choice in the deal. (Over the next four years, I would have more phone conversations with Al Davis than anyone else at another franchise. By the spring of 1993, when I told him, "You counseled me in the first two years," Al replied, "Whataya mean, counseled? I *made* you in the first two years." Actually there was an ongoing give and take where he schooled me about the methods and procedures in the league, but in return he picked my brain about players coming out of college.)

Moving down in the second round of 1989 didn't hurt us, because we got who we wanted, Daryl. But the sixth-round pick didn't help us, as we'd hoped. After the fifth round, we were dumbfounded to find that college coaching had left us woefully ignorant in one respect: We were used to being neck deep in prime prospects during the college recruiting process. And I mean neck deep in South Florida, let alone the rest of the nation, where we were on excellent recruiting footing because of our high visibility in so many national TV games.

It was scary as hell to find this out, working with a team that was so woefully shorthanded at the time, but after we got past the first five rounds of the draft, we really didn't see many guys on the board who we thought could help us.

We had gone in knowing it would take us time and a lot of work to turn the thing around. Now we knew we were in so deep, and the draft turned out to be so thin after the high rounds, that we couldn't rely on conventional methods of rebuilding. If we had gone the conventional way of waiting for our time to come in the draft, and using the choices as they fell, it was going to be a long haul. And I don't know if we could have ever turned it around.

We not only needed to scrape up more draft choices, but more high draft choices, in trades with other clubs. But with no more than we had to offer as bargaining chips from this brokendown old club, how were we going to pull it off?

IV

THE GREAT
TRAIN ROBBERY

Herschel Walker is a good football player. He is not a great football player. He can be made to look great, if you're willing to build your entire offense around him, as Vince Dooley was at the University of Georgia in the early 1980s and Tom Landry was at Dallas in 1988. I was not willing to do that.

If you give him the ball 30 or 35 times a game, then he's probably going to break some tackles and make some runs. But in the NFL, that's not going to be enough to win. It was enough for Georgia in 1980, playing a relatively mild Southeastern Conference schedule, to go 12–0 and win the national championship. But in 1988, Herschel rushed for

1,514 yards, caught 53 passes for 505 yards, led the NFL in all-purpose yardage and went to the Pro Bowl. And the Cowboys went 3–13 and finished dead last in the league.

Herschel is a straight-ahead power runner. He is strong enough in the open field to run over somebody, and he is fast enough to outrun virtually everybody. But he is not a nifty runner. That is, he cannot make the quick cuts and darts and fakes and wriggly moves that are necessary traits in any runner I would call great.

Herschel does some things extremely well. Then there are times when he doesn't make the cut and runs right up the rear end of an offensive tackle. Some people perceive that as a matter of Herschel not trying. I don't perceive that as dogging it as much as I perceive that he is just not very nifty. And when he misses a hole, it's just not a very good-looking play. He likes to turn his back, which in his case sometimes works, because tacklers sometimes do bounce off those big, wide pads of his. But when you turn your back, you can't see the hole.

Herschel's sort of Superman mystique has ebbed and flowed over the years. It began when he was in high school in little Wrightsville, Georgia, using his running style optimally. His senior year, half the people in the stands were college recruiters, from all over the country, and half the rest were sportswriters. So he was something of a national legend before he even graduated from Johnson County High. In his first game as a freshman at Georgia, he scored his first touchdown by literally running over Tennessee safety Bill Bates (later of the Cowboys) and stepping on him. He led Georgia to the national championship that year, and won the Heisman Trophy his junior year.

But after he came out of college early for the big money of the USFL, his mystique ebbed. He had his good days, but overall, the street talk was that wheeler-dealer owner of the New Jersey Generals Donald Trump had bought himself a power runner whose effort was questionable. As the USFL began to disintegrate and the NFL scouts began looking at Herschel, some didn't like him at all. For example, Tom Braatz, then player personnel director of the Atlanta Falcons (seemingly the natural NFL club for Herschel), wouldn't touch him, opining that Herschel had pretty well taken the big bucks and slacked off.

Gil Brandt of the Cowboys did like him, and brought him to Dallas in 1986. And by 1989, after Herschel's big season of 1988, the Superman mystique flowed again. He was perceived by many as the premier player in the NFL.

Three weeks into that first season we were 0–3, which was not at all unexpected. Early on, we'd made the decision that we didn't mind sacrificing some that year to get dividends down the road. One day my crew and I were walking back from our lunchtime jog, just bs-ing about what in the world we might do to "get this thing turned quicker," as Wannstedt put it. I said, "What asset do we have that would allow us to do something to get a jump start?"

My mind was clear from the jog. But what I was about to say would make the crew wonder if my mind was gone. I said: "We could trade Herschel Walker."

At first, Wannstedt, Wise, and Co. took that about the same way I'd taken it when Jerry Jones first told me he was interested in buying the Cowboys. I got a "yeah, right" response.

When they began to realize I was serious, they were kind of shocked that I would even think about it. They had several concerns. They knew we had no intention of building our offense around Herschel, but he had been productive and he was the only Pro Bowler, the only bona fide star, the Cowboys had left. And unlike Ed Jones and Randy White, Herschel probably still had some good years left. And, the crew figured, trading Herschel would send the public and the media into a new and greater fury, which was about all we needed. Jerry trusted me on the technical part of such a trade, but like the crew, his major concern was what the public reaction would be. Fans don't want to hear about the years to come. They want to win right now. And they like stars.

Herschel continued to espouse ambitions of being an FBI agent and of participating in the Olympics. A lot of that was just part of the whole Herschel mystique, and might have been a ploy to negotiate a contract. His contract was up, and at times he'd claimed to be considering retirement. That was all part of his baggage, which I could deal with. Everybody carries a little bit of baggage.

But the main points were 1) Herschel was our only real bargaining chip, and 2) that we weren't going to build our team around him anyway. I thought he was an asset. I thought he could help our team. But I didn't think he was nearly as good as what we were going to get on the other side of a trade. I felt we could get a lot more than we were giving.

I didn't even have to initiate discussions for the deal. A few days after our fateful jog, Ernie Accorsi, general manager of the Browns, called from Cleveland to talk about trading in general. Ernie brought up the possibility of Herschel Walker. I said, "Well, put together a package and let's talk." And that's how it all got started. Ernie and I got the deal going, and Art Modell, the Cleveland owner, was going to get involved.

I went to Jerry and said, "Hey, we've got this going with Cleveland, but I think we ought to call some other teams to see what else we could get." Mike Lynn, GM of the Minnesota Vikings, had called me earlier in the season and mentioned Herschel in passing.

We pretty well checked everybody in the league. There were mixed feelings. Some were like us and didn't want to build an offense around him. Some didn't like him at all. And there were some who thought he was the one who would take them to the Super Bowl. Minnesota was one.

Really, we were looking for a competitor for Cleveland, to get the Browns to sweeten the deal. There was a little bit of interest from the New York Giants, but we didn't want to trade within our division. From Atlanta, Tom Braatz, the Herschel skeptic, had moved on to Green Bay, and Atlanta was the team that I thought would step up and do it, because Herschel could help them fill their stadium. But Atlanta was concerned that this was the last year of his contract and that they'd have to hold contract talks with him. They figured he'd drive an awfully hard bargain with his crowd appeal in Georgia. Then too, what we were asking in return was too high for them.

Cleveland was our only serious offer at first. So I called Mike Lynn up in Minnesota and said, "Hey, I'm about to do a deal this afternoon for Herschel Walker. And if you're interested in doing something, here's what it's going to take." (The provisions, details, contingencies, conditional draft choices and eventual ramifications of that trade could in themselves make up an entire book. But I'll encapsulate that later). I told Mike, "I'm going to practice right now. You need to get back to me by 6:30, or else the deal will already be done."

I came off the practice field about 4:30, and there was a fax waiting for me from Mike. We negotiated for a few hours and, in essence, got it done that night. We finalized the way it was structured—or at least agreed to the structure.

I called Herschel in that night. I said, "Herschel, we've done something I think is really going to be good for you, and really good for the Cowboys. You're going to be able to go to a team that has the ability to go to the Super Bowl. We're going to get draft picks, players, et cetera. So both of us are going to come out well."

He was surprised. But I think more than anything, he wanted to get out of my office and call his agent, and that's what he did after staying only a few minutes. Then Jerry talked to Herschel's agent to make sure they were satisfied. We didn't want Herschel to balk at the trade. We wanted the publicity to be as positive as possible—if any positive publicity was possible.

Before the deal was signed, I had to rope-a-dope the media a little bit while the rumors were flying. This time they came up with a fresh gripe about me—that I'd lied to them. I didn't lie. One reporter made a statement intended as a question: "We understand that you are trading Herschel Walker to the Minnesota Vikings for Joey Browner, several other players, and draft picks."

"That is not true," I said. And it wasn't. Joey Browner was not part of the deal. Issiac Holt, David Howard, Darrin Nelson, Jesse Solomon and Alex Stewart were. But not Joey Browner. Oh, looking back, I guess it wasn't right to mislead the media that way. But I did not lie. I do not lie. The guy should have done his homework better and phrased his question more accurately. I kind of enjoy little mind games like that.

But what I enjoy even more is doing a deal. When people make a trade they always think they're getting more than they're giving. Mike Lynn actually thought he was getting the better end of the deal because he thought he was getting a player that was going to take him to the Super Bowl. And he was giving away—the way it was structured—some old, brokendown players and a couple of draft picks. As the years have passed since that deal, Mike Lynn has caught a lot of grief for doing it. It would turn out as a disaster for the Vikings for years to come, and a bonanza for the Cowboys. But at the time it was just the opposite. Mike truly thought he'd gotten a great deal. And virtually everybody else thought he'd pulled off a masterstroke on an idiot named Jimmy Johnson.

Here's the part nobody else, including Mike Lynn, figured out at the time: With the lone exception of Issiac Holt, who remained with us through the Super Bowl season of 1992–93, all the Vikings we brought to Dallas were essentially straw men, disguising what I really wanted.

On paper, on the surface, on October 12, 1989, the trade looked lopsided in Minnesota's favor: We traded Herschel Walker to the Vikings for a first-round draft choice in 1992. In addition, we got the five above-mentioned players. After reading that far in the press release, the media folks went ballistic.

BUT: Each of those five players was attached to a "conditional" draft choice or choices. By conditional draft choice, I mean that if we cut one of the old Minnesota players, we would get a predetermined draft choice from Minnesota instead. If we kept the player, we would not get the draft pick. Here's an example of how it would work: If veteran Alex Stewart, coming from the Vikings, didn't work out at Dallas and we cut him, then we would get a second-round pick in 1990. If we kept Alex Stewart, we wouldn't get that second-round pick in 1990. Each of the five veterans had a specific round and year for a conditional draft pick attached to his name. If any of them were not on the Cowboys roster as of February 1, 1990, Dallas would receive the corresponding draft choice or choices.

These conditional picks, if exercised, added up to a bonanza: first- and second-round choices in both 1990 and 1991, and first-, second-, and third-round choices in 1992.

Mike put a stipulation in the agreement that would prevent me from cutting the veterans, collecting the draft picks, and then re-signing the veterans. And we would not get the draft picks if we traded the veterans. To counter, we stipulated that if we cut the veterans, Mike couldn't sign them back on at Minnesota.

Mike, the media, and the public all made precisely the same mistake: They figured that I was so shorthanded that I'd have to keep all the old Minnesota players. And it was true that I intended to give all of them a thorough look. But it was also true that they would have to be spectacular, almost beyond the realm of possibility, to keep me from cutting them. Bringing them in was essentially a formality. I wanted the draft picks.

To follow our example of Alex Stewart, he turned out to be a lazy player with whom I immediately did not hit it off. I cut him and got the second-round pick instead. And that pick became part of a complex parlay of trading which would eventually allow us to move up in the order of the first round of 1990, and draft a fellow named Emmitt Smith.

As it turned out, instead of giving up a couple of picks and some brokendown players, Mike gave away a bunch of picks and a couple of so-so players. And Herschel never got him to the Super Bowl. Again, Herschel Walker is not a great football player. Let's put it this way, from the perspective of the years since: Herschel Walker is no Emmitt Smith. But in exchange for Herschel Walker and exercising those draft-choice options, I would eventually get Emmitt Smith. And Russell Maryland. And Kevin Smith. You might have noticed them in prominent roles in Super Bowl XXVII. And I got others.

The trade itself is mind-boggling. Nowadays, everybody talks about "The Trade." But if we hadn't taken the right players with those picks—if I had picked Joe Doe instead of Emmitt Smith—then it wouldn't have been a very good trade. The Los Angeles Rams, for example, got a very similar deal to ours when they traded Eric Dickerson to the Indianapolis Colts. But the Rams didn't use their picks well enough, and have been worse off since they traded Dickerson than they were before.

So at the time, with nothing showing on the table but a bunch of old Viking players and/or a few empty numbers on a sheet of paper, we had enough doubters to fill Texas Stadium. When I announced the trade and called it "The Great Train Robbery" in our favor, the media people just about hooted me out of Valley Ranch.

Then they blistered their keyboards. Here are samples:

Randy Galloway, Dallas *Morning News:* "The Vikings got Herschel Walker. The Cowboys got nothing more than a huge handful of Minnesota smoke. And who knows if there'll ever be any fire.

"Love that steal for Minnesota. See you in the end zone, Herschel. See you later, Dallas. Much later."

Frank Luksa, Dallas *Times-Herald:* "As the Cowboys continue their purge of treasured landmarks, the blessing is that they do not own John Neely Bryan's cabin. Else it, too, would be traded, probably for a bag of beans and a cow to be named later.

"Herschel Walker, the team's only offensive link with credibility, has joined the list of former Cowboys who by now outnumber present Cowboys. He was dealt Thursday to the Minnesota Vikings for five players named Joe and an assortment of draft choices."

Of the Jerry Jones–Jimmy Johnson regime, he concluded, "Turn out the lights. The party's over before anyone popped a top."

At least one person outside the Cowboys organization sniffed what I was up to.

Blackie Sherrod, Dallas *Morning News:* "There will be those saying the Jaybirds got taken like a couple of rubes at the carnival. But here again, there is suspicion there is more to the trade than the announced face value—five players and a No. 1 draft choice. Ah, there's the rub.

"We must wait to see if those five new players perform up to Jimmy Johnson's standards over the remainder of the season. If not, that may be where 'conditional draft choices' enter the picture.

". . . So the humble suggestion here is that the Jaybirds had to trade Mr. Walker—the sooner the better or watch his value decrease and, in the case of injury, vanish altogether. Whether they made a profit will not be immediately apparent. Like one detective said to the other on a stakeout: 'Might as well loosen our belts and get comfortable. We're gonna be here a while.' "

Blackie got the picture even better than two insiders, two key offensive coaches, Jerry Rhome and David Shula. They were very much against the trade. Both coaches had been with me such a short time that they just didn't know me very well. But neither did the Dallas public nor the American public in general.

Without that trade, I cannot say that we would now have a 1993 Super Bowl trophy on the table. And so if you ask, regarding the revival of America's Team, the standard question coaches get after games, "What was the turning point?" I would have to say it came on that early October jog with my crew.

But turning points are always determined in retrospect, and only if you've followed through thoroughly. All I've illustrated to you so far is that I'm a pretty fair commodities futures broker. But even after I obtained the hot commodities, Emmitt Smith, Russell Maryland, Kevin Smith, et al., I still could have botched the job, especially if I had treated those guys like commodities after they got to Dallas.

So the turning point only begins to tell you how we turned the thing around. As Winston Churchill told the British people after the North Africa campaign was won in 1942, it was not the beginning of the end, but it was the end of the beginning.

My crew, my old crew, from Miami, and Jerry Jones and I knew, at the moment we traded Herschel Walker, that the turn was then inevitable, that the beginning was ending. But nobody else knew or believed, because nobody else knew me. As I told the *New York Times* business writer in January 1993, I cannot hand you a 1-2-3-4-5 outline for success. It is not that simple. And it is a helluva lot more interesting than some instant formula from some hustler who claims he's going to make you a millionaire with easy steps 1-2-3-4-5.

How we did it in Dallas is inseparable from life experiences. It has to do with where I'm coming from, what I've been through, what I've learned, and most of all, the very careful ways in which I treat people. So to borrow from Blackie's detective, we might as well get comfortable. We're gonna be here a while.

V

PORT ARTHUR

You could say I owe it all to a guy called Bet-a-Million Gates. Without him, there might not have been a Jimmy Johnson. Or a Janis Joplin, or a Big Bopper, or a Tex Ritter—all of us out of Port Arthur. Certainly there would not have been the paradoxical environment (half-pious, half-hell-raising; shady-street respectable, seaport-exotic) that made us all what we became.

As for the whole state of Texas, it probably would have gotten rich anyway. But Bet-a-Million and his crowd gave it—well, you might say a vast version of the Herschel Walker trade—its jump start. Prior to 1901, Pennsylvania was the center of what little "lamp oil," petroleum, industry the United States had. Then the first Texas wildcatters hit the state's first gusher at Spindletop near Port Arthur, which was then a small railroad terminus on Sabine Lake near the Gulf of Mexico. Along came John W. Gates, to bet a million on the development of Port Arthur as a major deepwater port, wagering that someday, lamp oil would be a hot enough commodity worldwide for a need to ship it out of Texas. Bet-a-Million died in 1911, too soon to see World War I and its new mechanized, petroleum-fed warfare begin to prove him right.

Then came Model-T Fords and more gushers to feed them, and tankers to transport the crude. And there arose, over the decades, the industry that would make the state of Texas rich enough to have professional sports franchises such as the Dallas Cowboys, and make an Arkansas-born wildcatter named Jerry Jones rich enough to buy such a franchise. All of this probably would have happened without Bet-a-Million. But without him, the Cowboys of today very likely would be coached by someone other than Jimmy Johnson. I would have been born in Arkansas, if at all, and I probably would have been a different person than what I am.

Into the teeming Port Arthur of 1942 came young C.W. and Allene Johnson of Clarksville, Arkansas. World War II's thirst for petroleum had Port Arthur booming. Daddy immediately went to work at the Gulf Oil refinery and he, Mother, and my older brother Wayne, then two years old, settled in. Daddy had a brother and a sister who'd already migrated to Port Arthur. (And so, even growing up in Texas, I would hear no talk of football that didn't involve the Arkansas Razorbacks, from my earliest memories.) I was born on July 16, 1943. By the time I was six, Daddy had had enough of the refinery and went to work at Townsend Dairy, which provided him with a "company house," where I grew up.

He could walk out the back door and right into the dairy building where he supervised milk-packaging and ice cream–making. Not a bad job for a daddy to have. Wayne and I could walk out the front door onto DeQueen Boulevard, wide with a grassy median, nicely suited for pickup football games.

Port Arthur was segregated in those days, and the major black community was a couple of miles away from the corner of DeQueen and

Procter where we lived. But there were some black families in our area. I couldn't tell you when Baby Joe and I.E. became part of our pickup football games. It seemed they'd always been there. I'll always remember them simply as Baby Joe and I.E. You didn't learn other kids' last names until you got to school. I didn't know why Baby Joe and I.E. didn't go to DeQueen Elementary. That was before I realized there was such a thing as prejudice, or that anybody felt that way.

After fourth grade I got my first summer job, working for Daddy at the dairy. There were black and Mexican ladies working there. I rode a delivery truck as a route helper with a Cajun named Blackie. Ethnic interaction was so normal to me that I didn't actively think about it. Other than school hours, I associated with minorities all the time— afternoons, weekends, summers. And nothing negative was ever said or done.

It wasn't until I got older that I started hearing about prejudice. And by that time I had my mindset and my feelings. After I got to Thomas Jefferson High School, which was all-white, I would snap at anyone who made a prejudiced remark. Mostly it would come in the form of derogatory jokes, and I didn't understand why anybody would polk fun at anyone because they had different-colored skin.

Thirty years removed from Port Arthur, when the Cowboys played the Houston Oilers in 1991, I got to the Astrodome three hours early and was walking the field when I heard someone hollering from the edge of the stands, "Hey, Coach!" I tried to ignore it. If you walk over to the stands before a game, people will flock for autographs and just keep flocking, and it's hard to break away. But this guy kept yelling, "Hey, Coach! Hey, Coach!" From the corner of my eye I saw a black guy about my age. I kind of smiled and waved and looked back toward the field. Then he hollered, "Hey, Jimmy! It's Baby Joe!" I grinned and headed straight for him. What a moment. It was a name I hadn't heard since sixth grade, but a reminder of the freedom I was granted on DeQueen Boulevard, freedom from ethnic hangups. I met Baby Joe's wife, but I.E. wasn't there. Baby Joe said I.E. is a preacher now. Good. Maybe I.E. has been forgiven for putting scars on my head in street ball. Of those scars, some are the work of I.E., some from Baby Joe, some from Wayne and some from a white kid who joined our pickup games at about age 11, Jimmy Maxfield.

Maxfield and I became best friends as we began playing organized football together in the seventh grade. We would remain best friends through high school, and he would lead, and sometimes follow, me into a whole other form of, shall we say, cultural enlightenment. It led to something of a double life throughout my adolescence. My mother tells people to this day that "Jimmy was just a sweet lil' ol' boy who never gave us any trouble." My brother Wayne tells people, "Jimmy was a pretty good con artist. Probably still is."

Port Arthur in its day, our day, was an average, quiet American town on one end, and a very exotic place on the other. At one end of Procter Street, the main drag, lived the hard-working, church-going, everyday people. At the other end of Procter, down toward the docks, stood the whorehouses, the casinos, the brawling saloons, all catering to the merchant seamen who put into port from around the world. De-Queen bisected Procter, and we could get to the bad end as quickly as the good end.

Schoolwork came easy for Maxfield and me, so by sundown we were usually cruising Procter. Like most teenage boys of the 1950s, our fancies on those cruises turned to beer and girls. Texas had a legal drinking age of twenty-one. As we got a little older, we could drive "across the river," as we called it, into Louisiana where if you were fifteen and looked sixteen you could pass for eighteen, which was the legal drinking age over there. But early on, we found a hometown haven for beer-drinkers: the whorehouses.

There were eight or nine of them, and they sold beer, and they never questioned our age. Maxfield's daddy was in the oilfield pipe business, and some of the roughnecks who worked for him used to frequent the whorehouses, and helped us gain entree when we were fourteen or fifteen. The owners wouldn't let us go upstairs, but the parlors were great places for us to hang out and drink beer and look around—look at women who had very few clothes on. They would sit on our laps and kid around with us. The roughnecks and the whores thought we were pretty funny. As for the merchant seamen, hell, they'd seen everything, all over the world, so they probably didn't pay us any mind.

We started taking groups of our friends with us. Now, so many years later, Max has screwed up by telling people that we had a thriving little business, charging the other boys a quarter each to take them on tours of the bordellos. Well, *he* might have been charging them, but if he was, he was cheating me. He wasn't giving me my fair share. (That reminds me of a story—and this is awful—about two guys I knew years later at the University of Arkansas. They would hang out at a place called the Shamrock Club and pick up girls, and when the girls would go to the bathroom, these guys would take the money out of the girls' purses and split it. One night they were having a helluva time and two girls got in the car with them to go to another joint. One guy's driving and the girl in the front seat suddenly says, "Oh! Somebody took forty dollars out of my purse!" And the guy in the back seat says, "Richard, you sonofabitch, ya cheated me.")

It took me thirty-five years to find out, but Maxfield, ya sonofabitch, you cheated me on the whorehouse deal.

The really elite place of them all was called Marcella's. It was a little more restrictive than the others. One night Maxfield had too much to drink, and I think he might have wanted to go upstairs, and they wouldn't let him. He went outside and got a tire tool and proceeded to tear out their screen doors. The bouncers tracked him down and caught him, and made him come back up there to talk to the owner. Needless to say, Maxfield was scared shitless. The guy let him go because he was so afraid. But the incident almost ruined our nice little beer-drinking parties.

What did finally end the parties was this: One night I had a carload of guys and we were going down the main drag whooping it up, and Daddy was sitting on our front porch just a half block off Procter. He saw us and decided to follow us. We went into one of the bordellos and had a few beers, and when we walked out, Maxfield saw this car sitting in the street, idling. Maxfield said, "Jimmy! I think that's your dad's car!" I looked and said, "Oh, shit! That *is* my dad's car."

I walked out to the car. Daddy just looked at me, and then at Maxfield and the rest. "Boys," he said, "don't come to me if you need any shots." He didn't say another word. Just drove away.

Daddy could get your attention with a look and a line like that. He wasn't big on the belt. Didn't have to be. Once, though, my little sister, Lynda, and I were arguing over some leftover beans after supper, and I sort of popped her one. Lynda made a big deal out of it, as if her nose were bleeding. Daddy had his house slippers on, and took one off and popped me a few times on the back. It didn't hurt, but it left red footprints. When I took off my shirt in the football locker room the next day, one of the guys said, "Uh huh! The old man finally had enough of your act and knocked you down and *stomped* on you, didn't he?"

Port Arthur lay so close to the Louisiana line that the Texas Protestant reserve was spiced by the fun-loving, French-Catholic culture of the Cajuns—the "Coon-asses." (And that is not an ethnic slur; that is what they proudly call themselves. I'm not sure of the derivation, but the term may come from their centuries-old tradition of trapping in the swamps. Texas ladies refuse to use the term. My mother will say of someone, "She's French," and my sister Lynda might say, "She's a Coonie." But Louisiana ladies will tell you, "Ah'm a Coon-ass and proud of it.") Both geographical proximity and the oil economy—oil had been discovered in abundance in Louisiana in the 1930s—led to a back-and-forth migration. The old saying goes that "You're not a full-blooded Coon-ass until you've been to Poht Ahthuh twice." For every Johnson and Maxfield in the phone book, there was a Thibodaux and a Fontenot, and an Hebert and a Dupuis.

And so in a Port Arthur teenager's diet, there was more gumbo, crawfish, jambalaya, and boudin than there was barbecue and Tex-Mex. Especially boudin. To this day I can just about eat my weight in boudin, which is a sort of spicy rice concoction stuffed into sausage skins. The Cajuns came to Texas to work and open businesses, and we went into Louisiana to party.

On weekends there was mass migration "across the river," as we called crossing the Neches and Sabine rivers into Louisiana. If you were fifteen it was a lot harder to pass for twenty-one in Texas than to pass for eighteen across the river. In the high school corridors on Fridays, the most common question was, "Y'all going across the river this weekend?" On the Louisiana side there were all sorts of roadhouses and honky-tonks with live bands: pop, rock 'n' roll, Cajun, rhythm and blues, country. The Port Arthur area has produced an inordinate number of singers and musicians, from J.C. "The Big Bopper" Richardson who was older than us, to Janis Joplin, who was a year ahead of us in school, to the currently popular young Harry Connick Jr. The only explanation I can offer is the years of "across the river" weekends, when they were all exposed to such a wide variety of music.

Janis Lyn Joplin ran with what we called, in the late 1950s, the beatnik crowd. She wore black leotards, dark glasses, the whole bit. Her crowd was, to say the least, anti-jock. Our crowd was made up of jocks—most played several sports, not just football—and the cheerleaders and majorettes who hung out with us and wore our letter jackets. In the beatnik crowd there were rumors of marijuana and other drugs. Just rumors. I don't know. Beer was the only thing my crowd ever touched, so we didn't associate with the beatniks.

Janis looked and acted so weird that when we were around her, mostly in the hallways at school, we would give her a hard time. One of my football teammates nicknamed her "Beat Weeds." Beat was for beatnik. Weeds came to have an overall connotation of her disheveled, stringy appearance. But in the beginning "weeds" had a meaning rooted in the jock vernacular of Southeast Texas. Put it this way: In other areas of the country, she might have been known as "Beat Bush."

In Max's and my junior year, we had a history class that was required for graduation. Janis, a senior, had apparently put off taking the required course (she was bigger on art classes and that sort of thing). So by alphabetical order, Joplin sat behind Johnson in the history class. As I would take my seat, I might say, "Hey, Beat Weeds." And she would give me this haughty stare and sort of toss her head and look away. She graduated that spring of 1960, and we would never see each other again.

(Years later, when I was at the University of Arkansas and Maxfield was at the University of Texas, Max, whose sister had been friends with

Janis, said on the phone, "Hey, have you heard about Janis? She's the hottest singer in America." I said, "You mean Beat Weeds? Hell, I didn't even know she could sing." Then more years later, when she overdosed on drugs and died, nobody let me know. I just heard about it, somewhere along the line. I eventually bought some of her albums and listened to them. Her music was interesting, but not the kind of thing I would listen to on a regular basis.)

Buckshot Underwood was renowned as one of the best football coaches in the state of Texas. He won every year. Year in, year out, he was in the playoffs. It was almost unheard-of in those days, but Buckshot's Thomas Jefferson High School Yellow Jackets would draw between 15,000 and 20,000 people to their games. He had coached under Bear Bryant during Bryant's formative, tough-guy years at Kentucky, and they remained big buddies after Bryant moved to Texas A&M and then Alabama. When I was a little boy, my Daddy would go to those Jefferson High games and, although I didn't know it at the time, dream that his boys might just make the team. That was all he asked. Just that Wayne and/or I could dress out in the colors of the TJ Jackets and sit on the bench. That alone, Daddy promised himself, would make him happy.

By the time I started playing junior high football in the seventh grade, Wayne was in the tenth grade but hadn't made Buckshot's team. Daddy was always on Wayne about why he wasn't playing. Wayne said, "Buckshot just doesn't like me."

Daddy said, "Is it your grades?"

Wayne said, "Nah! My grades are fine." He showed Daddy his report card and it was all B's.

Daddy said, "I don't understand this. I'm going up there and find out why Buckshot's got it in for Wayne."

The principal said, "Well, Mr. Johnson, your son's grades are not good enough for him to be on the team. He just hasn't put enough effort into his school work."

Daddy said, "But he's got all B's."

The principal said, "Wait a minute. I don't think so."

It turned out that Wayne had changed his grades on his report card. Wayne was an outstanding athlete. He wound up as an all-state catcher in baseball, and Buckshot eventually told Daddy that maybe one athlete like Wayne came out of TJ every ten years or so. But the grades. Wayne just didn't care about school.

Wayne was into beer-drinking, hanging around, girls, and fast cars that he worked on himself. He was a little more mischievous than I was. And on top of being more mischievous, he got caught more often. That probably stemmed from the differences in our performance in school.

I was into beer-drinking, hanging around, girls, school, and football. I enjoyed school. Taking tests was fun to me. Academics came easy for me, throughout high school and college. I didn't spend a lot of time on it. My high school teachers used to talk to me about "your high IQ," and they'd get irritated because they wanted me to spend more time on academics than what I did. I never put much stock in IQs. First, I never actually had an individualized Stanford-Binet test. I only had standardized tests in the Port Arthur school system. Second, it didn't make any difference to me how high my IQ was, because I enjoyed studying people more than textbooks. Some of the most intelligent people in the world have a difficult time dealing with people. I was, and still am, always wondering what people are thinking. To me, dealing with people has always been a far better and more enjoyable learning experience than cramming for a test.

So I would hit—more accurately, glance off—the books just long enough to keep my grades good. That meant studying the material the night before a test, or writing a term paper the night before it was due. That worked just fine for me.

Football, I worked at. Clarence "Buckshot" Underwood, disciple of Bear Bryant, wouldn't have it any other way, no matter how much natural talent a player had. Buckshot was renowned not only for winning, but for hard-nosed, grind-it-out, physical football. He set firmly in my mind the ethic of true discipline. And we were rewarded for it. Every year, we were in the playoffs.

I was an offensive lineman and linebacker. In the tenth grade, on an offensive play, I got a front tooth knocked out. We were beginning to wear those old one-bar facemasks, but we didn't wear mouth guards. I looked on the ground and there lay my tooth, right in front of me. I picked it up and trotted toward the sideline, holding the tooth up so Buckshot could see it.

When I got to the sideline, Buckshot said, "Yeah, I see it, Johnson. Now get your ass back in there. We'll buy you another tooth."

That was in the days before coaches learned all the physics and kinesiology of using the hands and arms and shoulders for leverage. Under Buckshot, we used that ferocious, macho weapon known throughout Southern football as "the forearm." It was essentially a euphemism for an elbow to the chops, and nothing quite intimidated an opposing lineman like the knowledge that the guy across from him had a horrendous "forearm."

The macho thing to do on our team was to forearm everything in sight, on and off the field. In the summertime, working for Daddy at the dairy to earn money to buy my cars, I would do two things constantly. I would wear lead weights strapped to my ankles all day long, to improve my foot-quickness and speed. And I would forearm things. Instead of pushing the heavy doors at the dairy plant open, I would forearm them open.

My good grades, and my obvious dedication to disciplined football, probably went a long way toward giving Mother and Daddy the idea that I had some sort of halo around my head. I really was a good kid overall, especially at home. I never lied to them. But there were some things they never asked about. Until the night I threw one too many forearms.

Maxfield claims I used to forearm the bodywork of an automobile about once a week just to keep my hand in. It wasn't that often, but it did happen upon occasion. One night I'd had too much to drink, and this girl drove by the place where we were hanging out. Wayne knew her. I *wanted* to know her. I was standing beside her car trying to talk to her. We got crossways somehow, and out of irritation I forearmed the door of her car. Wham! Put a big dent in it. She got all upset and drove away.

I went home and went to bed. Within minutes the phone was ringing. Daddy answered. It was the girl's daddy. And he was really upset. After Daddy and Mother learned that I'd forearmed the car, they called me to the phone to apologize. If you've ever been a teenager up to the gills in beer, and gone to bed, and then had to get up, you can imagine how I felt. I staggered to the phone.

I couldn't even get the word "Hello" out without beginning to lose my stomach. After that the only sounds I could make to the girl's daddy were, "Aaaaagggg! Aaaaagggg!"

Daddy took it reasonably well, under the circumstances, considering that neither he nor Mother drank at all. Mother, on the other hand, had never had a clue that I'd ever touched a drop of alcohol. And so she went into the living room, sat down and began to cry bigtime. She was growing hysterical.

Luckily for me, at that point good old, poor old, Wayne, the family's known offender, walked in. Daddy turned toward him and said, "Oh! You're the one! You got Jimmy drunk!"

Wayne hadn't even seen me out that night, before I forearmed the car. After that, because he knew the girl, he'd tried to smooth things over with her. Then he'd come home. I didn't lie to them. They just assumed that Wayne had got me drunk, because I was so rarely bad. And, well, I guess I let them keep on assuming. So when my brother calls me a con artist, he says it not with malice but with a certain sincerity.

Buckshot Underwood wasn't a bad con artist himself, and one of his con jobs almost left me with a federal-offense record. Really. Buckshot announced to the team, as if he were doing us a big favor, that we were going to spend a big weekend at the beach house of one of Buckshot's doctor friends, over at Smith Point on Galveston Bay. About fifteen of us bit. What we got was a weekend of hard manual labor. Buckshot's doctor buddy, who was a big supporter of the Jefferson High football program, had an erosion problem around his beach house. Our dream weekend was to build him a new sea wall by sinking sections of telephone poles in the sand to support hundreds of huge chunks of concrete. We would obtain these materials at the site where the state construction crews had recently torn up an old concrete highway—not asphalt, but concrete. I mean, these chunks were boulders.

The highway site was about thirty miles from the doctor's beach house. Buckshot's work gang loaded the concrete onto a flatbed truck and off we went, with the players riding in back, on the piles of concrete. Going down the road, some of the players started taking smaller chunks and throwing them at road signs. Hit and miss.

I said, "Aw, bullshit! You guys are throwing these lil' ol' pebbles. I picked up a boulder, and I said, "Now watch this one." I heaved it, and it just tore the hell out of a road sign. Everybody cheered. I said, "Okay, next, we're gonna get mailboxes." So we started tearing the hell out of mailboxes. Other guys would try it, but they weren't nearly as accurate as I was. I just didn't miss. I hit road signs. I hit mailboxes. We left about a twenty-mile trail.

And somewhere back on that trail, one of the boulders rolled back out into the road, in front of a car towing a boat. It tore the hell out of the bottom of the car and turned over the boat. Which, I suppose, is the point at which the highway patrol became involved.

The flatbed truck was half empty when we got to the doctor's cabin, but I don't think Buckshot noticed. He'd been up in the cab, driving, and didn't even know what we'd been doing. We sat down to dinner, which was Buckshot's reward for us. It was one of those big, kind of country-at-the-beach, all-men dinners. Everybody was having a good time, when up rolled these two highway patrol cars.

Maxfield and the whole crew turned their heads and looked at me, and said, "Johnson, you've really got us into it."

Buckshot said, "Oh, shit, Johnson, what have you done now?"

The highway patrolmen said we were easy to find. They'd just followed the path of destruction. They loaded us all up, told us we would be charged with destroying federal property, and took us down and fingerprinted us. Finally Buckshot and the police got it worked out to where if we would all share in the costs of replacing the signs and mailboxes, our records would be expunged.

The other players, Maxfield being the leader, said, "The hell with this share stuff." Maxfield said I had hit more than everybody else, so I should take the bulk of the expense.

I said, "Screw you guys. We'll all share. Just because I hit more doesn't mean I should pay more. Y'all all tried to hit, and it just so happened that I was more accurate." Everybody ended up paying his share.

For all of the above incidents, Buckshot didn't get around to betting me that I would never graduate from high school until Maxfield and I got expelled. We'd had a history of incidents at school—all just minor, just michievous more than anything else—but what sent us over the edge was in fact a very good citizenship move on my part. I was studying the processes of American government, even if my method was a bit anarchistic.

To elect the president of the student body, the school held a mock presidential convention, with the format of the Democratic and Republican national conventions. Each home room was allowed to send only two delegates, and there were some guidelines in picking those delegates that eliminated Maxfield and me. I said, "The hell with this. I'm going to the convention."

So Maxfield and I cut classes and slid right through the security in the auditorium, where the convention was being held. It really was an interesting thing. Everybody holding their signs up, just like Democrats and Republicans. One of our buddies, Lamar Lawson, ended up as president. His father was some kind of county politician and Lamar understood how to go about these things, so he got elected, and we had a helluva good time.

The principal called us to the office the next day and said, "Y'all both expelled from school. For cutting class and crashing the convention."

To re-enroll, Max had to bring his daddy and I had to bring my mother. So much for the halo. That's when Buckshot called me in and said, "Johnson, I'll bet you a steak dinner you don't even graduate." I said, "Coach, you're on."

For all of my carousing, never once, on those mischievous nights and days, had I lost my bearings. Not only was I going to graduate, but I was going to be the first one in my family to go to college. That was a certainty. I had the grades, and I was playing my ass off for Buckshot. I was all-state in football. At the time, the football recruiters from the military academies got to make contact first, because of the extra time it took for them to get congressional appointments to the academies for the players. So I got my first recruiting inquiries from the Air Force Academy, and for a week or two I marched around the house and school, saluting everybody. I even had an interview with a congressman about the appointment. But after studying what academy life was like, I decided it wasn't for me.

I scheduled visits to Texas A&M and TCU. Buckshot said Bryant had called to see if I was interested in visiting Alabama. But when Arkansas came in, that was it. Hands down. All my life, I'd heard "Arkansas Razorbacks" from my parents, uncles, and aunts. Jim MacKenzie was an assistant coach at Arkansas and came down just after the high school season ended. He said, "We're going to offer you a scholarship. We want to set up a visit."

I said, "Coach, I don't need to visit. You say you're offering a scholarship? Okay, I'm coming."

He said, "You've never been to Fayetteville, Arkansas, in your life."

I said, "I don't care. I'm committed. Where do I sign?"

He said, "You can't even sign yet. You have to wait until the proper time."

I said, "Let me know." I didn't even schedule a visit to Alabama, and I canceled the visits to A&M and TCU.

Doug Dickey, later to be head coach at Tennessee and Florida, was a young assistant at Arkansas, and he came down to sign me. It was one of those good old-fashioned, big-deal-in-the-community signings, complete with a picture in the Port Arthur *News*.

That fall, on one of the proudest nights of their lives, C.W. and Allene Johnson drove me to up to Fayetteville.

VI

FAYETTEVILLE

F rank Broyles's Arkansas coaching staff of the early 1960s was a nest of young giants. For example, Arkansas had two pretty fair freshman coaches named Barry Switzer and Fred Akers, future head coaches at the universities of Oklahoma and Texas, respectively. Defensive coordinator Jim MacKenzie would become head coach at Oklahoma before Switzer, but would die suddenly. Doug Dickey was bound to be head coach at Tennessee and then Florida. Hayden Fry would be head coach at SMU, North Texas State, and Iowa. Bill Pace would be head coach at Vanderbilt. And there was Johnny Majors, later head coach at Iowa State, the University of Pittsburgh, and Tennessee.

Twenty-six years later, at a press conference just before his Oklahoma Sooners and my Miami Hurricanes played for the national championship in the Orange Bowl (we kicked their ass, of course), Switzer would be asked if he could remember when he first heard of Jimmy Johnson. "It was," said Switzer, "when Jim MacKenzie told me they'd signed some little old squatty-body lineman out of Port Arthur, Texas."

The early sixties were the heyday of Bear Bryant's "po' lil' ol' boys," who'd knock your jock off, over at Alabama. The trend of the small, strong, quick linemen swept the South. Johnny Vaught, who ran one of the national powerhouses of the time at Ole Miss, maintained that any kid who weighed 225 pounds could play any position on the field. Vaught used to love to sign a truckload of fullbacks and scatter them into various positions. At Arkansas the thinking wasn't much different. In fact, that fall of 1961, Broyles was in the process of switching a 200-pound redshirt freshman fullback named Jerry Jones to the offensive line.

Even for that era, I was small. I played at 195 pounds. (Switzer would one day write in his autobiography that there was no way that Switzer the Arkansas player of the late 1950s could have made Switzer the coach's Oklahoma teams of the seventies and eighties, considering Switzer's size and speed in his youth. In size, certainly, Jimmy Johnson the player could not have made my Miami teams of the eighties. But in speed and quickness, hell, yes, I could have played at Miami—probably at linebacker. I was fast and talented and I have to believe it was genetic, looking at the enormous potential my brother Wayne never chose to fulfill.) Like Bryant's po' lil' ol' boys I was quick as a cat, strong, had the good ferocious forearm, and I was hyper. The Arkansas coaches took to calling me "Smiley" because I was always happy, and "Jimmy Jumpup" because I was always hyper, jumping up immediately, even after I'd been knocked flat. I played both ways: nose guard on defense, and guard on offense. That's where I met Jerry. We were both offensive guards.

Academically, I had no idea what I was going to major in. I enrolled in the college of arts and sciences and took physics, chemistry, and biology, all courses I really liked, as a freshman. They were hardly jock courses. I was in classes with premed majors. I thought I might major in zoology, because I liked the sciences and I liked animals. At age eighteen, even around a lot of uptight premed majors, I was in no way sweating the word "career."

Then came the worst, and the best, and the most formative semester I had in college, the spring semester of my sophomore year. It was the only time I ever flunked a course. I'd gotten to where I was really enjoying college. I would sit in the student union building most of the day playing bridge with what in those days were called eggheads—guys definitely on the opposite extreme of jocks. Really intelligent guys who liked to play bridge for a penny a point. I picked up a few extra bucks playing bridge in the union and got to where I didn't go to class very often unless there was a test, or the course was one I really liked.

I was taking an invertebrate zoology class. I'd hardly been to class all semester. I did go to take the final exam, and made a C. I figured I had a C in the course. I happened to be walking through the biology building one day and noticed the grades posted for that course. Beside "Johnson, James W.," there was an F. So I went to talk to the professor. I said, "What F? I made low Bs and Cs on all my tests."

He said, "Well, Mr. Johnson, you only came to my class to take the tests. You weren't here and I can't give you a passing grade." It was the only failing grade I ever had. It ticked me off and got my attention. I had to have a better game plan for college, in order to, if nothing else, keep the bridge bucks coming.

I was taking an introductory psychology course that same semester. In the psychology department, they did not count class cuts. And I really enjoyed the course. I made up my mind that I was going to take courses I enjoyed. So I switched my major to psychology, because I enjoyed going to class. And, if I wanted to play bridge, I could play bridge. (My decision to major in psychology was also the decision that would eventually make the difference between a good, solid, Xs-and-Os college coach and a national championship coach; between a good, solid NFL coach and a Super Bowl coach. I hadn't a clue of the magnitude at the time. Hell, I had no idea I would end up as a coach.)

That was the same semester the dean of men took my car away.

If you were in college in the sixties, this might bring back memories: In the spring, people would get a big tub and mix up a batch of Purple Passions—you started with grain alcohol and grape juice, and threw in any and every other ingredient you could think of. Well, we were having one helluva time.

My buddy Stan Sparks, who was my roommate, and I were at the epicenter of this particular Purple Passions function. (If, in 1989, Stan Sparks had bought the Dallas Cowboys and made me the coach, *then* the world could have raised some justified hell about a guy buying his old roomie a play pretty.) I had a '56 Ford I'd bought with summer-job money from Townsend Dairy back home. There are sidewalks all through the University of Arkansas campus. They weave not only among the buildings but through the wooded areas. It was such a lovely spring day, Stan and I decided to tour the sidewalks, by car. I jumped the curb and away we went. The dean of men didn't appreciate that. So he took the keys to my car.

Which was but a minor inconvenience. I had just started dating a girl from eastern Arkansas, over by the Mississippi River near Memphis, Tennessee. She had her own car, so I simply began driving hers.

It was a tradition in the South for campus beauties to participate in ROTC as "sponsors." They wore cute little uniforms and marched along with the companies on drill days. I was in Air Force ROTC. Linda Kay Cooper of Marked Tree, Arkansas, was in "Angel Flight." I saw her on a drill day. I didn't know her. But I called her up and asked her for a date. I think she did some checking around to find out who in the world I was. My references must have checked out, because we went out on a date. I spent lavishly. Football players had special passes that got us into the drive-in movie free. Our guests were charged twenty-five cents. I took Linda Kay Cooper, campus beauty and star of Angel Flight, to the drive-in. For a quarter.

I must have impressed her with my mind. She definitely impressed me with hers. I just never had been the type to go for airhead girls, no matter how pretty. Linda Kay was pretty and smart and sophisticated and dignified—just my type. We got married that summer, and moved into an off-campus apartment.

Jerry Jones was a year older than me, and a year ahead academically, but since he had redshirted his freshman year, we had the same amount of football eligibility left. Jerry also got married as an undergraduate to one of Linda Kay's sorority sisters. Gene was also a campus beauty. We all settled into the realities of married-student life, and so Jerry and I were friendly neighbors in Fayetteville, and roommates on football Friday nights. But Jerry and I came from very different backgrounds. Jerry's family was already well-to-do. His father, J.W. "Pat" Jones, was a successful entrepreneur in supermarkets and insurance. Jerry had always known plenty of money. Linda Kay and I supported ourselves, she by teaching school after our first year of marriage, and I later on by going home in the summers to work in the Port Arthur shipyards.

After a couple of years in psychology, I got to thinking: What was I going to do to make a living? It was difficult to do much with a psychology degree other than teach, and I didn't want to teach. I realized I would have to go an extra step: I planned to get a master's degree in psychology and then go to work for some company as an industrial psychologist. Such specialists evaluate the personalities and aptitudes of employees, develop ways to teach them their jobs more efficiently, and generally try to keep them happy on the job. Any good CEO knows that such corporate caring makes the company more efficient and profitable. (And so does any good football coach, though again, I wasn't at all thinking in terms of coaching. I hadn't hit on the right job yet, but I was definitely on the right track: making people happy, making people fit into a plan, making people proficient and efficient.)

The Razorbacks of 1964 went 11–0, beat Nebraska in the Cotton Bowl, and won the national championship. You won't find us ranked No. 1 in the final AP and UPI standings, because that was the last year the wire services took their final polls prior to the bowl games. But by today's criteria, we were national champions hands down. Alabama, featuring Joe Namath, was voted into the national championship before losing in the Orange Bowl to Texas, a team we had beaten in regular season. The national championship awards that weren't locked up before the bowls, the Grantland Rice and MacArthur Bowl trophies, went to Arkansas.

We beat Texas in a thriller at Austin, and I made the crucial play of the game. We'd gone up 14–7 on a punt return, but Texas had come back to score a late touchdown, and was lining up to try a two-point conversion to win the game. When we saw that they'd taken out Ernie Coy, their big running back, we anticipated a pass. I moved out to linebacker in coverage, but it was a sprint-out pass so I rushed the quarterback, forced an incompletion, and we won, 14–13.

We had five games left after the Texas game, and went on to shut out every opponent. In the Cotton Bowl, Nebraska had an even more massive offensive line than usual. That was my last game in a uniform, and I got flattened on the first play, but went on to have an excellent game, with twelve tackles. Considering the size differential between me and the Nebraska blockers, I will always consider that my career game.

That was the first season of free substitution in the NCAA, so I had stopped playing both ways and gone strictly to defense. Our overall defensive performance, plus my work against Texas and Nebraska, were probably why I was voted All-Southwest Conference nose guard that season, and later named to the All-Decade team of the 1960s at Arkansas.

I got my first taste of the concept of winning it all—at least, everything within our power. With the success of the team, and the personal accolades, I thought, "Now that's the way to end a playing career." I was too small for the NFL, and so it was time to think about finding a job and going to work.

The Hogs' season-long onslaught of 1964 drew the attention of a lot of other coaching staffs, particularly in the South and Southwest, to our defensive scheme, nationally known as the "Arkansas Monster Slide Defense." It was a 3–4 defense that stunted to, in essence, a wide-tackle 6 with an 8-man front. During my senior year, coaching staffs from other schools would visit Fayetteville to talk defense, and as a professional courtesy, the Arkansas staff would let them sit in on our meetings.

One day at such a meeting, there were representatives from several other staffs. I didn't know it then, but some Louisiana Tech people had come in from Ruston. For some reason, MacKenzie decided to send me, rather than one of the assistant coaches, to the blackboard to explain our defense—our style of defense, what everybody played and what everybody did—to the visiting coaches. It was an insignificant meeting, I thought, at the time.

That summer I went back to Port Arthur and worked as a welder's helper at Burton Shipyard, to make some money for graduate school and to help support our little family, which now included toddler Brent. In Port Arthur, I got a phone call from Jim MacKenzie, asking if I'd be interested in coaching the next semester at Louisiana Tech. It seemed those coaches had been impressed with the way a squatty-body lineman understood and could teach the entire Arkansas defensive scheme.

George Dougherty, Louisiana Tech's defensive coordinator, recently had suffered a heart attack. His doctors told him he should be fine, if he would take one season off from coaching to recuperate. Louisiana Tech certainly wanted George back for the long haul, but they had to find a replacement for him for the season of 1965. They wouldn't be able to hire an established coach for such an interim job. And, they ran the Arkansas Monster Slide Defense and needed someone who knew our system.

They said they'd pay me one thousand dollars a month for three months, and give me a courtesy car and an apartment. One thousand dollars a month, in 1965! I said, "Hey, I'll be there."

So here was our plan: Linda Kay and Brent would stay in Fayetteville, where she was teaching school, and I would go down to Ruston, make the quick three thousand, and hightail it back to Fayetteville. And we would be all set for me to finish graduate school and become an industrial psychologist. We had our lives all mapped out.

Yeah. Right.

VII

THE TRENCHES

I got my three thousand bucks out of Ruston. And I got three months of revelation. In coaching, I could apply all the formal psychology training and all the informal people skills that James William Johnson, industrial psychologist, could ever hope to apply. Plus, my knack for Xs and Os and my love of the game wouldn't go to waste. Plus, I began to develop some new defensive concepts of my own. I began to wonder why, for example, defensive linemen were always coached to wait and read the offensive blocks before taking action. Why weren't they attacking, right from the snap? Why was defense so defensive? Why couldn't defense be offensive? In coaching, I could innovate.

I'd had a taste of it. I decided, "This is what I want to do."

I went back to Fayetteville in the spring of 1966 as a graduate assistant on Broyles's staff, and began looking around for a fulltime coaching job. With the connections that Broyles, MacKenzie, Switzer, Majors, and Co. had around the nation, Arkansas had what you might call an excellent job-placement system for young coaches in the sixties. Bill Peterson called from Florida State, and I went to Tallahassee and had an interview with him. Bill indicated that I was going to get the job. FSU was just beginning to come into football prominence, and it looked like something of a ground-floor opportunity, so I put a lot of stock in going to Tallahassee. But the situation dragged on . . . it still seems like forever . . . all summer . . . and I never could get an answer. Finally, Peterson called and said he'd decided to hire another guy who had more experience.

So I was stuck without a job. Johnny Majors told me about an opening in Picayune, Mississippi. He'd coached at Mississippi State for four years and knew virtually every high school coach in the state. He said, "They need an assistant down there at the high school. It's down in South Mis'ippi (when you've coached in Mis'ippi, you pronounce it like the natives do), and I know the head coach. Guy by the name of Frank Skipper."

I said, "Fine." I called Frank Skipper. He hired me on the phone. I loaded up Linda Kay and Brent and all our belongings in a U-Haul trailer and drove to Picayune, Mis'ippi. Frank was the head coach, a guy named Buck Kennedy ran the offense, and I ran the defense. That was the coaching staff.

The very first day, I was riding with Frank in his car down the only main street. I said, "How'd y'all do last year?"

He said, "Oh, you don't know?"

I said, "No."

He said, "Well, you might say, in some ways, that we had a perfect record."

I said, "What do you mean, a perfect record?"

He said, "We didn't win a single game last year. In fact, Picayune hasn't won a game in a couple of years."

In the fall of 1966, Mississippi high school football was in its last hurrah. Soon it would disintegrate because of lingering resistance to desegregation. Diehard segregationists would open dozens of private academies, completely fragmenting both education and football.

But when I got there, Picayune was the smallest school in the most powerful division of what was then a strong high school football system. Mississippi in those days churned out enough players to keep Ole Miss a national power, and to provide extra blue-chippers to augment the might of Alabama and LSU.

Now then: With all my, hrrrumph, expertise in coaching, we came *close* to winning a game in my season there. It was the season-opener against Ocean Springs. They were a division below us, and that's why we thought we might have a chance. But they turned out to be one of the best teams in that lower division, and beat us. After that, when we started playing Biloxi, Moss Point, and all that crew, they just killed us. We didn't win a game. Our ten losses were the most I would suffer through, in a single season, until I got to the Dallas Cowboys in 1989.

And I got into a little scrape at Picayune High. I didn't have a teacher's license and the budget didn't provide for a fulltime coach. I had to do some other duty to justify being on the payroll. So they got me a temporary certification so that I could keep study hall. They said I didn't have to do anything other than keep the kids quiet.

It was a big study hall, and I would sit up at the front, going over defensive schemes on paper. And if anybody talked, I'd call them up to the front and give them a paddling. If anybody even acted like they were going to talk, I'd paddle them. Boys or girls. I didn't discriminate. It got so that if I so much as pointed to them and motioned them to the front, the girls would start crying.

(I have since wondered if any of the graduates of Picayune High School, Class of '67, ever read or heard any of the media accounts in the 1980s wherein I was accused of being lax on discipline. They would have gotten a pretty good laugh out of that.)

One day I was called to the principal's office. This lady was waiting for me, upset, because, she said, I had put welts on her daughter's rear end. The matter upset me because I'd been doing what the principal had asked me to do, which was keep them quiet. And the principal had said it was okay to paddle them.

In the meeting with the mother, the principal wasn't too upset, and pretty soon everybody calmed down. But I thought then and there, "I'm not cut out for this." If I'd had to stay at Picayune and keep study hall, I'd have been back in industrial psychology the next year.

Fortunately, Switzer called. He'd had a helluva time locating me. "They need a defensive line coach at Wichita State," he said. "They can only pay six thousand dollars a year. You interested?"

"Who do I talk to?" I said.

The Arkansas network got me out of Picayune. Switzer's longtime buddy, Larry Lacewell, had just taken the job as defensive coordinator at Wichita. Head coach Boyd Converse had assigned Lacewell to look for a young guy willing to work hard for low pay. Lacewell had called Switzer and MacKenzie for recommendations. They had recommended me, but hadn't a clue where I was. Switzer conducted the search by phone.

I was out of Picayune High in January 1967, after only one semester, but Lacewell wanted me to stay in Mississippi for a while to recruit some junior college players. I sent a few up to Wichita, then loaded another U-Haul, and moved Linda Kay and Brent, and now Chad, born in Picayune, to Kansas, where we would live so briefly that Chad's first memories would be of Ames, Iowa. We stayed a season in Wichita, and I suppose the main thing I accomplished was to impress Lacewell with my enthusiasm in a tough, low-budget situation.

In 1968 Johnny Majors got his first head-coaching job, at Iowa State, and called and asked if I'd come to Ames as his defensive line coach. When I got there it was cold beyond anything I'd experienced. Johnny was still assembling the staff and I made a total of four coaches, including Johnny.

He'd brought in a defensive coordinator named Swede Lee, who'd been out of football and in the insurance business in Arkansas for a couple of years. Swede was constantly bitching about Ames and the situation. This was going to be a tough enough deal even for guys like Johnny and me who were determined to make the best of it. All my life I've kept a positive attitude even when I had to work at it. Being around

Swede, I really had to work at it. He was so negative I was afraid it was going to be contagious.

One day we were sitting in a motel room, our headquarters, and it was about 20 below outside. Johnny brought out a road map of Iowa. He said, "For now, I'm going to divide the state into four parts." Interstate 80 ran east and west, and I-35 north and south, pretty well marking geographic quadrants. Each of us was to recruit in one of the quadrants. Swede said, "Coach, you'd better divide Iowa into three recruiting areas. I'm going back to Arkansas."

Johnny and I looked at each other. Johnny didn't say one word trying to change Swede's mind. Johnny took his car keys from his pocket, threw them to me, and said, "Jimmy, will you take Swede to the airport?" I grabbed the keys and didn't say a word myself. There was almost no conversation as I drove Swede to the airport. That was one of the quietest and most pleasant drives I've ever had.

When I got back to the motel, Johnny, Gordon Smith, and I congratulated one another on getting rid of that black cloud over our efforts to do the best we could with what we had. But now, what the hell was Majors going to do for a defensive coordinator? I didn't have the experience to take on that job. But I'd been talking with Lacewell on the phone and knew he wanted out of Wichita State.

I said, "Johnny, there's a guy named Larry Lacewell. He'll talk your head off, but he's a helluva coach." Lacewell came in immediately, stayed a year there and then left for Oklahoma, and Majors made me defensive coordinator. During Majors's time at Iowa State, a pretty star-studded nest developed there, too. Majors brought in a young, bright guy named Jackie Sherrill to work under me on defense. Jackie would go on to be head coach at Washington State, Pitt, Texas A&M, and Mississippi State. Majors brought in George Haffner on offense. Haffner would go on to be offensive coordinator at Pitt, where he and Majors would build a running game around Tony Dorsett that would take them to a national championship in 1976; then to Florida State, where he and Bobby Bowden would build the now notorious Seminole passing attack; then to Georgia, to build another ground attack, around Herschel Walker, for Vince Dooley.

Oh, and one other tradition was born at Iowa State. I started my notorious Halloween parties which, in the future, would bring some awfully downcast coaching staffs out of the dumps. Linda Kay and I got out into the community in Ames, and didn't confine our social lives solely to the coaches and their families. Our first Halloween night there, some of our townie neighbors came roaring into our house at midnight, dressed up in wild costumes and having a *good* time. They woke us out of a sound sleep, but it's never taken a helluva lot to get me into a party mood. I grabbed a blanket off the bed—it bore some resemblance to an Indian blanket—and painted up my face with some of Linda Kay's lipstick, and off we went. The deal was that Linda Kay and I had to pick the next households the party would hit, so naturally we directed the raiding party to the coaches' houses. We scared the hell out of Lacewell and his new bride Chris.

Ames was a small town, but we made the best of it and managed to have a pretty good time as a coaching staff. We were pretty big down at the Elks Club every night after work. I came home one midnight and woke Linda Kay up to inform her that I had just dethroned the longtime shuffleboard champion of the Elks Club. Somehow she didn't seem as excited as I was.

We looked for all sorts of things to keep ourselves cheered up. Majors loves recalling one of our fabricated social events so much that I'll let him tell this one the way he often does:

"The city recreation department would flood the tennis courts and take down the nets in the winter to make ice-skating rinks. My staff was mostly Southern boys who'd never ice-skated in their lives, and, hell, I hadn't even learned to roller skate as a kid in Lynchburg, Tennessee. But we decided we were going to reserve one of these tennis court ice rinks and have ourselves a big staff ice-skating party.

"For the occasion we had ourselves, shall we say, plenty of 'punch'—some serious beverages. Then we went out to skate. I got a big goose egg on my head and Gordon Smith wound up with a separated shoulder. But Jimmy Johnson, out of Port Arthur, Texas, looked like Dick Button out there. Jimmy was confident as hell.

"The next morning the rest of us came dragging into the office, hurting, and got to wondering just how Jimmy got to be such an ice-skater. We got to checking around and found out the little son of a gun had been taking lessons and practicing for three or four days before our party, to get an edge on us."

You can't turn competitiveness on and off. Even at shuffleboard or ice-skating, I wanted to win and was willing to work to get there.

We had a lot of fun in Ames, but I was making $12,000 a year and it was cold. Just after the 1969 season I got a call from Hootie Ingram, the Clemson coach, offering me a whopping $14,500 a year. Johnny scrambled around with the administration and offered to match the salary. But South Carolina was warm, and there was somebody at Clemson I wanted to meet.

In January and February of 1970 I had the shortest coaching job I've ever held, and yet in some ways the most delightful. Beyond doubt, I received the most unusual welcome of my career. I damn sure didn't leave because I didn't like the place, or because they didn't like me. I left after only six weeks, to take a higher profile job at higher pay. But at Clemson University in South Carolina, they rarely harbor ill feelings. They manage to find humor everywhere in football and in life. That tradition had a prominent founder.

Coach Frank Howard, the grand old man of Clemson, is as legendary a wit within the realm of football as Mark Twain was to the general public. My respect for Coach Howard is indescribable. Like Bear Bryant, Howard was a product of Coach Frank Thomas's magnificent Alabama program of the 1930s. In the 1940s and 1950s, Howard took a small agricultural college's football program to national prominence, and he managed to turn Clemson's country-cow-college image into a positive promotional tool. Unlike Bryant, Howard retired from coaching in time to have fun fulltime.

By 1970, Howard had become Clemson's athletic director, had made Hootie Ingram his head coach, and was touring the country telling audiences, "What the American public don't understand is that Bear is about the dumbest 'un that ever come out of the University of Alabammer, and I'm about the smartest. There he is over in Tuscaloosa workin' hisself sick, and here I am makin' a fortune tellin' jokes on him."

When Ingram offered me a job, one reason I took it was that I had always wanted to meet, and get to know, the legendary, crusty, hilarious Frank Howard. For those of you unfortunate enough to be uninitiated, here are a couple of Frank Howard stories in the way of background.

In 1947, Howard had a team which many in the South felt was quite worthy of an Orange Bowl bid. But Clemson as a school was still small and obscure enough to be snubbed by the Orange Bowl Committee. Furman Bisher, later to be the grand old columnist of the South at the Atlanta *Journal,* was then a young sportswriter with the Charlotte *News.* The story goes that Bisher went to interview Howard about the Orange Bowl snub. "The Orange Bowl," said Howard, "can kiss my ass and go to hell." The next day, Howard read Bisher's column. It stated that "Frank Howard says the Orange Bowl can drown in its own juices." Howard snatched up the telephone and called Charlotte. "Bisher, you misquoted me," Howard said. "I want you to print a retraction and a correction." Young Bisher nervously said he didn't understand. "I did not say anything nearly as stupid as 'the Orange Bowl can drown in its own juices,' " said Howard. "I told you, just as plain as I know how, that the Orange Bowl can kiss my ass and go to hell."

In the mid-fifties, another story goes, Howard and his big running mate, Wake Forest head coach Douglas Clyde "Peahead" Walker, were in New York for the Football Hall of Fame banquet. The featured speaker was General Douglas MacArthur. Peahead and Howard had been drinking a bit, and Peahead had to go to the bathroom. "Hell, Peahead, you can't get up and go to the bathroom right in the middle of the General's speech," Howard whispered. Peahead said he was about to die. "Well, just do what all these refined people are doing," said Howard. "Just take one of these empty glasses, hold it under the table, and pee in it." Peahead did so, and set the full glass on the table. As Peahead turned his full attention back to five-star General of the Army Douglas MacArthur, Howard slipped a few ice cubes into the glass in question. MacArthur was rolling on about how Teddy Roosevelt had said to him fifty years earlier, "Douglas, I'd rather be in the Harvard backfield than in the White House." Now engrossed in the speech, Peahead absently took a sip, and blurted out, "Howard! You poured salt in my drink!" Howard grabbed him by the arm and whispered, "Pea-head, you're drinkin' your own piss! Now quit makin' a fool of yourself and pay attention to the General!"

Peahead, after moving on to coach at Yale (I swear it) and then the Montreal Alouettes of the Canadian Football League, got Howard back in the sixties, in the form of an open letter to the Charlotte *Observer*. Howard was going to Europe to lecture American military men on football, and Peahead wrote publicly that "I thought the age of miracles had come when they started talking of a man going to the moon. That isn't near as ridiculous as turning you loose in Paris." Peahead advised him on manners and protocol in Europe: "In France there will be occasions when an introduction calls for you to kiss the lady's hand. Try not to be chewing tobacco at this time." And, "Don't call the Italians dagos, like you do some of your recruits from Pennsylvania." And, "If you should dine with royalty and should unexpectedly belch, say, 'Excuse me, your highness,' and not, 'dawg but them taters wuz good.'"

And so it had gone, for decades.

Anyway, when I got to Clemson, we went immediately to work in the offseason conditioning program. After I'd been on the job for several days, I still hadn't met Coach Howard.

Old football coaches find it hard to break their longtime routines, and Coach Howard would shower every afternoon in the team facilities. One day after a conditioning session, I walked into the shower and saw Coach Howard soaping up in the steam. I really didn't think it the proper occasion to introduce myself. I got over in the shower next to him and was shampooing my hair, and suddenly I felt something warm on my leg.

I looked around, and he was peeing on my leg.

He said, "H-e-e-y, little buddy! Welcome to Clemson!"

Now, before anyone thinks "how disgusting!" let me make this perfectly clear: He did not pee on my leg to insult me. It was just his unique way, as unique as I've ever seen, of saying hello. We got to be great friends. He called me "Pepsi Generation" because I was young and enthusiastic and he liked the way I coached.

But in March 1970, Lacewell called from Oklahoma and said

Chuck Fairbanks, the head coach, was interested in hiring me. Clemson at the time was struggling in football, and Oklahoma offered a higher profile program at a better salary. I began calling around the country asking for advice. A number of people, including Frank Broyles, advised me that leaving Clemson so suddenly would damage my career. So I turned down the Oklahoma offer. But then Fairbanks called me back and said he would pay me, as defensive line coach, $2,000 a year more than Lacewell was making as defensive coordinator. The staff salaries were published, so Fairbanks offered the $2,000 in cash, so it wouldn't show up in the newspapers that I was making more than the defensive coordinator. Fairbanks made me an offer I couldn't refuse.

Hootie understood completely. But then I had to face the big boss, the athletic director: Coach Howard.

"Well, little buddy, you've got to take an offer like that," he said. He mused, with that blinking, bald eagle gaze of his. "You know, I never signed a contract here. I've had offers to go various other places. (Hell, the man was qualified in his day to coach Notre Dame or Southern Cal.) But I was always afraid that in those other places, people would get upset if I said shit, or piss, or hell, or damn. So I just stayed right here at Clemson. But you're young, little buddy, and you've got a great opportunity. You go ahead."

After that, we would see each other occasionally at coaches' conventions, and I always made it a point to spend time with him, to learn, and to listen to his stories.

Twenty-three years later, in February 1993, of all the letters of congratulation I got, the most delightful one was from Coach Howard, by then nearly eighty-four years old. He asked for a Dallas Cowboys jacket and said he'd pay for it. The letter concluded:

> Now that you've won the Super Bowl, I promise to call you Mister Football.
> Best regards,
> Frank Howard
> P.S.—I also promise never to pee on your leg again.

Several of my old crowd from the Arkansas staff had landed at Oklahoma by 1970, and they'd pretty well found themselves in the soup.

Jim MacKenzie had gone to Norman in 1966 and had taken Switzer with him. After only one season, MacKenzie died suddenly of a heart attack, and one of his assistants, Fairbanks, was promoted to head coach. Oklahoma had gone 10–1 under Fairbanks in 1967, but then had fallen off to 7–4 and 6–4. The Sooners still weren't out of the doldrums they'd been in since Bud Wilkinson, who'd taken Oklahoma to the national championships of 1950, 1955, and 1956, quit after the 1963 season to make an unsuccessful bid for the U.S. Senate.

At least, the Sooners weren't out of the woods in the eyes of their "Chinamen," as they called their insatiable alumni and fans. The term goes back to an old sportswriter's line about Sooner fans' lust for high point totals: "How much rice can a Chinaman eat?" Oklahoma had never been known for defense, and the Chinamen didn't care, as long as the offense kept running up and down the field. But in 1969, every farmer in Nebraska and Kansas, and all around the Big Eight Conference, was gobbling up the Chinamen's rice. Oklahoma's opponents were the ones running up and down the field.

In 1969 the Sooners gave up the most points in a season in Oklahoma history. After that season, their defensive coordinator resigned, and gave Lacewell his job. That meant the defensive line coaching job was open. Switzer and Lacewell talked Fairbanks into hiring me. Lacewell knows now that Fairbanks paid me more to come than Lacewell was making. But Lacewell, bless his heart, tells people it was worth it.

"Really, from that moment on," Lacewell says, "I think we turned the thing around." Larry says that in retrospect. At the time, he and I argued like hell over defensive philosophy. There were days on end when Lacewell and I wouldn't even speak to each other—well, saying Lacewell didn't speak is like saying he didn't breathe. So the truth is, there were days when I wouldn't speak to him.

My problem was that I had truly come to despise this matter of defense being so damn defensive. Coaches persisted in ordering defensive linemen to sit back, wait, and read the blocks. It seemed that everybody in college football, including Lacewell, was teaching that but me. I believed, and still do, in creating upfield pressure from a 4–3 stack formation, that is, four down linemen, with three linebackers (true linebackers, back off the line of scrimmage, rather than hybrid "up ends"). Let the linebackers do the waiting and the reading of blocks. Let the down linemen fire off the snap, and charge upfield, creating havoc in the offense. Put simply, *attack* on defense. I called it "upfield pressure." Lacewell and the traditionalists considered it tantamount to sending the defensive front on kamikaze missions, committing them too soon, too totally.

After all that arguing, Lacewell looks back now and says, "But we played pretty good defense in 1970, and saved our jobs. Jimmy had us ahead of our time."

Back then, my defensive philosophy was in the formative years. But at Oklahoma that year, I saw an opportunity to prove my theories by taking advantage of the quickness of three defensive linemen: Lucious Selmon, Derland Moore and Sugar Bear Hamilton. Lucious was a squatty fullback that we turned into a nose guard, and he became an All-America lineman. Derland was a walk-on who'd come to Oklahoma on a track scholarship, as a shot-putter. They were going to give him a look on offense and I asked if I could try him on the defensive front. Derland also made All-America, and went on to a decade or so as a mainstay of the New Orleans Saints' defensive front. Sugar Bear was undersized but very quick, and would go on to a great career with the New England Patriots. After that first year, my backup linemen included Lucious's younger brothers, Lee Roy and Dewey Selmon, both of whom would go on to star at Tampa Bay.

And so those guys were the framework of my prototype upfield pressure defense which is now standard in college and the NFL.

What brought Oklahoma back into the spotlight? I think it was a combination. On the technical side, it was the combination of adding the up-the-field defense, and putting in the wishbone offense. But on the mental side, the aggressive style of play we went to in the defensive line carried over to the entire team.

In 1972, we shut out five opponents. Fairbanks and I both left Oklahoma after that season, he for the NFL and I to return to Arkansas as defensive coordinator. But from 1972 on, Oklahoma was known as a heckuva defensive football program. And Lacewell, as the most renowned defensive coordinator ever at Oklahoma, would tell people, "We were left with the things Jimmy taught us, that style of play. I got a lot of the credit. But Jimmy Johnson had a lot to do with it."

This is a style of defense I've carried with me ever since, right through Miami and now with the Cowboys. It's more than technical strategy. It's a frame of mind that starts with the defensive line. If they're sitting in their stances waiting to react to the offensive linemen's blocks, it takes away their aggressiveness. So the thing we've tried to instill in all of them, at all the places I've been, is that as soon as that ball moves, we are charging up the field. Why be satisfied with the line of scrimmage the offense has established? Why not establish our own line of scrimmage, back in the offensive backfield? It's very disruptive to any offensive system. But more than anything else, it establishes an attitude that we are attacking, rather than sitting back and reacting. And that style of play carries over to the entire football team. There has been no finer or more obvious example of all of this than the way my Miami defensive front of 1986, led by guys like Jerome Brown and Daniel Stubbs, set the tone of all-out attack for the entire team.

Also at Oklahoma, I suppose I did my part in the way of attitude adjustment among the coaching staff, although guys like Lacewell and Switzer were by no means difficult to get into a party mood.

Switzer, Lacewell, and the whole bunch still love to tell the story of our "Beat Colorado" party of 1970, which was sort of an outgrowth of my Halloween parties at Iowa State. Lacewell and I were still bickering over up-the-field defense, and Fairbanks and Switzer had just installed the wishbone offense, which Texas had just welcomed to the wishbone family with a 40–14 kicking of our ass in Dallas. Lacewell has since called that part of the season "like living on a cliff."

Having been humiliated by Texas, and being on the way up to Colorado for the game that just might do us in as a staff, we decided that Thursday night to . . . well, let Lacewell open the story:

"Things looked tough. We were in trouble. Our asses were about to get fired. But no matter what, Jimmy was a fun-loving, hyper guy who always wanted to do something, always had a plan. That Thursday night, I'd gone on to bed. And, hell, here they came. They got me again, just like that first Halloween party at Iowa State. Woke me up. This time they were dressed up like women. God, it was a nightmare."

I seem to recall wearing a big old bra, stuffed. But most of us were just dressed silly. The one who surprised even me was Fairbanks, who went into the closet and got one of his wife's really nice designer dresses and put it on. I know he must have split the rear end out of it.

I don't remember the late details of the party as well as Switzer and Lacewell claim to. But the story goes that another assistant, Gene Hochevar, and I left the party in the same car and were still wearing our wives' clothes. (Nowadays, Lacewell claims he and Switzer were in the car too. The legend grows.) Supposedly we stopped at a traffic light and two rednecks in a pickup started making wolf calls at us, thinking we really were women, and that I rolled down the window and said in an obviously masculine voice, "Go fuck yourself!" This supposedly nearly gave the rednecks the big one. Then, the staff supposedly got to thinking that that was all we needed—about to get fired anyway, and then having it get out in the media that we were not only involved in a wee-hours altercation, but that we were in drag.

I don't know that all that happened. But I don't know that it didn't happen. All I know is, that party pulled an entire coaching staff out of the dumps, and that we beat Colorado 23–15 the following Saturday and kept on coaching at Oklahoma.

In 1973 I still had nothing but positive feelings toward my alma mater. When Frank Broyles asked me back to Arkansas as defensive coordinator, my mentor Jim MacKenzie's old job, I readily accepted, and returned to Fayetteville with the notion, in the back of my mind, of staying for keeps. In 1975 we won the Southwest Conference and beat Nebraska in the Cotton Bowl. There was a growing sense that Broyles might soon retire as head coach, and I harbored aspirations of replacing him.

Then the 1976 season collapsed. We'd had expectations of another really good season, and had started out fine. But then we had problems on offense and really struggled in the last half of the season. And Frank Broyles retired, to become athletic director fulltime.

Frank called us all into a staff meeting after the season was over. He told us that he had made the decision early in the year that he would retire, and that at that time we were doing fine and he had privately anticipated giving me the job. (My heart beat faster—I had actively expressed my desire for the job.) But, he continued, because we'd struggled so at the end of the season, he felt responsible, as athletic director, to open up the search for a big-name, established coach. From the outside.

I was deeply disappointed, but I was not bitter or angry toward Frank. It was not as if he'd promised me the job and reneged. He simply admitted, after the fact, that he had anticipated giving me the job, but hadn't been able to follow through. That was fine. (And, looking back: at age thirty-three I was not ready to be a head coach of a major program.)

So Broyles hired Lou Holtz. Lou came in and talked to me about staying on as defensive coordinator. I told Lou that because of the way things had gone—nothing against Lou—I just felt I would have been less than enthusiastic if I had stayed on with the thought in the back of my mind that I could have been the head coach. I told him I felt I should leave, and he understood.

Furthermore, my Halloween party tradition had met its end in Fayetteville. When Eddie Sutton pulled a gun on us, I decided it was time to call off the house-to-house raids. Sutton was the head basketball coach at Arkansas, and later at Kentucky. Those round-ball guys are scary sometimes.

During my last stint at Arkansas, we played Oklahoma State home-and-home. Once in the mid-1970s, the night before the Arkansas–Oklahoma State game in Little Rock, a guy I rarely saw anymore, Jerry Jones, had a party at his house. He invited me and some of the other Arkansas coaches. Being in the oil-and-gas business, Jerry did a lot of work in Oklahoma City, and so at that party we met some of his friends and business associates who were Oklahoma State alumni. I met one of the most influential OSU alumni, Kevin Leonard. We had a pleasant conversation, and that was about it. We wouldn't meet again for about four years.

As I prepared to leave Fayetteville for the last time—at the moment, for points unknown—there was a lot of movement in the program that had just won the 1976 national championship, the University of Pittsburgh. Johnny Majors left Pitt at the pinnacle, to go home to coach at his alma mater, Tennessee. Jackie Sherrill became head coach at Pitt.

Sherrill, who used to work for me, called me to work for him. It was a very attractive position: defensive coordinator and assistant head coach. Jackie would give me some of the duties normally associated with a head coach, a lot of the public speaking engagements, etc. It would be great preparation for head coaching.

(I know a lot of people have questions about Jackie. And I don't always agree with his methods. Sometimes he might try to take short-cuts, one way or the other. And Jackie tends to embellish on occasion, which leads to some people mistrusting him. But I had a chance to work with him from day one of his coaching career at Iowa State, and the bottom line about Jackie is, he'll win. And I've always admired that.)

In Pittsburgh, I got my first taste of living in a big city, and liked it. (In fact, of all the places I've ever lived, Pittsburgh still ranks second to Miami in the pleasant-memories column.) After you've lived in towns like Fayetteville, Picayune, and Norman, it's refreshing to find so much to do, so many people to meet, in a city like Pittsburgh.

And at Pitt, I formed some great friendships, especially with players—one of them being Hugh Green, the great defensive lineman who would go on to play linebacker in the NFL, at Miami and Tampa Bay. Hugh had come to Pittsburgh from Natchez, Mississippi, where he'd been raised by an aunt. His freshman year we became close, and that first summer he was a long way from home and kind of needed someone. He spent the summer with me and really got close to Brent and Chad and Linda Kay. We actually talked about legally adopting him, but he was a grown man by then, so we dismissed the idea. But we formed a bond with Hugh that went on for many years. (When I got to the Cowboys, Hugh wanted me to work out a trade so that he could come and play for me. But by then he was near the end of his career, and I didn't want to be the one to tell him it was over.)

My first year at Pitt, the Air Force Academy called and I interviewed for the head-coaching job. But after looking at the situation, and realizing that the environment for players was so different than what I was used to, I cooled toward that job.

After my second season at Pitt in 1978, Jim Stanley was fired at Oklahoma State, which had found itself in a world of trouble with the NCAA for recruiting irregularities. Kevin Leonard, the guy I'd met at Jerry Jones's party in Little Rock, was on the selection committee for a new head coach. One day in Oklahoma City, Kevin and Jerry were talking about the situation in Stillwater, and Jerry said, "The guy you ought to call is Jimmy Johnson."

Kevin called me in Pittsburgh and asked if I would send a résumé and apply for the Oklahoma State job. But because of their situation—not only were they on probation but another NCAA investigation was ongoing, and *Sports Illustrated* had printed a big expose—it wasn't a very attractive job. I decided not to pursue it.

Then Jerry called me on their behalf, and I got a second call from Kevin, telling me that the deadline was approaching for applicants. Would I please send a résumé and at least take a look at the job? I did that, with only a passing interest.

After Pitt's last game of the regular season, and prior to going to the Tangerine Bowl (now the Citrus Bowl) in Orlando, I went down to Stillwater for an interview. Kevin picked up Linda Kay and me at the Oklahoma City airport, and all the way out to Stillwater, about an hour's drive, he schooled me on the selection committee, on all the individuals who would be at the table. He really gave me insights into the concerns of each individual.

I really had a great interview, and they offered me the job. After spending a lot of time looking into it, I felt it might be an opportunity, since Oklahoma State was in the Big Eight Conference—albeit at the bottom of the Big Eight, and on probation. I didn't realize what kind of chore we'd have in playing Oklahoma and Nebraska, but I felt that if we were able to accomplish something, people would take notice.

I met with the board of regents that night. I met the president of the University, Dr. Larry Boger, who remains without question the finest administrator I have ever been around. I accepted the job.

The biggest mistake I made was a decision I let my heart and ego make for me, rather than my head. Even though I accepted the Oklahoma State job, I felt obligated to stay with Pitt through the Tangerine Bowl. By the time I accepted the new job, less than a week remained before the bowl game, and I didn't want to leave Jackie on such short notice. The reason it was a mistake was that so many of the Pitt assistants—Dave Wannstedt, Tony Wise, Pat Jones and others—had approached me saying they wanted to go with me to Oklahoma State.

On the bowl trip, Jackie was pretty upset. There wasn't a whole lot of conversation. I was trying to avoid any confrontation, and every day after practice it was almost comical to see which assistants would ride together on the way back to the hotel. It was as if there were a Pitt staff, and an Oklahoma State staff. The players sensed this, and there were players, including Hugh Green, who approached me about transferring to Oklahoma State.

It was all extremely disruptive. It caused not only a miserable bowl trip but a miserable performance by our team, and we lost to North Carolina State. And it caused a strained relationship with Jackie, at least for a year or so.

So looking back, I should have gone straight to Stillwater rather than detouring through Orlando. After all, I was a head coach at last.

VIII

STILLWATER

I t seemed that Oklahoma State was synonymous with probation for years. Because Oklahoma State was always a step behind the University of Oklahoma in football, some of the coaches and some of the alumni were, out of frustration, overzealous in their recruiting of players. And that caused all kinds of well-documented infractions, slush funds, et cetera.

And so in 1979, I walked into an Oklahoma State program that was under NCAA arrest, on its knees, bound, shackled, closely monitored, with further investigations continuing into allegations about the past. I met a second time with Dr. Larry Boger, the school president, and he told me, "Jimmy, this is not your doing. Let the administration deal with it. Completely block it out of your mind. Operate the program in a first-class manner."

Which we did. My crew, my original crew, which came in with me from Pittsburgh, understood, without being told, that we would not cheat to win. For those who didn't yet know me well enough, I told them my position. During my five years at Oklahoma State, I didn't get involved in many "heavy recruiting battles," for the simple reason that we weren't going to break the rules.

That said, we should deal up front with this: It has always hurt me when people have associated me with a probation OSU went through after I left. When that investigation went on, there were no allegations or infractions associated with me, other than my hiring of an individual to whom I was just trying to give a second chance, and who ended up breaking the rules after I left. Here is exactly what happened:

After my fourth year at Oklahoma State, I lost one of my black coaches to Southern Cal. I wanted another quality black coach to replace him. I started calling around for recommendations. One of the head coaches I called was Danny Ford at Clemson. I'd heard about a coach by the name of Willie Anderson who was very aggressive, very intelligent, and was an outstanding coach. But he'd had problems with the NCAA because of recruiting violations. He was coaching at Clemson, but was not allowed by the NCAA to recruit for Clemson.

I called the NCAA enforcement office and asked their opinion. They said that if Willie Anderson accepted a job with me at Oklahoma State, he would be able to recruit, but he would be monitored. They emphasized to me that I must make sure that I monitored him myself, and must make sure that he abided by the rules. Which I really felt I could do, and, in visiting with Willie and with Danny Ford, I felt Willie would do.

The first year Willie was at Oklahoma State, everything went fine. After that season, I left to take the Miami job. Pat Jones was named head coach at OSU, and he named Willie Anderson recruiting coordinator. The next recruiting season, 1984–1985, while I was at Miami, there was a player named Hart Lee Dykes from Bay City, Texas, whom everybody was recruiting. In fact, we at Miami even had some contact with him.

Hart Lee was involved in some recruiting sanctions at both Oklahoma and Oklahoma State. He played at Oklahoma State and ended up being an outstanding player. But because of recruiting infractions, both Oklahoma State and Oklahoma were placed on probation. My error in judgment had been in hiring Willie Anderson, who recruited Hart Lee Dykes and who, because of Willie's enthusiasm, broke the rules in the process. But a lot of people, looking back, have associated me with the probation that OSU eventually went on, when in fact I wasn't even there when the infraction occurred.

One of the problems on rules infractions is that a lot of times, people and schools are penalized for things that others had a hand in doing. And too many times, in my opinion, the player himself has a big part in the rules infraction. And more times than not, the player goes unpenalized.

Occasionally you run into players in recruiting who are looking for something extra. As long as you state right up front that the rules aren't going to be broken, you can nip it in the bud. But if you don't stop it right then, sometimes through very competitive recruiting rules are broken.

Generally speaking, I think most rumors about recruiting violations are either exaggerations or outright fabrications. A lot of times the players themselves, just to make themselves look good to their friends or a recruiter, will even fabricate stories about what some other recruiter might have insinuated. One prime and sad example of how far these things can go occurred in 1992, when a University of Georgia player claimed that the University of Alabama had broken the rules during his recruiting process. He was so convincing that the Atlanta papers ran his story. Alabama issued such a sound, clear rebuttal, including the Alabama recruiter's offer to take a lie-detector test, that the player's story fell apart, and the newspapers had to recant when the player finally admitted he'd been "just jerking (the reporter's) chain." Some joke. And it was a classic case of there being no guarantee that everyone who originally read of the charge also read of the exoneration of Alabama, in what turned out to be a national championship year for the Crimson Tide.

Assistant coaches out on the road recruiting tend to gossip among themselves, and the rumors fly back and forth. And if a recruiter fails to get a player, then it's an easy out to tell the head coach that the other guys were cheating. That's why more college head coaches are adopting the policy that if their recruiters discover another school cheating and can document it, fine. They'll turn in the offenders to the NCAA. But head coaches no longer want to hear any whining excuses based on gossip over a beer with assistants from other schools.

In light of the University of Oklahoma's history of problems with the NCAA, people sometimes ask me if I thought Oklahoma was cheating while I was at Oklahoma State. Oh, there were always rumors back and forth, but again, when you're out recruiting anywhere, you hear rumors almost on a daily basis. Ninety percent of those rumors don't have any substance.

Besides, believe it or not, we didn't go head-to-head with Oklahoma in recruiting very much, for the simple reason that we knew we were the underdogs. We would take players that Oklahoma wasn't offering scholarships to, and we knew we weren't going to get the players Oklahoma wanted. On a very few occasions, we got players Oklahoma was after, but it was always because of unusual circumstances, such as family members having already played at OSU, or the family being diehard OSU fans or alumni.

Okay, that's my speech on recruiting. Now to the five very pleasant and sometimes zany years I spent in Stillwater, Oklahoma.

Our first year there, 1979, was as exciting a year for me and my crew as any we've had in coaching. I can state that even now, in the light of 1993.

Because of the NCAA sanctions, and because of poor academic performance leading to individuals' ineligibility, we had about 55 players on football scholarship that year. By comparison, the normal NCAA limit on scholarship players was 95. So we were playing Big Eight opponents with 95-man scholarship rosters, and either Nebraska's or Oklahoma's 95 were going to be better than anybody else's 95 in the conference anyway.

So we instituted a walk-on program, just to get bodies on the field.

It truly was comical, because anybody who wanted to play for the Oklahoma State Cowboys would be given a suit. A lot of those guys hadn't even played high school football. But we needed them just to practice.

One year we had over two hundred players—let me correct that: two hundred bodies and half a dozen players. There were so many that we didn't have enough equipment to outfit them. One of our equipment managers found a deal on soccer shoes for three bucks a pair. So the bottom-of-the-barrel walk-ons got these awful-looking black soccer shoes.

Sideline space on the practice field was so limited that we built a three-tiered bench. We'd have two hundred bodies perched up there, and if we would have a tackling drill, we'd call a group of them over and use them as tackling dummies. They understood their roles, and I gained a lot of respect for all of those who did all that we asked of them, and stuck it out, and received no financial aid whatsoever in return.

They benefited from it because they could walk around campus and say they were on the Oklahoma State football team. We benefited from it because, through numbers, we were able to be competitive with some of the Big Eight opponents, even with our 55 scholarship players to their 95.

It created some great spirit at the school. And it gave everybody a chance to play college football, which was the way the game was originally meant to be. (I say everybody—the issue of women playing football hadn't yet come up. But if a coed had come out, I guess we'd have put her in pads and soccer shoes and let her have at it.) And through that bunch, some pretty competitive players emerged.

That first year, we won seven games. And in Stillwater, Oklahoma, you'd have thought we'd just won the Super Bowl.

We weren't allowed to go to a bowl game. But that's when I started my "crew trips" to reward my coaching staff. It's become something of a tradition throughout my head-coaching career. I've loaded up my guys and their wives or girlfriends and taken them on trips, at my expense.

That first year, we had a couple of private planes take us out to Las

Vegas. We were on the economy plan since I didn't make a whole lot of money at the time. (After I started making a little more money, I worked some deals with the airlines and alumni, and our trips have gone everywhere from St. Martin to Puerto Rico to the Bahamas to skiing in Colorado. From Stillwater to Miami to Dallas, I think those outings have been vitally important for the unity of the staff, and I think even more important for the wives. They're able to form a bond that they can hold on to when you go through very trying and demanding seasons, when their husbands are working late hours and are seldom at home with their families. On those outings, we can be an inner circle, enjoy one another, let our hair down, and not be on stage like we are with alumni or media or outsiders.)

Still, recuperating from the probation and the severe scholarship limits was not a breezy process. We dropped off to 3–7–1 my second year in Stillwater, but in 1981 we went 7–4 again and were able to go to our first bowl, the Independence, in Shreveport, Louisiana. We had another rough year in 1982, going 4–5–2, but at that point we turned the thing around.

In 1983 we won eight games, including the Bluebonnet Bowl in Houston, which was as close to home as I'd ever coached a game. We had it going. We were on our way. We were no Oklahoma or Nebraska, but we were now ready to win our class, the rest of the Big Eight, regularly for a while to come. Then in recruiting season of 1983–1984, we managed to sign a breakthrough player, running back Thurman Thomas. So who knew? Maybe we could even knock off the Cornhuskers sometime, or even the red monster from down on the other side of Oklahoma City.

Savoring all of this, I was at my favorite club, Oak Tree Country Club in Edmond, Oklahoma, between Stillwater and Oklahoma City. I had spent many a day at Oak Tree, not only for the golf but for the good camaraderie. It was an all-men's club and a place where you could really let your hair down and have a good time. I had just finished a round of golf with Pat Jones, Kevin Leonard, and another friend and supporter, Don Childress. We were sitting around the clubhouse when the news came on television that Howard Schnellenberger had resigned at the

University of Miami to take a job with the United States Football League.

Kevin said, "Who in the world would want to take that job?" And everybody else joined in the conversation. Except me. They said Miami was a crime-infested city. They said nobody could follow the act of Howard Schnellenberger, who'd just won the national championship, especially when most of Miami's top players in their Orange Bowl upset of Nebraska were departing seniors.

I said, "Hey, I'd love to have that job. That's what I've always dreamed about in college coaching: being at a place where you've got the talent to win the national championship, being in a city where there's a lot of things to do (two years of coaching in Pittsburgh had opened up my feelings to that kind of atmosphere), especially in a city with warm weather, close to beaches." I mean, it had everything I wanted, both professionally and personally. It was a unique situation.

But that was the extent of our conversation. I didn't pursue the job. I really didn't think a whole lot more about it . . . for a while.

Then I had a phone call from Frank Broyles, to see if I was interested in the Arkansas job. Lou Holtz, who'd had a great run there, had been fired—well, there were different reports coming out. One side said Lou had resigned and the other side said he'd been fired. Either way, he'd left and gone to Minnesota. Frank wanted to know if I was interested in coming over to Fayetteville and talking about the job. I said yes, but I wasn't 100 percent excited about it. I felt very good at Oklahoma State, and I felt very good about the team we had coming back. But Arkansas was my alma mater. It was a place that was special to me.

I went through the interview with Frank the evening after I got there—well, Broyles talked to me, but we didn't actually have an interview. We went to Herman's Rib House, a local barbecue institution, had some ribs and talked for a little while. Then the next morning, the trainer, Dean Webber, picked me up before I had any further conversation with Broyles, and took me to the airport. I was just sort of hustled away.

Then I found out the job had already been offered to, and evidently accepted by, Ken Hatfield. In fact, Orville Henry, a renowned Little Rock sportswriter who is very close to Frank, had spoken at a luncheon while I was in Fayetteville for the interview, and said that Ken Hatfield had been given the job.

Consider the sequence of events: At lunchtime in Springdale, only ten miles from Fayetteville, Orville says Ken Hatfield is the new Arkansas coach; then that afternoon, I do a TV interview because I'm supposedly in town to talk about the job; so the public finds out that Hatfield has the job, and that I'm in town to interview for the job, at the same time; so just about everybody but me knows that Hatfield has it before I go to dinner that night with Frank; and I *still* don't know about it *after* dinner with Frank. And so you can imagine my embarrassment and outrage upon finding out the truth.

As it turned out, Jerry Jones, as one of the school's most generous and influential alumni, had called Frank to recommend me. Larry Lace-well later told me he had received a call from Frank, asking which guy he, Lacewell, would recommend. Larry told Frank he felt he would be getting a good football coach either way, but that "I really believe Jimmy would be the better all-around recruiter. I think Jimmy could appeal to any kind of kid. With Ken's FCA (Fellowship of Christian Athletes) background, there may be only one side of the street he's going to walk on. I think Jimmy prides himself in taking a certain kind of kid and turning him around."

Image is very important to Frank, and his choice could have gone all the way back to when Ken and I were players for him at Arkansas. I had always been a bit of a roustabout, always on the edge of mischief. Ken was in the FCA and walked the straight and narrow. I don't mean that disrespectfully; I respect Kenny Hatfield's beliefs.

Now if Frank had just given the job to Hatfield without ever calling me, that would have been fine. I already had a good job, and that job looked like it was about to get a lot better. Or, if Frank had just called me and said, "Look, Jimmy, some of our alumni want you, but you've always been a bit of a hellraiser, and I'm going to give the job to Kenny because I like his image better," then fine. (Funny how it turned out: Kenny was so good that a lot of the Arkansas faithful felt uncomfortable around him.) Or even if Broyles had given me a little image speech over our barbecue ribs, and told me he'd felt compelled to go through the motions of an interview to appease Jerry Jones's crowd, it wouldn't have been quite so bad.

But to lure me into the picture, let word of it get out to the public at the same time that word of Hatfield's hiring got out, make me look like a reject to both Arkansas and Oklahoma State followers—that bothered me. And for him not even to tell me the truth in a private conversation—that really bothered me. And to top it all off, after I got back to Stillwater, Frank had his administrative assistant, Lon Ferrell, call and tell me to remove my name from consideration publicly, because Frank had given the job to Hatfield. I said, "I'm not removing anything. And Frank can stick it where the sun doesn't shine." He hadn't even had the courtesy to call me himself.

After that, I talked to a few people at Arkansas and asked, "Why, if you were a friend, didn't you at least tell me that the job had been offered to someone else?" They didn't really have an answer.

And for that reason, I've had very little contact with the people at my alma mater, especially Frank Broyles, since.

That spring of 1984, still smarting from the slap in the face from my alma mater but trying to get over it, I went to a national coaches' convention in Dallas. It was at the Hyatt Regency downtown. At one of the functions, Sam Jankovich, the University of Miami's athletic director, asked if we could talk privately. He was searching for a new head coach to replace Schnellenberger. Sam wanted my opinions on some guys he was considering, one of them being John Cooper, head coach at Tulsa (and later at Arizona State and Ohio State). I don't recall the others he was interested in, because before Sam could get many questions out of his mouth, I said:

"Sam, I wouldn't mind living on the beach myself."

He said, "You mean you would be interested? Let's talk."

We had some very intensive interviews right there at the Hyatt. One of my biggest concerns about taking the job was that Sam demanded that whoever replaced Schnellenberger retain his old staff.

Schnellenberger had pretty much left his staff flatfooted, and it was June, too late in the year for them to find anyplace else to go. So Sam was going to take care of them, and guarantee that they would be retained for a year. I admired Sam's decency about it. But that sort of thing is highly unusual. When you see a new head coach come into any program, clean house and bring in his own people, it isn't just because he wants to give all his old buddies jobs. I repeat, and I cannot say it enough times, that coaching staffs must be bonded to function properly. They must know one another well, like one another (hell, even their wives and girlfriends have to like one another), and be able to communicate very efficiently. When coaches say of one another, "I would go to war beside him," they mean it. They must.

Sam was adamant. If I took the Miami job, my crew would have to stay behind, at least for a year. That was no problem for them, because my assistant head coach was Pat Jones, one of my closest friends, going back to our assistant coaching days together at Arkansas and Pitt. If I took the Miami job I was going to do whatever I could to help Pat become my successor as head coach at Oklahoma State, and that meant my crew, and his crew, would remain intact as a staff.

The problem was all mine. During a break from the meetings with Sam, I polled seven or eight different coaches at the convention about whether I should take the job. We'd finally gotten the Oklahoma State program turned around. With Thurman Thomas and that group coming in, it looked like we were going to have some very good teams.

Almost every friend I asked, including Gil Brandt, scouting director of the Dallas Cowboys, advised me to turn down the Miami job. Everybody said Schnellenberger's 1983 national championship would be a tough act to follow with so many players graduating, nine defensive starters, and my going in at that late date without my own staff.

After I'd listened until I was just sick, I went to my room alone and sat on the bed, thinking. My dream job had a catch. I wanted it so bad, and I was probably going to take it anyway, but it really bothered me that everybody I talked to said, "Don't." I picked up the phone and called Lacewell's room.

When he answered, I said, "Come on down to the room." He was there in a few minutes. I told him I'd been offered the Miami job and told him the catches. I asked, "What would you do?"

"Jimmy," he said, "I'd go."

"You're the first person at this whole damn convention who's said that," I said.

He said, "Jimmy, you also coached at Oklahoma one time, remember? You know their firepower. You know what you're battling every year. You can't win a national championship at Oklahoma State. But you can win one at Miami. It's been proven. It's been done. I think you ought to go."

We stayed up late. The catch still nagged at me. I said, "But Larry, I'll have to inherit a staff."

He said, "Well, sooner or later you'll straighten that out."

The next day, I told Sam Jankovich he had himself a head coach. (Later, I would lobby on Pat Jones's behalf at Oklahoma State, school him on what the board of regents would expect from his interview, and even set up a one-on-one meeting between Pat and one regent, Ed Ketchum, who'd been negative toward him. Pat got the job and the crew had some security.)

Immediately after telling Sam of my decision, I left Dallas, drove back to Stillwater, and Linda Kay and I packed some clothes and went straight to the Oklahoma City airport. We checked into a hotel and tried to get a few hours' sleep before an early flight to Miami. But I was as excited as I'd ever been.

IX

AMBUSH

C orey Johnson, Miami's recruiting coordinator, met our flight and diverted us through an emergency exit of the jetway and down a stairway onto the tarmac, where a car was waiting for us. We bypassed the gate area and the terminal so we could avoid the initial rush of media people. The press conference was scheduled for 1 p.m., a couple of hours away. Out in the helter-skelter traffic of the airport exit area, just past the first lush palm trees, the car turned suddenly onto LeJeune Road and headed for the Miami Airport Marriott.

Sam Jankovich was waiting in the lobby. If you've ever had anything to do with bigtime football in Miami as a fan, coach, player, or journalist, college or NFL, chances are you know that lobby: buzzing with conversations in several languages; busy people outbound to Caracas or Tel Aviv or London or New York, with no time to notice anyone else, certainly not a hairsprayed little coach out of Stillwater, Oklahoma, nor a middle-aged athletic director from the University of Miami. (Besides: Considering what the cosmopolitan metropolis of Miami knew or thought of me at that point, anyone looking for the new Miami coach would have been on the lookout for some guy from out on the range, in a cowboy hat and boots.)

On the way to the hotel meeting room, Sam told me he wanted me to meet the staff and talk with them for an hour or so before the press conference.

Walking down the corridor, Sam said he had told them the night before that none of them would be promoted to replace Schnellenberger, and that the job had been given to an outside guy from Oklahoma State.

Walking down the corridor, I told myself that obviously they were outstanding assistant coaches. Hell, they'd just won the national championship. I didn't know who they were, but I felt like we could get along and adjust.

Walking down the corridor, I did not realize that three of them had applied, and had been considered, for the head coaching job: Tom Olivadotti, the defensive coordinator; Gary Stevens, the offensive coordinator; and Bill Trout, who'd been Schnellenberger's administrative assistant. Olivadotti had been far and away the leading candidate in the minds of the Miami media, and therefore, I suppose, in his own mind. (Don't ever let any coach or player kid you by saying he doesn't pay attention to the media. We all do.)

Walking down the corridor, Sam did not tell me that each had been told that he was to make an evaluation of me, and if he wanted to stay on fine, but if he decided he did not want to coach under me, then he would still receive his salary for a year.

When I walked into the room, it was like a gust of cold air hit me right in the face. Every coach was sitting around a conference table with a stern look on his face. I'd only had a few hours' sleep the night before, anticipating the press conference but not a meeting with the coaches.

Sam did not introduce us. He just said, "Everybody, this is Jimmy Johnson, who we'll be naming as head coach at a press conference in about an hour and a half."

Sam turned to me and said, "I'll leave you with them." He left the room.

And there was:

Dead . . . silence.

I sat down at their table. There were ten of them. I was stammering and struggling for words. Remember, I didn't know they had an option. I thought we were all supposed to make the best of this. I said, "Well, to get things started, why don't we go around the table, you introduce yourself, tell me who you are and what you coach, and a little bit about yourself."

The whole time I was talking, Olivadotti was sitting there with a set of keys in his hand, continually dropping the keys on the table, picking them up, and dropping them. Picking them up . . . And dropping them . . . picking them up . . . and dropping them. Clink . . . clink . . . clink . . . clink . . . as he, and every other coach, just sat there, staring down at the table.

I got up and began to walk from man to man. I would stop and shake his hand, ask his name, ask what he coached, try to make conversation. And I got one- and two-word answers. And all the time, Olivadotti with his keys: Clink . . . clink . . . clink.

I tried again to talk to the group, and there were two or three guys talking to each other, low, not loud, just enough to aggravate the piss out of me.

Finally, Olivadotti spoke up and said, "I've seen your teams play, and I really don't think our philosophies could coexist. I can't coach defense the way your teams play defense." He picked out a game where we'd played poorly and been upset a couple of years before by a weak opponent, and threw it in my face. He said, "I saw the film of that game, and your teams don't play the way we want to play."

He might as well have said, "I think you're a horseshit coach from out on the range, with cowshit stuck to your boots, and I just got through coaching a national championship defense in the big time in a big town. And how you got this job over me, I have not the slightest clue."

And some guys in my shoes might have just lost it then and there and said, "Look, asshole: the Selmon brothers were making All-America in an upfield-pressure defense at Oklahoma while you were coaching at some place called Salesianum Prep School in fucking *Delaware*. Did you ever happen to wonder who might have thought up the Oklahoma upfield-pressure defense that got the football world's attention, all the way to Salesianum Prep School in fucking *Delaware?* The point is, my scheme, with the right talent to execute it, can disrupt any offense. Now, I know you believe in a three-man front that tied up blockers for the linebackers, and did well enough to let Schnellenberger's offense win the national championship for you. But don't say we can't coexist if I show you a four-man front with upfield pressure that, I guarantee you, is going to make Miami the most ferocious and feared defense in Division I. I happen to think you're a helluva coach, no matter what you think of me. And I know you can't think clearly about me, because I know *exactly* how disappointed you feel, not getting this job. I went through exactly the same thing at Arkansas in 1976, when I was defensive coordinator of a major program and you were coaching linebackers at fucking *Princeton*. But when *my* athletic director decided to go outside, and gave Lou Holtz the job I was dying for, I treated Lou with courtesy and decency, and told him honestly what my real problem was, and I kept my frigging *car keys* in my pocket! Now then: Does anybody else smell any horseshit in this room?"

But I didn't. Wouldn't. I was trying to win them over because Sam had told me I *had* to retain the staff, and I wanted to be at Miami so bad, and I really felt that I could overcome anything, survive anything, and make adjustments after that first year.

I stammered again. I said, "I'm sure that we can work with each other."

I was pressed for time because I had to go to the press conference, and so I excused myself. I was stunned. Thinking what in the world have

I done? How am I going to be able to coach an entire year with a group that can't stand my guts, just because I happen to be the guy who got the job that they wanted?

They all filed out of the room. Most said, "I haven't decided what I'm going to do. I'll let you know." Some, including Olivadotti, said, "I really don't think I can work with you. But I'll meet with you in an individual meeting this week." A couple actually said, "I'll stay and work with you."

I left the room to go to the press conference and try to fake being enthusiastic, positive, and upbeat about accepting the Miami job.

The first press conference in Miami was not hostile or even negative. If the Olivadotti proponents were there, they kept their opinions to themselves. And, as the months wore on, I would realize that the loss of Schnellenberger was actually what continued to bother the media people. Some of them, particularly the most prominent columnist in town, Miami *Herald* sports editor Edwin Pope, were great believers in Schnellenberger and were close to him.

And that is all very understandable, when you consider what had been the recent history of Miami football. As late as 1976, intercollegiate football was almost abolished at the university. The Dolphins were at the peak of their popularity, and nobody seemed to care about the Hurricanes, who weren't in a conference, played a bonecrushing national independent schedule, and couldn't even draw decent crowds when Notre Dame came to town. After going 3–8 in 1976, Carl Selmer was fired as coach. Poor guy had had to face Colorado, Nebraska, national-champions-to-be Pittsburgh, Penn State, Notre Dame, the University of Houston in its heyday, and Florida. His three wins had come against TCU, Boston College, and a then struggling Florida State team which a new coach named Bobby Bowden was in his first year of rebuilding.

The administration was at the brink of dropping football when a handful of ultrarich alumni poured in a lot of money to keep the program alive. They brought in Lou Saban, a coach who'd had success in the NFL with the Buffalo Bills. He stayed at Miami only two seasons, the best of which he went 6–5, but he got the financial juices flowing again and the vital signs back near normal.

In 1979 the university hired Schnellenberger, Don Shula's long-time offensive coordinator with the Dolphins. Even he had a losing season, 5–6, his first year. But what Schnellenberger established was "The State of Miami." For decades, Miami had gone North to recruit. It was an expensive private school which could attract some northern players to the warm climate. Historically, that had been enough to let Miami start any given season as a good team—about one-deep at each position. Then the murderous schedule would take its toll in injuries week-by-week. For depth, Schnellenberger, with long established Miami-area high school coaches such as Joe Brodsky and Don Soldinger on his staff, would come up with a different plan.

Outside powers such as Oklahoma often came in and raided the blue-chippers of South Florida high schools, and the University of Florida skimmed off the rest. (And by 1979, Bowden was beginning to make inroads from suddenly successful Florida State.) But Schnellenberger and his staff looked around and realized that with the enormous wealth of talent in South Florida, even if a national power came in and got the best player at a position, and Florida got the next best, then even the third best player was a pretty damn good football player. So Schnellenberger established, for recruiting purposes, "The State of Miami," which ran geographically south from an east-west line through Orlando and the Cocoa-Cape Canaveral area. From that region, they would take the player who might be an inch shorter and ten pounds lighter but was still a good player. They would still go North for some players, especially quarterbacks, but South Florida would be their base. Such were the beginnings of mighty Miami.

Schnellenberger went 9–3 in 1980, 9–2 in 1981, and 7–4 in 1982. But the only thing those teams had to do with the national championship was to begin the now notorious Miami tradition of almost annually screwing up poor old Bobby Bowden's national championship hopes at Florida State.

(Hardly anybody else in the nation beats Bobby; but Howard beat Bobby, I beat Bobby, and now Dennis Erickson beats Bobby. In 1992, after yet another one, Bobby rubbed his brow and said, "They're going to carve this on my tombstone: '. . . but he had to play Miami.' " No man in coaching deserves to have won a national championship more than Bobby Bowden. If it weren't for Miami, he almost certainly would have several national championships under his belt by now—he could pretty well handle the Ohio States and Nebraskas and Michigans and Notre Dames. I respect and admire him enormously as a coach and as a person, and I like to think the feeling is mutual. In 1993, I got a letter from him which he closed by writing, "I meant the things I said [the last time we'd visited]. I don't think there is a better football coach in America—you should fit right up there with the Bear Bryants and Vince Lombardis when you finish up." And it's a very bittersweet thought to me that if it weren't for Miami, Bobby would already be well established in those legendary ranks himself. He fits there. All that's missing is enough recognition, and those 1's in all his 11–1 records are the reason.)

Also, those early-1980s Miami teams managed to begin an absolute, bitter, year-to-year war with the University of Florida that spread right up into the stands. Florida State and Florida for years already had hated each other's guts, but now the intrastate rivalries were in the free-for-all that was the beginning of the modern-day fact that the best college football in America is concentrated in the state of Florida. One thing was certain, going into 1983: Greater Miami's interest in the 'Canes was back.

After being blown out in the season-opening war, 28–3, at Gainesville, by Florida, Schnellenberger's 1983 Hurricanes fell behind early in the polls and it took them all season to catch up. In the last game of the regular season they beat FSU in Tallahassee on a last-second field goal, 17–16.

And so Miami went into the Orange Bowl 10–1, but as an underdog to undefeated, untied, consensus Number One Nebraska. And the rest, truly, is history. Schnellenberger's offense matched awesome Nebraska blow for blow, right down to the wire, and as the clock ran out, Nebraska went for a desperation two-point conversion to win or lose it all. The play failed, Miami won 31–30, won the national championship, and the power structure of national college football would not be the same to this day. Since that Orange Bowl upset of Nebraska, more years than not, and more consistently than any other program, Miami has been the most feared college football team in America.

So no wonder they loved Schnellenberger in Miami. And so for all the early pounding I took in the media, I realized it was mainly because I was not Schnellenberger. And that pounding, hurt though it might, was a minor matter indeed compared to the pounding I took for not being Schnellenberger in the hallways and meeting rooms of the University of Miami football offices.

As it turned out, Olivadotti would be the only one to leave the staff immediately. He took his salary and stayed out of coaching for a season. (He is now defensive coordinator of the Miami Dolphins and doing a good job bringing along a defense peppered with young players. In the years between, I have gotten to know Tom fairly well and we have a fine—well, an okay relationship.)

You'd think the rest of the guys on the staff would have held their little fraternity hell week for the new guy, me, and been done with it. But no. Oh, no. It didn't get better. It got worse. And it was almost like everywhere I went, I had a bunch of eyes following me, whether from the strength coach who later resigned, or the trainer who later resigned, or the defensive coordinator (I moved Bill Trout into that job) who later resigned, or the offensive line coach who later resigned.

The staff took the entire month of June and part of July off, and when they came back, we had to face an early opening game without even knowing one another. As Miami had been voted national champions of 1983, the other team touted by the speculators and re-hashers as the one that had deserved the championship was Auburn. In 1984, the Kickoff Classic game, at the Meadowlands in East Rutherford, New Jersey, was at the peak of its influence, and so chose to pair Miami and Auburn.

When the team came back for preseason practice, the kids were a lot quicker to adapt and accept me than the coaching staff. Years later, Michael Irvin, then a freshman receiver who'd signed with Schnellenberger with high hopes of catching lots of passes, would tell the story that he was at first worried about me. And so were the other players in Schnellenberger's pro-set offensive scheme. You see, the people of Miami were afraid I was going to run the ball on every down. In fact, at Oklahoma State, we'd been second in the Big Eight in passing, and had thrown the ball more than the Miami people realized. But they thought Oklahoma State was on the other side of the moon, and all they knew of the Big Eight was run-run-run. The Miami players read the papers and were worried about who would fit in and who wouldn't.

But as Irvin tells it, everything was fine with the players after I walked in and said, first thing, "Hey, it's a lot easier for one guy to change than for one hundred guys to change. I'll change. You guys don't have to."

And I truly liked what I saw on offense. Who wouldn't, with Bernie Kosar at quarterback, Eddie Brown at receiver, Alonzo Highsmith at fullback, and on and on? We had run the I-formation at Oklahoma State, but I was absolutely open to the talent-laden pro set that had had such success already. I'm a defensive coach by background and that's where my strong beliefs and expertise lie, but I'm flexible on offense.

That first year, I left the defense in a 3–4 scheme. No point in going to a four-man front when Trout and the other defensive coaches weren't exactly what you'd call disciples. With the Olivadotti vacancy I was able to bring in one of my crew from Oklahoma State, Butch Davis, as my defensive line coach.

Other than Butch, one of the few guys who would talk to me, and who I was able to befriend, was Hubbard Alexander. And "Ax," as we call him (he's in Dallas with us today) would jog with me at lunchtime and provide a friendly shoulder that I really needed.

Despite the mess within the staff, the season started very positively. We went to the Meadowlands to play Auburn who, with Bo Jackson, had been ranked Number One in the preseason wire service polls. We won, 20–18, on a Monday night.

We flew back from New Jersey, practiced for a couple of days and then went to Tampa to play Florida on a Saturday night. Some might call that a neutral site, but playing Florida in Tampa is about like playing Notre Dame in Chicago. Through the great play of Bernie Kosar, Eddie Brown, and Willie Smith, we passed our way to a great comeback win against an outstanding Florida team. So we'd beaten two of the best teams in the country, on the road, in less than a week.

A third straight game on the road was too much for us. Bernie threw one too many interceptions at Michigan, and we lost 22–14. The fourth straight week on the road, we beat Purdue, 28–17.

Finally, we came back to Miami and prepared for our first home game, against Bobby Bowden and Florida State. By that time, our players were beat to hell physically and mentally, even though we were 3–1. And we were still trying to feel each other out as a staff. We were still having trying times, having arguments back and forth, and they were still wondering what kind of guy I was.

Florida State not only won, but embarrassed us, 38–3. (After that, I was bound and determined not to lose to Florida State, and never did again. We won four straight from them. In fact, after that embarrassing game, I would always spend extra time on Florida State during our spring and summer practices, to make sure we were able to get an edge on one of our major rivals.)

We went up to Notre Dame and had very few problems with their football team in a 31–13 win. What we had problems with was that little leprechaun mascot of theirs, and his crowd. Police control of the sidelines was virtually nonexistent. The Notre Dame alumni band was even spilling over into our bench area. And while I was trying to coach a football game, that obnoxious little student in the Irish getup kept running up to me and getting in my face. Anybody else might have knocked him on his ass. And I can't tell you it didn't cross my mind. All things considered, 31–13 wasn't as strong an ass-kicking as the Notre Dame crowd deserved that day. We would see them later.

Even with my little darlings on the staff remaining their surly, leering, silent selves, we were 8–2 heading into the last two games of regular season.

Then, the house came tumbling down.

All teams suffer memorable losses. Some suffer nationally famous losses. But I can recall no team that has put together a run of nationally famous losses to equal that of the Miami Hurricanes of 1984.

The disaster began just after halftime of the Maryland game at Miami. We led 31–0 at the half, and had the ball early in the third quarter. And then everything that could go wrong did go wrong. Our big power fullback, Alonzo Highsmith, who was our whole running game, went down with an injury. Then we were stopped on a third-down conversion and had to kick. After that, everything, from fumbles to interceptions to botched kickoff returns to defensive backs underplaying the ball, went wrong. And even though we tried to hold on, and went for a two-point conversion that would have tied it, we lost to Maryland 42–40. National headlines: MIAMI BLOWS 31–0 HALFTIME LEAD. Or, MARYLAND STAGES ALL-TIME COMEBACK.

And that was when, because of lack of unity, lack of a bond, lack of trust, lack of respect on the coaching staff, we totally came unraveled. That was the day I said, "Just please, somehow, let me survive the rest of this year." Conversations with the assistant coaches after that game were nonexistent. I pretty well stayed in my office, except to jump into a meeting and watch some tape occasionally.

Despite all that, we had accepted a Fiesta Bowl bid. We were still a nationally prominent team, still had a decent overall record, and the selection committee figured we could handle Boston College at home in our final game of regular season. During Boston College week, I had indications that Bill Trout, who'd replaced Olivadotti as defensive coordinator, and his part of the staff were going elsewhere. I of course had no objections to that, because after the season I was going to put together my own staff. Bill told me just prior to the Boston College game that he was resigning, effective after the game. In fact, he'd cleaned out his office the night before.

Well, you can imagine what kind of frame of mind our whole defensive structure was in for that game. Even so, with our great offense, we stayed with Boston College in a scoring race and it looked like we had the game wrapped up with a few seconds to go. From what I've been told, Trout had left the coaches' booth in the press box and gone down on the elevator when BC quarterback Doug Flutie scrambled out of the pocket and threw the Hail Mary pass that virtually every football fan remembers, to win the game. Trout's presence in the coaches' booth probably wouldn't have made any difference, because our defensive backs underplayed the ball. Whatever: National headlines: HAIL, FLUTIE!

Then, it was a matter of, what can go wrong now? I hadn't seen anything yet. We had an obligation to play in the Fiesta Bowl, but I don't think anybody was excited about going out there. Prior to leaving for Phoenix, a lot of the coaches announced their resignations. In fact, we made the trip without a defensive coordinator and without an offensive line coach. And we went to Arizona with a lame-duck trainer, strength coach, quarterbacks coach and two graduate assistants, all of whom had given me their resignations. Some fiesta.

And so, of course, in the game, we moved the ball offensively but lost a close, high-scoring game to UCLA, 39–37. The morning after the game, I held a press conference not to rehash the Fiesta Bowl, but to announce the restructuring of my staff. Never, ever again, in college or the NFL, was I going to have a staff that was not bonded. With loyalty as a key concern, I felt it was important to bring in coaches who had worked with me before. From Syracuse I brought in Tony Wise, who'd been with me at Oklahoma State, as my offensive line coach. I brought in Paul Jett, who'd also been with me at Oklahoma State, as my defensive coordinator—one thing was for damn sure: We were going to the 4–3 defense the next year. Gary Stevens remained as offensive coordinator, and I added coaching quarterbacks to his duties. Gary had worked with quarterbacks in the past, and I have always felt that the coordinator and play-caller should coach quarterbacks directly, so they could be on the same page. This step would make our already outstanding quarterbacks even better.

From the first meeting of my new staff and for the next four years, the remainder of my stay at Miami, we would lose four games. We would win forty-four. If you'd told me that in January 1985, I would have guaranteed you Jimmy Johnson and the Miami Hurricanes would have had no more problems as long as I was there.

But then, at that point, I wouldn't have taken seriously what Walter Highsmith, Alonzo's dad, had told me that first season. The Highsmiths are black. Walter was coaching a high school team in Miami, and one day I was visiting with him on the sidelines. We were talking about the cool reception I'd received when I got to Miami.

Coach Highsmith said, "Well, Coach, you know one of the biggest reasons why you got a cold reception is that people are concerned that you're going to recruit too many black players."

I looked at him with a stunned look. I was taken aback.

He said, "Yeah, that's kind of your reputation. And I think some people probably don't want that." It hadn't even registered on me that Miami, an expensive private school, previously had had a predominantly white football team. It hadn't registered on me that some people chose to assume that black players from hard backgrounds were ill-prepared to handle the academic work at Miami.

And so, in response to Walter Highsmith's warning, I laughed. I said, "Well, I'll guarantee you this: I'm not going to keep count of how many black players I recruit. I'm going to recruit the best football players. I could care less what color they are."

X

MY BLACK HAT: A GIFT FROM ST. ARA

Wright Bazemore made Valdosta High in south Georgia a perennial contender for the national championship of high school football, and he blew out many an opponent in the process. In the moments following a 40- or 50-point Valdosta cakewalk, as he shook hands with the opposing coach in the middle of the field, Bazemore might get a less-than-appreciative look or comment from the loser. And Bazemore, it is said, would reply: "Hey, I can't help it if you've got a bad football team."

I like that. There is a right way to play this game, and it isn't half-speed or half-ass. It is not a 30-minute game. It is not a 45-minute game. It is a 60-minute game. I coach one mode of football: attack. It is aggressive, all-out, all the time, and you can't turn it off and on. Wright Bazemore understood that in Georgia, where General Sherman had shown the culture firsthand that war is hell. (And after all, what is football in the American culture if not vicarious war? Bob Oates wrote an excellent piece in the Los Angeles *Times* in 1980, arguing quite successfully that that year was the true centennial of American football. In 1880, the line of scrimmage was instituted, forever separating the game from English rugby, and giving football the battle line, the tactical and strategic planning, the diverse modes of attack, and the element of surprise—in other words, the characteristics that have made American football so popular. I'm not the war analogist and student of military history that some coaches, most notably the late Woody Hayes of Ohio State, have been. But I do suspect that as football coaches, William Tecumseh Sherman, Stonewall Jackson, and George S. Patton, all of whom believed in attacking, all the time, without letup, would have subscribed to Bazemore's and my philosophy. Hold-your-ground generals like George McClellan, James Longstreet, and Omar Bradley wouldn't have fit in very well on my staff.)

I don't sit on a lead. With a fat one, I might adjust the strategy to lessen the number of passes, and I'll put the substitutes in, but I won't bridle them. They can keep ringing up touchdowns until the scoreboard lights blow out, if the opponent fails, or, as often happens, gives up. I don't ever want my players to know what it feels like to let up. If they feel the sensation once, they might feel it again at an inappropriate time. And nobody is going to take the attack initiative from us. Our offensive players are taught to run their attack according to the defense's alignment. For example, as long as a defense insists on blitzing us, we're going to throw on them, to take advantage of their gamble, which places their defensive backs in single coverage. If they blitz, we throw, whatever the score.

As for the notion of a comfortable lead, I've never believed in going into a shell and letting the opponent catch up with you. Look at what happened to us against Maryland in 1984, after we'd led 31–0 at the half. If I see 51 points on our side of the scoreboard, I want 58 up there.

And every Notre Dame fan in America will know precisely where I'm headed, in recalling the season of 1985.

That summer, Bernie Kosar, who'd graduated early, had come out in the NFL's supplemental draft and gone to the Cleveland Browns. So we made Vinny Testaverde our starting quarterback, and had a squadron of gifted receivers such as Brian Blades, Mike Irvin and Brett Perriman. We had Alonzo Highsmith and Melvin Bratton back, to balance our attack with excellent rushing. We installed the 4–3 defense and turned loose guys like Jerome Brown and Daniel Stubbs, guys who had not only the physical talent but the right mindset for aggressive upfield pressure. And my coaching staff was a unit. Now, we were getting somewhere.

We lost the opening game to Florida in Miami, 35–23, but I actually saw some things I liked in that game. I actually came out of that game with a decent feeling. (And as it has turned out, that was the last game Miami lost in the Orange Bowl, to this day.) Then we rolled over some fair-to-middling opponents and were 4–1 when we headed to Norman, Oklahoma, for the big showdown of midseason. At Oklahoma State, I had never beaten Barry Switzer. At Miami, I would never lose to him.

We were rated as an underdog in Norman, but we went into the game with a lot of confidence because we really didn't feel that Oklahoma's defensive style of play (they were geared heavily toward defending against the run) and their pass defense could hold up with us throwing the ball.

And I knew their wishbone offense. I had been at Oklahoma when Switzer, then offensive coordinator, had instituted the wishbone in 1970. So I felt like I knew the wishbone as well as they did. And we had the defensive speed to stop the wishbone.

We had a virtual lock, and all that remained was to play it out. And we did. And how, 27–14. And it wasn't that close. Jerome Brown, for his play in that game, would be named Defensive Player of the Week by AP, UPI, and *Sports Illustrated*. He had sixteen tackles, two sacks, caused a fumble, and blocked a field goal. And Jerome was in on the play that would, long range, net the Dallas Cowboys and me a Super Bowl–winning quarterback. I had known Troy Aikman since he was in high school, and hated that he got his leg broken under our pass rush that day. Jerome Brown and John McVeigh rushed him, and Oklahoma's pass protection was terrible because they were so unaccustomed to it, and were breaking out of character in desperation. But the sack by McVeigh and Brown got Troy Aikman out of the wishbone offense where he didn't belong, got him to transfer to UCLA where he could throw the ball effectively, and so, in the long run, it all prepared Troy much better for the National Football League.

Two weeks later we went to Tallahassee for, ho-hum, just another thriller with Florida State, which we won, 35–27. Then we redeemed ourselves against Maryland in College Park, 29–22. After we disposed of Colorado State 24–3, we were 9–1, and around the country people were beginning to notice that the Miami Hurricanes were again a contender for the national championship.

We had one more game remaining in regular season, at home against Notre Dame. As surely as Howard Schnellenberger's Orange Bowl upset of Nebraska had established Miami in the nation's mind as a football power, our game with Notre Dame would place a nationally perceived black hat on Miami's head, and specifically on mine.

Like Wright Bazemore, Gerry Faust had run a legendary, superpower high school football program at Moeller in Cincinnati. After Dan Devine resigned as head coach at Notre Dame following the 1980 season to go to the Green Bay Packers, Faust was named Notre Dame coach by the school's president, the Rev. Theodore M. Hesburgh, and the executive vice president in charge of athletics, the Rev. Edmund P. Joyce ("Father Joyce," as he's known throughout all of football).

Faust's arrival in 1981 was the most celebrated for a Notre Dame coach since 1941, when Frank Leahy was brought in from a highly successful tenure at another Catholic school, Boston College. Faust was and is a devout man (and, as with Ken Hatfield, I respect that). So Faust's arrival was much more than a secular celebration. It was a nationwide religious experience. He was Mister Catholic, and he came from a superpower Catholic high school to coach Old Notre Dame. *Sports Illustrated* ran a picture of Faust kneeling at a little shrine, accompanied by some of his players.

It just never worked out like they'd hoped. Faust's years at Notre Dame were troubled indeed. In 1981 he coached the Irish to their first losing season since 1963 under Hugh Devore, who had only lasted that one season as head coach. In 1982, 1983, and 1984, Faust went 6–4, 7–5, and 7–5 respectively—this in a program whose followers were disappointed any year they weren't in the running for a national championship.

Here are some circumstances, leading up to our game with Notre Dame on November 30, 1985, that I would not learn about until many years later, from journalists:

By the week of Notre Dame's final home game of the 1985 season, on November 23 against LSU, the Faust regime was coming apart at the seams, and deeply disillusioned Notre Dame players were beginning to speak out vehemently against Faust—they claimed he and his staff were inept and that the squad was simply miserable and fed up with him, except possibly for a few players to whom favoritism had been shown.

That week, there was a heavy undercurrent of feeling that Faust was about to resign under pressure, but Fathers Hesburgh and Joyce weren't confirming. Before the LSU game, the Atlanta *Constitution* got some players to talk. With their stories of misery and incompetence came wryly spoken references to "Mister Catholic" and how, in crucial game situations, Faust would yell down the bench, "Okay! Everybody say a Hail Mary that we'll make this first down!" This on a staff which, when offensive linemen would come off the field reporting that the blocking scheme was futile and suggesting adjustments, would reply, "You do the playing and be quiet, and we'll do the coaching." And the onslaught from the opposing defensive front would continue.

The players who talked were adamant that the *Constitution* hold the story until the morning of the LSU game, to assure that they wouldn't be held out of their final home game in South Bend for speaking out. The story was picked up by CNN and South Bend was abuzz with it during the game, which Notre Dame lost to a mediocre LSU team, 10–7.

Notre Dame alumni in Atlanta wrote thankful and congratulatory notes to the *Constitution,* and added that they'd Fed-Exed the story straight to Father Joyce's desk, to make sure he got those kids' messages loud and clear.

The following week, Gerry Faust announced his resignation, effective after the last game of the season, which would be played on the road. That road trip, a nice one, amounted to one huge sigh of relief from the Notre Dame players. They wanted to go to Miami, to lie in the sun for a few days, after such a miserable season, and, in some cases, such miserable college careers.

And that was the Notre Dame team Miami faced on November 30, 1985. I knew that Faust had announced his resignation, but I had no idea of just how bad the situation was within the Notre Dame team. I'd been totally focused on coaching—we'd won nine games in a row—and hadn't picked up on the news stories.

In fact, getting ready for Notre Dame, I was scared to death. With the pride and the tradition of Notre Dame, and the quality of their players, I thought Faust's resignation might be a rallying point for them. I could envision us walking into a buzzsaw, with them at a fever pitch emotionally to win one last game for Gerry.

Silly me.

On game week, the only hint that I had that they might not be ready to play was that a few of the media people had told us Notre Dame had come down a few days early, and that their players were up in Fort Lauderdale having a big time enjoying the sunshine and the beaches.

Well, of all the games that I have ever coached in my career, I don't know that one of my teams has ever played another game as flawlessly as that Miami team did against Notre Dame. We scored on defense, we scored in the kicking game, we scored on every possession up until the last part of the game, and it was a complete rout, 58–7.

Now: Little did I know that with us playing so flawlessly and the rout being what it was, Ara Parseghian was up in the CBS broadcast booth almost in tears, saying that we didn't have any compassion.

Parseghian was there as color commentator. This was the same Ara Parseghian who'd spent eleven years as Notre Dame's head coach, 1964 through 1974, and who during that time had made a common practice of humiliating opponents. He coached so many routs that his mere over-40 totals would take too long to list, but here are highlights of Irish rampages on Parseghian's watch: On November 6, 1965, he beat Pittsburgh 69–13; on November 12, 1966, he beat Duke 64–0; on October 7, 1967, he beat Iowa 56–6; on October 19, 1968, he beat Illinois 58–8; in the 1970 season alone he beat Army 51–10, Navy 56–7, Purdue 48–0 and Pittsburgh 46–14; in 1971 he beat Northwestern 50–7 and Pittsburgh 56–7; on October 20, 1973, he beat Army 62–3. And on December 1, 1973, he beat the University of Miami 44–0.

And Parseghian's ruthlessness was not at all a departure from Notre Dame tradition. Their current unbroken history of football began in 1892 (they had dabbled at it off and on previously) when the Irish opened the season by edging that renowned powerhouse of the Midwest, South Bend High School, 56–0. From 1902 through 1905 they carried on a heated rivalry with mighty American Medical, and escaped with wins of 92–0, 52–0, 44–0 and 142–0. Knute Rockne himself wasn't above hanging, oh, for example, a 74–0 on Kalamazoo here and a 77–0 on Beloit there.

In 1977, Parseghian's successor, Dan Devine, didn't particularly like Georgia Tech coach Pepper Rodgers, so Devine decided to express himself in public. In the fourth quarter at South Bend, with the scoreboard whirring like a digital computer with Irish points, Devine let the bombs-away passing assault continue. And with each Notre Dame touchdown, on their sidelines, right biceps would be grasped with left hands and right arms thrust into the air in gestures that said, "Stick *another* one up your ass, Rodgers!" The clock ran out before Devine could get past 69 points.

And even poor old Gerry Faust hung a 52–6 on Purdue in 1983.

And never once, by November 30, 1985, had I criticized Notre Dame for running up a score. I still don't. Again: it's a 60-minute game. I just point out some of their routs to illustrate to you what an absolute hypocrite St. Ara the Tearful was being when he criticized me, saying emotionally to a national television audience, "It's time for Jimmy Johnson to show some compassion."

Well, even down on the sidelines, I guess I should have known. I'd learned way back on DeQueen Boulevard in Port Arthur, Texas, that nobody cries louder and more pitifully than a bully who's just had the shit stomped out of him. But later, when I watched and listened to the videotape of the telecast, I was incredulous.

Not only had Parseghian shown his gold underwear and been an obvious hypocrite to anyone with an objective knowledge of football history, but he had failed to do his job as color commentator, and Brent Musburger had failed to do his as a play-by-play man. What, after all, are broadcasters there for? They are there to spot with expert eyes, and explain with expert tongues, things that the layman viewer has not spotted. One thing they said was absolutely ridiculous: "How can they [Miami] be blocking punts when the game is completely out of hand?" That was probably the line that made Miami a name that would live in infamy in Notre Dame hearts, and therefore in many, many American hearts in general. But here is exactly what happened on the punt block:

By that point, we had so many second- and third-string players in the game that we were having problems getting our substitutions straight. All the starters had been pulled. Notre Dame was punting out of their own end zone, and we set up to return the punt, but it wasn't even our regular punt return unit. We called for a return right. By no stretch of the imagination did we have a punt-block called. And, in the substitution confusion, we only got ten men on the field for the play.

And then Bill Hawkins, one of our backup defensive tackles, strolled untouched into their backfield and blocked the punt for a touchdown. Now if we'd sent some first-string strong safety firing through a gap or around the outside to block the punt, that would have been one thing. But as it was, any junior high coach could have sat up there in the broadcast booth and seen that there was no punt block on and that Bill Hawkins had just waltzed in. What was Bill supposed to do? Take five giant steps backward and bow while the punter got it off?

And any color commentator or play-by-play man with anything remotely resembling an objective eye would have seen that and would have said so. But this was Parseghian and this was Notre Dame. Very few American souls are objective about Notre Dame. Most people either love them or hate them, and the lovers vastly outnumber the haters. And to compound it, this was Gerry Faust's last game and everybody felt for him—everybody, it seems, except his players. Those players were truly just putting in time that day, and my team happened to play flawlessly.

I had never seen anything like the reaction we got the next week. We had stacks and stacks of letters, most of them negative. But some of them were very positive: "Hey, Notre Dame has been doing that to us for years. I'm glad you did what you did."

But that was the day Miami got the black hat, a gift from St. Ara, placed squarely on my head. And to this day a lot of people think I'm negative toward Notre Dame. Just the opposite is true. I've always had tremendous respect for Notre Dame, and actually, it's one of my favorite schools. It's just that we happened to put a score on them that they'd put on other people for years and years.

And to borrow again from Wright Bazemore: Hey, I couldn't help it if Gerry Faust had a demoralized football team.

We finished the regular season 10–1 with one of the youngest teams in the country. We had only one senior starter, Kevin Fagan (now a defensive end with the San Francisco 49ers). People were really beginning to talk about this being a national championship–caliber team. Or, considering our new image, maybe people were beginning to *fear* that this could be a national championship team. The team America now loved to hate was going to the Sugar Bowl, and cast in the role of the good guys were an old friend and colleague of mine Johnny Majors and his Tennessee Volunteers.

That bowl season we clearly had a chance to win the national championship, even though we'd had the opening loss in regular season. There were two other contenders for the title. Penn State was ranked No. 1 going into their Orange Bowl pairing with Oklahoma. I figured Switzer's speed merchants could outburn Joe Paterno's team. And we'd beaten Oklahoma soundly in regular season. So Oklahoma likely would beat Penn State, and all we had to do was take care of our end and we'd win the final wire-service balloting.

While Switzer's burners were indeed taking care of Penn State, Majors did me the most dubious favor he'd done since he'd gotten me the job at Picayune, Mis'ippi. Tennessee showed us we didn't have the experience to win it all. We went into the game planning to run a bunch of audibles with our offense. Well, the Superdome was filled with Tennessee Vols, and I've never been so sick of hearing "Rocky Top" in my life. Their band must have played it once a minute.

I'd told Vinny Testaverde, "If you can't hear, don't pull away from the line of scrimmage, because it'll only make the noise get louder." And on the first play of the game, Vinny called time out because he couldn't call his signals. An orange-colored hell came down around us, and it just got worse and worse. And we really played poorly. We turned the ball over and had a poor outing, and Tennessee took advantage of it and played well, and they kicked our ass, 35–7. Hey: Johnny Majors couldn't help it if I had a young and nervous football team.

XI

US AGAINST A WORLD LED BY OUR OWN PRESIDENT

L oving the ethnic swirl of Greater Miami as I did (and do), it was a joy to realize by 1986 that we were drawing a true cross section of the community to the Orange Bowl for our home games. We were filling the stadium, something even Schnellenberger's teams hadn't managed, even in the national championship season. Now it was great, and a little ironic: Here was an expensive private school that had produced Everyman's team. Florida State and Florida could fill their stadia virtually with their alumni alone. Miami's alumni weren't nearly as numerous nor as fanatic. We needed the public. And we got them.

Since my talk with Coach Highsmith at his practice, I had looked around and realized that, in the middle of all the talent in South Florida, we'd had a predominantly white team, and that a lot of talent had been bypassed. I wasn't going to bypass anybody, as long as he was a good player and could handle the academics. By 1986 the number of black players at Miami had significantly increased.

We were an exceptionally close-knit team which happened to be made up of African-American, European-American, and Latin-American players. It was not an issue with us, and it was not an issue with the people of Greater Miami. I only wish I was more certain about the rest of America's perceptions of the Miami Hurricanes of 1986.

We had some players who came from very deprived backgrounds. That in no way hindered their quality as men and as citizens. It did, in some cases, leave them with insecurities they had to work out and overcome. If you've grown up in the hard environments of Pahokee or Homestead, and suddenly find yourself walking the well-to-do environs of the University of Miami campus in Coral Gables, there is some adjustment to be made. And so to mask nervousness, anxiety, and insecurity, some of our players behaved quite the opposite way on the football field: cool, supremely confident, joyful. They exulted in their success, and they were demonstrative about it.

Confidence is necessary to play football. Different players have different ways of building confidence. Both my formal training in psychology and my decades of firsthand experience with human beings told me that if I stymied and handcuffed the players who needed to be demonstrative, I would stymie and handcuff their confidence. Because of a lot of our players' backgrounds, we had to be somewhat flamboyant.

And so we the Miami Hurricanes got our national reputation as "hot dogs." The tragic irony is that if America had understood the true reasons our players were demonstrative on the field, we might have been more popular, or at least less criticized.

Take, for example, Michael Irvin. If you watched my Miami teams play on television, you may recall how, after catching touchdown passes in home games at the Orange Bowl, Mike would run right up into the lower end zone seats, pointing at fans seated there. Just watching on TV, you might think, "What a hot dog!" But the truth is that that group, which was ethnically diverse, turned out especially to see Mike play. And when he pointed at each of them, he would look them in the eyes individually and they knew that the gesture meant, "This is for you, and you, and you, and you, and you, and you . . ."

Michael Jerome Irvin grew up in a family of seventeen children in Fort Lauderdale. His father died in 1983, and Mike dedicated his football career to his dad's memory. He went on to graduate from Miami in four years with a business management degree, in an era when much of the general student population of the United States requires five years to graduate from college.

And now that he's an All-Pro receiver with the Cowboys, people in the Dallas–Fort Worth area know Michael Irvin. He hosts a popular television show, and he is one of the most popular figures and truly class acts in the community, transcending sports. I daresay nobody in the area begrudges him his big salary, because they know much of it goes to help support his family back in Florida.

But in 1986, all that America knew was that we had a lot of flamboyant players, that we'd blown out Notre Dame the year before and been heavily criticized for it, and that we had a lot of black players out front, many of whom tended to be demonstrative.

That 1986 team was one of the finest football teams I had ever seen anywhere, at any level. We really just rolled through every opponent in regular season. But as our success snowballed so did the criticism. If 1984 and 1989 were the hardest years of my life, and 1987 and 1992 were the happiest, then 1986 certainly qualifies as the most bittersweet.

We opened at South Carolina with a 34–14 win, beat Florida 23–15 at Gainesville, and really started showing our offensive firepower when we beat Texas Tech 61–11 in our home opener.

We were 3–0 when we headed into the big Number One versus Number Two showdown of Oklahoma versus Miami, at Miami. Brian Bosworth, Oklahoma's big, fast, mouthy, super cool, demonstrative, flamboyant, controversial linebacker, had come out and said all sorts of things about what they were going to do to us. He also was quoted as saying playing us was like "playing the University of San Quentin." The Boz, who happened to be white, was being touted in the media as a new-wave role model and just about the coolest guy ever to hit college football—entire suburban peewee football teams were getting "The Boz" haircuts, and weren't they cute? The Boz would end that season banned from the Orange Bowl game for suspected steroid use, would make an ass of himself over it by wearing that NATIONAL COMMUNISTS AGAINST ATHLETES t-shirt on national TV, and he and Barry Switzer would go on hurling verbal bombs at each other, everywhere from press conferences to books, for years. Some role model.

(I know, I know. I had a linebacker, George Mira, Jr., banned by the NCAA from the next Orange Bowl after urinalysis detected a diuretic that could be used to mask steroid use. He sued in court for reinstatement. And I said way ahead of time that he was not going to play, no matter what the courts ruled. And I meant it. And he didn't play.)

Well, The Boz and all the other Oklahoma defenders ended up just exhausted, trying to catch Vinny Testaverde, who put on a show. On one play Vinny scrambled all over the field and threw a touchdown pass to Alonzo Highsmith. We beat Oklahoma 28–16.

Because of the reaction of the media to the Notre Dame blowout the year before, gradually we had started to get more and more negative publicity with our players. They were very, very good and they knew they were good, and they were aggressive, enthusiastic, sometimes loud and boisterous, and without question, by general America's definition, cocky. This caused negative reactions on a lot of fronts, not only from the media but from our college administration.

That year we had several off-the-field incidents, any of which, isolated, would have been considered minor. Out of any group of ninety-five college men, on any campus, you're not exactly going to get one continuous Eagle Scout meeting. But we were the Miami Hurricanes, and because of the scrutiny of the administration and the media, the incidents started to pile up. University of Miami President Edward Thaddeus Foote II was as good as anyone at forming critical opinions first and learning the full story later—if at all.

Here are some examples of the whole stories:

Melvin Bratton was charged with shoplifting. He had gone into a J.C. Penney store with his mother and sister. He had tried on a pair of sunglasses, which, according to the fashion of the time, included putting the sunglasses up on his head. He continued browsing and talking with his mother and sister, forgot the sunglasses were on top of his head, and walked out of the store. He was quickly acquitted of the charge when the truth was determined, but you know how that goes—the charge makes headlines and the acquittal is buried somewhere in the "Sports Briefly" roundup.

Michael Irvin allegedly ran over a law student's toes with his car. Michael was leaving the cafeteria, the law student walked right in front of his car, and Michael honked his horn. The student challenged him, standing firm, apparently showing off what he'd learned in law school about pedestrian rights. Michael was both exasperated and trying to drive around the confrontation.

A regular student found a lost telephone credit card and wrote the number on the wall by the public phone in his dorm. He thought it was great fun to leave the number for use by all comers. Several football players came along at various times and used the number. But a much larger number of non-athlete students from the general campus population used the number. It was by no means right for our guys to use it, but it was no less wrong for the other students to use it. And if the incident had involved all non-athletes, I wonder how much local, let alone national, media attention it would have gotten.

The Miami *News* ran a story about three or four of our players driving expensive cars. They staked out parking lots and wrote down license plate numbers and traced them. Alonzo Highsmith was one of the players who had a nice car. A check of the registration showed that his father, a high school coach, and his mother, who worked in a hospital, had indeed bought him the car. They had for years been saving money for Alonzo's college education, and when he got a full football scholarship to Miami they didn't need the money for his tuition, so they bought him a car. Only one registration check turned up something I had to deal with. Winston Moss, one of our star linebackers, had borrowed a car from a guy who claimed to be an agent. For this, I suspended Winston from the opening game against South Carolina. That turned out to be the most serious proven offense and punishment on our team all year.

Greater Miami at the time was a battleground for several heavily competitive newspapers, as well as a television market that ranks in the top dozen or so in America and is highly competitive. There's nothing wrong with that. (Hell, we eventually began to use it as a recruiting tool: "If you come here to school, you *will* make news—one way or another.") It's just that other major-colleges football programs, mostly located in smaller towns such as Tuscaloosa, Alabama, or State College, Pennsylvania, or Norman, Oklahoma, or Lincoln, Nebraska, don't know media competition and therefore don't know the kind of scrutiny we knew. Such incidents as ours, had they occurred in a smaller market, would have been less likely to come to light at all, let alone become big issues.

A Miami player could barely belch after lunch without public knowledge. Everything was a story in a media greyhound race. The Miami *News*, for example, was fighting for its life (and would later lose) in the face of the dominant Miami *Herald*. Throw into the fray the papers from up the coast (Fort Lauderdale, Hollywood, Palm Beach, et al.) and even all the way out to Orlando and St. Petersburg and Tampa. From across the peninsula, the Fort Myers paper had a beat reporter assigned to us daily, and his stories were fed to the enormous Gannett chain that included *USA Today*. Then add local television.

No other college team, not even Southern Cal or UCLA, was under that kind of media miscroscope. In Los Angeles, media attention is heavily diverted to the professional Dodgers, Angels, Raiders, Rams, and Lakers. In Miami at the time, we and the Dolphins were the only games in town. The Dolphins' public and media appeal was past its prime, and we were on the rise.

I readily admit that we had our share of campus incidents in 1986, but I honestly believe that we had no more than our share, either for a football team or for any other random sampling of ninety-five college men on any campus in a year. It's just that we were highly visible, in a highly competitive media market where reporters were pursuing their jobs all-out, and so we stood out.

The stories of our missteps went nationwide, and we found ourselves tagged with the title of a popular network television series of the time, *Miami Vice*. The regular season was rapidly building into what our sports information director, Rich Dalrymple, would call "the undefeated season from hell."

And so there developed almost an "Us against the world" mentality, not only among our players but among our fans.

Now add to that the American public's perceptions whenever we played on national television. I don't know that there was racism in general America's perceptions of us in 1986, but I do think the circumstantial evidence is pretty strong that there was ignorance involved—not enough people in white America having had real relationships with minority individuals. And I don't mean having someone clean your house. I mean real relationships. If there hadn't been ignorance out there, then there would have been a better understanding of our players' emotions.

By no means am I going to be like some of the holier-than-thou people I come across on occasion, who say, "I understand what black people went through and I understand how they were treated—I understand." I don't understand, because I didn't go through it. I do take a person for who he is, and I do think I have some compassion for an individual who has gone through adversity because of the color of his skin. But my dealing with players is not a black-white thing. It's a matter of treating each player individually. And I think having feeling for the individual is what helps me bring out the best in all of them.

So if dropping the ball to the end zone turf and trotting stoically off the field brought out the best in one, fine. And if prancing in the end zone with arms thrust to high heaven and then running into the stands brought out the best in another, fine. And so I began to take heat for "failing to control" them.

Our black players knew what was going on and were feeling bad about it. One day, Michael Irvin walked into my office and sat down. I looked up and said, "Mike, what do you need?"

"I don't need anything, Coach," he said. "I just came to make sure you're okay this time. Because Coach, you put up with so much. Man, how do you put up with so much? People giving you such a hard time about us and the way we play. Is there anything the players can do for you?"

I said, "Mike, you just keep playing and winning. I'll put up with all that."

The team was very close, and our white players didn't like the rain of negativism anymore than the black players. It wasn't a black-white thing with us. Mess with one guy and you'd messed with them all.

The late Jerome Brown was a tremendous leader to the day he died, and beyond. Just look at the inspired season his Philadelphia Eagles teammates played in his memory in 1992, after he was killed in an automobile accident.

So we finished the 1986 season 11–0, and were so dominant in college football that we actually got to choose which bowl the national championship game would be played in. Our theme, as led by Jerome Brown, then our All-America defensive tackle, was "We're on a mission."

Undefeated Penn State was ranked No. 2 and, like Miami, was not in a conference at that time. Because we were both independents, an opportunity fell open for some second-echelon bowl to snare itself a national championship game. The big bowls where these things were normally decided were all tied up with conference contracts. The Rose must take the Pac-10 and Big 10 champions, the Sugar the SEC champion, the Orange the Big Eight champion and the Cotton the Southwest Conference champion. None of those champions were in the hunt for the national championship that year. And so there arose a bidding war for the title game, and the final two combatants were the Fiesta Bowl in

Tempe, Arizona, and the Citrus Bowl in Orlando. Landing this matchup would permanently improve the stature of either bowl.

Penn State agreed to play wherever we chose, since we were Number One. I usually say I never look back. But about this matter, I do. Larry Guest, sports columnist at the Orlando *Sentinel*, kept trying to get me to have the game in Orlando. Sam Jankovich, as athletic director, was pretty well making this call. But, I guess through cockiness or overconfidence, I took the stance that I didn't care where we played or who we played—we'd beat anybody we played.

Looking back, it would have been a lot better home field advantage had we played in Orlando rather than going all the way out to Arizona. And very likely, as a Florida team, we would have gotten much better treatment from the Citrus than the Fiesta, which is to say, we would at least have been treated decently.

We chose the Fiesta Bowl, and even though we were the ones who made the decision, the Fiesta, after they got us committed, really gave us backdoor treatment. They went completely the other way with their attention because of the prestige of Penn State, the number of fans they were going to bring (we didn't have a strong enough alumni backing to bring a lot of fans on such an expensive trip), and the prestige of Joe Paterno, who'd just been named Sportsman of the Year on the cover of *Sports Illustrated*.

After they got us locked in, we ended up becoming the visitors and getting the visitors' dressing room. And where Joe was touted—they couldn't do enough things for Joe; they waited on him hand and foot—we were treated as the black sheep or the ugly sister. I had a couple of run-ins with Bruce Skinner, Fiesta Bowl director at that time, over the treatment of our people. The discussions were pretty heated. I was upset, and there wasn't much reply he could make. Even though we could have taken the game to Orlando, the Fiesta had locked us in and now was blatantly bowing to Sportsman of the Year Paterno and to that tremendous number of fans Penn State would bring.

In January 1983, the Washington Redskins had arrived in Pasadena for Super Bowl XVII, dressed in combat fatigues. John Riggins, their big, flamboyant, controversial fullback, who happened to be white, led the fatigue movement and was sort of the team spokesman for it. And America and its media thought, Well, isn't that cute? In ensuing years, spurred on by the Rambo movies, American youth from junior high to college age had adopted the fad of wearing combat fatigues.

By January 1986, not only was the fad not controversial, it was not even new. But it did fit in with our "We're on a mission" theme. When our team stepped off the plane at Sky Harbor International Airport in Phoenix wearing combat fatigues, led by Jerome Brown, who happened to be black, the nation reacted as if it had been invaded by a hostile power.

I had flown out to the Fiesta Bowl early for a function two days before the team flew out. I had scheduled a team meeting their very first night after they got off the plane, and here came the players, walking in in combat fatigues. It was a surprise to me. I knew nothing about what their attire was going to be. When the media began to ask me about it, some of them thought it was comical and some thought it was interesting, but I played it that the players had a serious approach, that they were on a mission: they were going to win the national championship. I didn't know who had instigated it—Jerome, Alonzo Highsmith, Winston Moss, or who—but we had a lot of senior leaders and I realized immediately that this was just their thing and I went along with it completely. I found out later that the entire team had gotten together and talked about it and decided to show unity that way.

But the question to me, constantly, was: "How are you going to deal with it?" Deal with it? Hell, I didn't even see a lot of harm in it. Little did I know that it was going to cause such a negative reaction, especially after the game was over with. Regardless, I wasn't about to come down on our players and chastise them just a few days before the biggest game of their lives and the biggest game I'd ever coached in. I was going to keep everything upbeat and positive.

It was sometimes hard to bite my tongue in public considering the treatment we were getting from the Fiesta Bowl, but I intended to go along with everything with a positive public face. The Fiesta Bowl annually hosts a Steak Fry for both teams. It is held in some tourist attraction, a sort of pioneer town way the hell in the middle of nowhere, and the drive out there seems to take forever. Joe Paterno did not require the Penn State players to go. I required my players to go. Joe Paterno did not even show up at the Steak Fry. I went, and sat through the whole thing, until Jerome Brown decided it was time for all of us to leave.

After dinner, our guys were asking me, "Coach, can we leave?" I said, "No, no, no. We're here now; we might as well stay for the whole thing."

Each team was supposed to put on a comedy skit. Penn State's players, the ones who were there, went first. We were supposed to do ours last.

But the Penn State punter got up and made an off-color joke. He said Penn State was supposed to be lily white, and that they had the white hats and Miami had the black hats. He said, "Hey, we have black players at Penn State. In fact, on occasion we even let our black players sit down at the table and eat with us."

Well, that didn't sit too well with Jerome and our other black players. It probably didn't sit too well with the black players from Penn State, either, but they didn't say anything. Joe didn't have many black players. The majority of our players were black.

I was standing in the back, beside Jerome, and Jerome was cussing. The racial remark had set him off, but he wasn't moving yet, just standing there, cussing. Then the Penn State punter made a joke about my hair.

Jerome said, "Coach, we joke all the time about your hair, but that doesn't give those motherfuckers the right to joke about your hair."

Then Jerome got up and gave his now famous little speech: "We didn't sit down to dinner with the Japanese the night before Pearl Harbor, and we're not going to get up here and act like a bunch of monkeys to entertain you people. We're going to war."

Jerome walked out and everyone else from the University of Miami, including me, followed.

The vast majority of the national media people didn't arrive in Phoenix until the next day. Many hustled to catch up after they heard about the Steak Fry Incident. They got the quotes from Jerome's speech from others, but didn't get much else as they hit their keyboards on the fly. And so America was told, essentially, that big, bad Jerome Brown had led the bad, bad Miami Hurricanes stomping out of a dinner party with Joe Paterno's little darlings. Just another episode of *Miami Vice*, right?

Then there was a Fiesta Bowl luncheon, even more tedious and even more visible, in downtown Phoenix. For this one, Paterno showed up and brought every one of his players in coats and ties. Most of them matched: blue blazers and striped ties. Many of our players didn't even own coats and ties, let alone blazers that matched for the entire team. Miami is simply not a coat-and-tie town, especially for young people. And, frankly, some of our players couldn't afford coats and ties. Team blazers used to be the norm for Division I teams in the 1960s, but the NCAA has long since stopped allowing schools to make such purchases for their players. One of the things the Fiesta Bowl did allow us to do was buy each player a nice warmup suit. We thought the black warmups looked sharpest, and chose them. And so for the luncheon, Paterno's perfectly groomed, immaculately dressed players paraded across the stage making their speeches. And in the back of the room, dressed all in black, sat the mostly black Miami Hurricanes.

I went up to the podium to make a few remarks. What I was about to say was half in jest, but half a matter of not being able to bite my tongue any longer. Over the microphone, to at least a thousand people that included many media representatives, I referred to Paterno as Saint Joe. Sure enough: Another episode of *Miami Vice*. The arrogant King Renegade, Jimmy Johnson, had blasphemed the Sportsman of the Year.

As game day approached, the media buildup was a clear consensus: It was the duel in the Arizona desert between the good guys and the bad guys.

Vinny Testaverde, our quarterback, had been in a motor scooter accident—he'd been eating a hamburger while driving, and lost control of the scooter—just prior to our final regular season game. He'd skinned up his arms and legs and face, and hadn't been able to play in that last game against East Carolina. And he had missed most of bowl practice due to the injuries and all the time he spent traveling around the country to accept the Heisman Trophy, the Maxwell Trophy, and the various other awards he was getting. He was a great player, but he simply was not prepared well enough for the game against Penn State.

We played fantastic defense the entire game. Penn State got only eight first-downs total. And we had about 450 yards on offense. In retrospect, we probably could have done nothing but give the ball to Alonzo Highsmith and Melvin Bratton and run it down their throats, and we would have won the national championship. But our offense was based on balance, and we mixed it up. Vinny was not sharp. Paterno's defense did a good job of disguising and rotating their coverages, and even their big linebackers would come lumbering out of nowhere to pick off passes. Vinny threw five interceptions and we lost the game, 14–10.

It was the most devastating loss I've had. It remains so to this day. I went to the locker room and players were crying. Emotions were rampant. And I myself was devastated. I knew that we'd just lost a chance at being remembered as one of the best teams of all time. And I knew that it was the best team that I'd ever coached. And we had come up short.

I went to the press conference the next morning and fielded still more questions about our black-hat image. I kept repeating that I thought it stemmed from the *Miami Vice* notion. I was heartsick about the loss, and up to the gills in questions about our image, but I kept my cool. Paterno sat there beside me, admittedly a bit hungover from the celebration.

"A couple of players came by my room looking for a case of beer, and I helped 'em find it," Paterno said. Everybody laughed. The Good Guys had won.

I got on a plane in Phoenix and headed not back to Miami with my players, but to Tokyo to coach in the Japan Bowl all-star game. I couldn't get over my devastation, even on the other side of the world. My old and dear friend Pat Jones, head coach at Oklahoma State, was there. Pat had been my friend since Arkansas and Pittsburgh in the seventies. He provided a friendly shoulder that I badly needed. Pat and

I stuck pretty much to ourselves that week, while I hashed and rehashed the Fiesta Bowl. And slowly I began to feel a little better, or rather, a little less awful.

Then I got a long-distance call from Nick Christin, my attorney and best friend outside of coaching, in Miami. Nick asked if I knew what was going on back in Miami, and actually back around the country—the reaction to the Steak Fry Incident and the fatigues—and the negative reaction by our administration and by President Foote. I said I was completely unaware of it.

Nick said, "You'd better be prepared, because there's been a daily onslaught." My trusted attorney didn't sound like there was any letup in sight.

Prior to the game with Penn State, there had been a lot of speculation that I might be going to Southern Cal as head coach. (And USC did have a lot of the same attractive qualities as Miami: warm weather, big city, bright lights, beaches, national championship capability.) Edward Thaddeus Foote II, the University of Miami's president, had always postured himself as an educator who wasn't actively in favor of bigtime football. Tad Foote missed his calling when he wasn't a politician. In fact, I wonder if he wasn't a wannabe politician. He's the son-in-law of the renowned former Senator J. William Fulbright, and is by training a lawyer and a journalist. And I won't be surprised if Foote does land in politics some day.

While the Southern Cal rumors were flying, at our football banquet just after the end of regular season, Edward Thaddeus Foote II, non-advocate of bigtime football, talked to me over at the side of the banquet room about how he wanted me to stay, et cetera, et cetera, et cetera. And although I really didn't care a lot for some of his views, I still could have dealt with him. He said he wanted to extend my contract, and that he would rework my contract (the implication was a more attractive package). So I agreed.

Tad Foote then went up to the podium at the football banquet and made the announcement that I had decided to sign a new contract, that I would be staying with the University of Miami Hurricanes, and so the

This building used to be Townsend's Dairy (on Proctor Street), a place where my father worked and I spent a lot of my time. The building is now abandoned. DALLAS COWBOYS WEEKLY

Age 8 in Port Arthur.

C.W. and Allene Johnson—Daddy and Mother. DALLAS COWBOYS WEEKLY

University of Arkansas days. UNIVERSITY OF ARKANSAS

A pregame walk was an Arkansas team tradition. Here, in 1963, I'm joined by *(left to right):* Ronnie Mack Smith, my roommate Stan Sparks, and Jim Williams (currently the president of the Cotton Bowl). Notice the only guy who is wearing a tie and has his sport coat buttoned. I guess I've always been a neatness freak.

Buckshot Underwood, our high school head coach, was the first strong football influence in my life. J.C. WATKINS PHOTOGRAPHY

University of Oklahoma, 1970

FRONT ROW *(left to right):* Barry Switzer, Jimmy Dickey, Gaylen Hall, Don Boyce, Chuck Fairbanks, Warren Harper, Larry Lacewell, Jimmy Johnson, Billy Michael. SECOND ROW: Gene Hochevar, Don Jimerson, Leon Cross, Jerry Pettibone, Bobby Warmack.

Iowa State, 1968

(Left to right): Larry Lacewell, Jimmy Johnson, Gordie Smith, Jackie Sherrill, Johnny Majors, Lew Erber, King Block, Joe Madden, Arch Steele.

Iowa State, 1969

FRONT ROW *(left to right):* Joe Madden, Jackie Sherrill, Jimmy Johnson, King Block, Johnny Majors. BACK ROW: Gordie Smith, George Haffner, George Dyer, Ray Greene, Joe Avezzano, Ollie Keller, athletic trainer, Arch Steele.

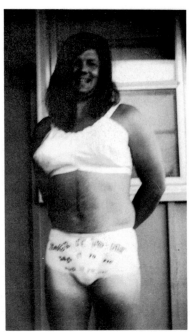

Linda Kay and I in Acapulco.

In drag in Ames, Iowa.

A victory rise in 1981, after we beat Iowa State (27–7) at Ames to earn an
Independence Bowl bid. OKLAHOMA STATE UNIVERSITY

Woody Hayes was the guest speaker at one of our Oklahoma State football banquets.

Dexter Manley after a big win at Oklahoma State. OKLAHOMA STATE UNIVERSITY

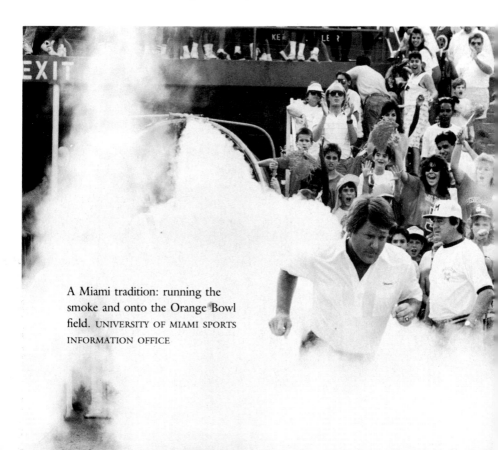

A Miami tradition: running the smoke and onto the Orange Bowl field. UNIVERSITY OF MIAMI SPORTS INFORMATION OFFICE

The victory celebration following parade to honor the 1987 national champions. UNIVERSITY OF MIAMI SPORTS INFORMATION OFFICE

The bronze bust that was sculpted for a celebrity roast in Port Arthur following the 1987 national championship. DALLAS COWBOYS WEEKLY

At the White House with the Hurricanes and President Reagan. WHITE HOUSE PHOTO

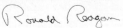

To Jimmy Johnson with best wishes, Ronald Reagan

Relaxing with Rhonda at a
gulfside restaurant in Galveston.

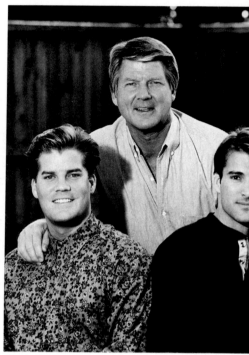

Chad *(left)* and Brent *(right)*. PETER READ
MILLER

Clowning around with Barry Switzer at a press conference prior to the
national championship game with Oklahoma in 1988 at the Orange
Bowl. UNIVERSITY OF MIAMI SPORTS INFORMATION OFFICE

University of Miami quarterbacks. I coached four of them in college and coached against four of them in the NFL. This photo was taken at a golf outing in 1990. Jim Kelly (12), Steve Walsh (4), Bernie Kosar (20), Vinny Testaverde (14), George Mira (10), and Craig Erickson (7). © J. SCOTT KELLY

A victory ride following the 20–14 win over Oklahoma in the Orange Bowl that gave Miami the 1987 national championship. UPI/BETTMANN

An extremely tense first press conference—February 28, 1989. DALLAS COWBOYS
WEEKLY

Our daily prepractice talk. This was during two-a-days in Austin in July 1991. THE
DALLAS MORNING NEWS

Troy Aikman doing what he does best.

Trying to sort things out with Jesse Solomon. Not the easiest thing to do.

DALLAS COWBOYS WEEKLY

A staff party at my house in 1991. This singing quartet includes *(left to right)* assistant coaches Dave Campo, Tony Wise, and Ron Meeks.

Draft day 1989: Troy Aikman, the first overall pick in the draft. To his left: Jerry, Leigh Steinberg (Troy's agent), and Mike McCoy (Cowboys' vp). © RON ST. ANGELO

Our first Cowboys' training camp in Thousand Oaks, California (July 1989). DALLAS COWBOYS WEEKLY

Facing the reality of a 31–17 loss to the Giants in 1990. DALLAS COWBOYS WEEKLY

One of the very few smiles of 1989 while talking to ESPN after our only win, a 13–3 victory over the Redskins at RFK. DALLAS COWBOYS WEEKLY

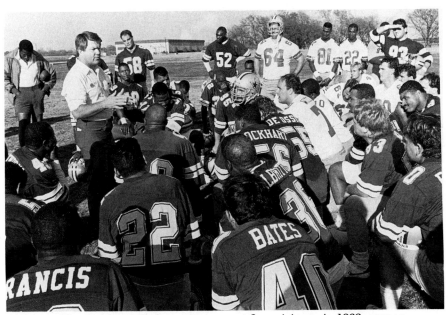

A post-practice meeting with the veterans at our first minicamp in 1989. DALLAS COWBOYS WEEKLY

THE 1992 WORLD CHAMPION DALLAS COWBOYS

 TOMMIE AGEE
 TROY AIKMAN
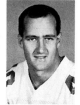 BILL BATES
 STEVE BEUERLEIN
 RICKY BLAKE

 LARRY BROWN
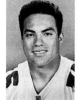 TONY CASILLAS
 FRANK CORNISH
 DIXON EDWARDS
 LIN ELLIOTT

 MELVIN EVANS
 THOMAS EVERETT
 KENNETH GANT
 JOHN GESEK
 KEVIN GOGAN

 CHARLES HALEY
 ALVIN HARPER
 DALE HELLESTRAE
 CHAD HENNINGS
 TONY HILL

 CLAYTON HOLMES
 ISSIAC HOLT
 RAY HORTON
 MICHAEL IRVIN
 LEON LETT

 KELVIN MARTIN
 RUSSELL MARYLAND
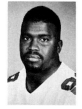 GODFREY MYLES
 NATE NEWTON
 KEN NORTON

THE 1992 WORLD CHAMPION DALLAS COWBOYS

JAY NOVACEK

CURVIN RICHARDS

ALFREDO ROBERTS

MIKE SAXON

EMMITT SMITH

JIMMY SMITH

KEVIN SMITH

VINSON SMITH

MARK STEPNOSKI

TONY TOLBERT

MARK TUINEI

ALAN VEINGRAD

JAMES WASHINGTON

ERIK WILLIAMS

ROBERT WILLIAMS

DARREN WOODSON

ALEXANDER WRIGHT

JERRY JONES

JOE AVEZZANO

JOE BRODSKY

DAVE CAMPO

BUTCH DAVIS

ROBERT FORD

STEVE HOFFMAN

BOB SLOWIK

TONY WISE

JIMMY JOHNSON

DAVE WANNSTEDT

NORV TURNER

HUBBARD ALEXANDER

Encouraging Eugene Lockhart *(middle)* and Nate Newton *(right)* to finish a grueling 110-yard conditioning sprint. DALLAS COWBOYS WEEKLY

The same pair they tried to run out of town less than four years earlier. The post–Super Bowl locker room celebration. DALLAS COWBOYS WEEKLY

Telling the President that he'll have to jog a little faster if he's going to play for the Cowboys. DALLAS COWBOYS WEEKLY

football program was going to have continuity and be stable. And everybody applauded. At the moment, it suited Tad Foote's purposes and ambitions to be an advocate of bigtime football.

Then we went to Arizona. We lost, and then I went off to Japan.

And while I was gone, Edward Thaddeus Foote II deftly danced back to the posture of an anti–bigtime-football educator who was downright embarrassed by the actions of the University of Miami's football team. Hey, if America wanted to clean out this nest of renegades, Edward Thaddeus Foote II had his saber drawn, ready to lead the charge.

When I got back to Miami, I'd been in the air from Tokyo for about seventeen hours. It was night in Miami. Rich Dalrymple met me at the airport. He said, "Coach, it's ugly."

I went home and slept a few hours, then went to Sam Jankovich's office. Sam told me we had to go straight to Foote's office, because he, Foote, had set up a press conference for me to apologize to the nation for my players' actions. And I mean right then. We were to go directly from Foote's office to the press conference.

In Foote's office, we had some initial conversation, and I was definitely not in a good mood by this point. I'd had little sleep, and here he was telling me all this stuff. And my players had done nothing wrong at the Fiesta Bowl, except in the half-baked opinion of an ambitious president who'd seen some half-baked media reports and had, typically for him, decided to play to the grandstand again without even trying to find out the whole truth. (I had some nifty runners and some grandstanders on that team, but none could compare with Edward Thaddeus Foote II, who could find the hole, make the quick cut, run right over ninety-five football players, accelerate to the end zone, throw up his arms and get off on the crowd roar better than anyone I've ever seen.)

Still, in my fatigued mind, I prepared. I was going to apologize for the reaction that the public had, and apologize for the public not understanding exactly what had happened. I can play semantics with anybody. I didn't tell Foote this, but I was, in effect, going to apologize to my players for the half-ass reporting job that had been done on them, and the half-ass reaction from Foote. And I was going to make Foote, a half-ass listener, walk out of that press conference satisfied that I had apologized the way he wanted me to apologize. But in his office, for the moment, I held my tongue, just as I'd held my tongue in that Marriott meeting room with Schnellenberger's old staff two years earlier.

There were four people in Foote's office, including Sam and university attorney Paul Dee. I held my tongue, and held it, and held it. And then I asked, "Well, President Foote, what does this do to my contract status? And when are we going to sign that?" For some reason, I just had a feeling, because he was being so negative.

All that had changed between December and now was that 1) Foote had made sure I didn't go to Southern Cal, 2) our players had worn some Army surplus clothes, 3) our players had walked away from an insult, and 4) we'd lost the national championship in a way that had nothing to do with our team's actions and everything to do with the fact that one player, Vinny Testaverde, had been thrown into tough circumstances and had a tough game.

But Edward Thaddeus Foote II said: "Oh. We can't do anything about your contract *now*. We're not going to add anything to your contract *now*. We're not going to redo your contract *now*."

I said, "What?"

I said, "You just stood up publicly and said to everybody that you were redoing my contract and I was going to stay and I was going to be on for five years. And you're telling me now that you're the CEO of a major operation and you're not a man of your word? How is that going to look?"

He said, "That's not something we're going to talk about [at the press conference]. We won't even address this."

And I was about to explode. I looked at Paul Dee. I looked at Sam Jankovich. And they were both just staring at the floor, embarrassed. I really felt sorry that Paul had to witness this, because Paul reflected 99 percent of the people at the University of Miami—first-class, and a really good person.

I said, "Let me get this straight: You've gone out publicly and said you're extending my contract, that you're redoing my contract, how happy you were that I was going to stay at the University of Miami, and now you're telling me that you're not a man of your word. Is that correct?"

He said, "Well, we're just not going to do anything about this contract. We'll have to address this at a later date."

I walked out of his office and slammed the door so hard it just about came off its hinges. Sam came running down the hall after me. I said, "Sam, go back in there and get him to settle on what years I've got left. I want out of here!"

I was heading to that press conference intending to say, "I'm out of here," and to tell the truth about how our players had been screwed, and what Foote had just done.

Sam kept saying, "Just settle down, just settle down, just settle down."

I said, "Hey: I can't work with someone who's not a man of his word."

Sam said, "Just settle down, just settle down, just settle down."

I calmed down. Sam Jankovich had brought me to the place I wanted to be. Our players had endured this crap for two weeks while I was in Japan. I couldn't desert them now.

I went to the press conference. I was a man of few words. Foote did most of the apologizing and most of the talking. I did not apologize for our players or their actions. I placed blame where it was due, but made it semantically smooth, as I'd planned: I apologized for the public's mistaken perception of our players.

I would deal with Edward Thaddeus Foote II later. I knew I was going to find the right time.

XII

WE BEAT THE WORLD: FLORIDA, FSU, ARKANSAS, NOTRE DAME, OKLAHOMA, AND FOOTE

About the only villains' role we'd missed in 1986 was a rematch with Notre Dame. The schedule, made years in advance, had us skipping a year in the series. That, of course, was merely delaying the inevitable. By the 1987 season, Irish hearts had had a year to fester with the wound of the "58–7" branded on them. And Lou Holtz, hired to replace Gerry Faust after the 1985 season, had had his year, and two recruiting seasons, to rebuild. Lou had gone through a 5–6 season in 1986 but now was ready to win a lot of games. Whether he was ready for us, well, we would see.

Our nationally anticipated rematch would be Notre Dame's last regular season game, and our next to last. Another quirk of scheduling had placed the game in Miami again. Considering those winters in South Bend, I can see how they weren't hard to convince to play in Miami. But this time, they had a lot more on their minds than lying in the sun.

In preseason of 1987, we had to replace a lot of players. Vinny Testaverde, Jerome Brown, and Alonzo Highsmith had departed for the NFL, all three going in the first nine picks of the draft. We were in a rebuilding year, but that, for us, was relative. We were by no means hurting for personnel. I expected a good year, but didn't count on fielding the sort of all-time team we'd had in 1986.

Steve Walsh took over at quarterback. He wasn't as gifted physically as Vinny or the other great Miami quarterbacks of the recent past, such as Jim Kelly and Bernie Kosar. But Walsh had tremendous field-awareness, that is, he could take in everything going on around him in a matter of split-seconds, and take advantage of it. Steve Walsh didn't make mistakes. And that turned out to be the keynote for the Hurricanes of 1987.

Florida by that point had announced they were dropping Miami from their schedule due to commitments to play more Southeastern Conference games. Our fans jeered the Gators, saying they were ducking us because the rivalry had become too much of a strain on them. Our rivalry with Florida State and Bobby Bowden, though intense, was never vicious. With Florida, things could get ugly. Their campus security had once uncovered a student plot to pelt Miami Hurricanes not just with oranges but with frozen oranges, which could be dangerous. Now, to open the 1987 season, we would play the last game in a long and bitter series with Florida. And we would play them in Miami.

And we crushed them. We beat them 31–4. Their only points came on two safeties when we lined up to punt and made bad long-snaps which went out of our own end zone. The unproven sophomore Steve Walsh chilled out the entire Orange Bowl with his icy poise. He wound up completing 17 of 27 passes, with only one interception. We didn't have a Superman this time, but we had a helluva quarterback to go with two seasoned wideouts in Mike Irvin and Brian Blades, and with one of the best backs in the country at catching the ball out of the backfield,

Melvin Bratton. Miami was a national championship contender again.

Then we went to, and I still get a little hyper, just remembering, Little Rock, Arkansas. By now in his fourth year of coaching the Razorbacks, Ken Hatfield had yet to lose in Little Rock. Our players knew my feelings about the University of Arkansas. They also knew I wanted them to play extremely well there.

Arkansas had been picked in preseason as one of the top teams in the country. So had we. It was billed as a bona fide early-season heavyweight bout. If so, it was like the legendary fight between Joe Louis and Max Schmeling. Bam. Bam. Bam. KO. Walsh threw. Irvin caught. Warren Williams ran. Williams's 49-yard touchdown run made it 14–0 in the first quarter. It was so clearly a rout, so early, that I started pouring in reserves in the second quarter. Didn't matter. Leonard Conley, a freshman, scored our third touchdown on a 15-yard run. Bam. Bam. Bam. We led them 38–0 at the half. I would imagine that by that point, up in Frank Broyles's VIP box, they got my message from the scoreboard. We led them 51–0 in the fourth quarter before they finally scored with three minutes left in the game to make it 51–7.

Ahhhhhhhhh. I needed that. To paraphrase General Sherman, war is hell and the other side started it. My players gathered around me in the locker room and Warren Williams gave me the game ball.

There was just enough time for a celebratory Heineken or two before we headed into a real fight at Tallahassee. When Florida State breaks out of its beloved night-game tradition and plays in the afternoon, you know the game is big enough to bring the national TV money pouring in. The national attention was much more intense than the pairing of No. 3 Miami and No. 4 Florida State now looks in the records. And in the Southeast, the game was just about all anyone was talking about, even distracting the usually SEC-obsessed fanatics in Georgia, Alabama, and Tennessee. It was much more like a No. 1 versus No. 2 game. Bobby Bowden probably had his best team to that point, and even this early in the season, speculation was that the winner of the game would go on to the national championship. Doak Campbell Stadium may just be the most underrated noise factory in the country. Florida State used to enjoy excellent success in the most notorious noise canyon of them all, LSU's Tiger Stadium in Baton Rouge. The Seminoles, because of their own facility, simply felt right at home in the ear-splitting noise of Tiger Stadium. But, just like the fans at Tiger Stadium, the fans in Tallahassee are at their loudest at night, in an eerie and beverage-fueled atmosphere. So playing in early afternoon, with the FSU fanatics (the original tomahawk-choppers and war-chanters) juiced only by the occasional Bloody Mary, helped a little.

The Seminoles were all over us in the second quarter and early in the third, and had us down 19–3. And bless Bobby Bowden's heart, I know that felt good. But I also know he knew it wasn't over. Bratton got us back in it with a 49-yard catch and run for a touchdown, after which we made a two-point conversion to make it 19–11 going into the fourth quarter.

And then Michael Irvin went wild. This was the quarter that would seal him as a household name (in any household that knows much about football). His 26-yard touchdown catch, followed by our second two-point conversion, tied the game. Then came the game-winner: The Play. From our 27, Walsh threw. At about midfield, Irvin caught. To this day, Deion Sanders, FSU's All-America cornerback (and later All-Pro with the Atlanta Falcons), will shout down anyone who implies that he, Sanders, was in any way responsible for what happened. All I know is, Michael ran by everybody. It was a total 73-yard catch-and-run for a touchdown. We led 26–19. But Bowden's offense drove right back, 83 yards, and scored with 42 seconds left in the game.

Bobby despises the notion of a tie as much or more than anyone I've ever known. And for a good sincere Southern Baptist, he's got more gambler's instinct than anyone I've ever known. If he walked away from that game, that early in the season, with a tie, he had a good chance to recover week-by-week in the polls and still win the national championship. But with 42 seconds left, he lined up his offense to do what came as natural to him as breathing: Go for two, to win or lose. But he tipped his hand. He called time out to make sure his team had its act together, and we were able to look at their substitutions. He took Sammie Smith, his big, topnotch running back, out of the game. So we figured they were going to throw. They put the ball over on the left hashmark, so we rotated our coverage to the right side of the field. Sure enough, they tried to throw the ball to the corner of the end zone to the wide side of the field. They threw to their big tight end, Pat Carter, who'd been hurting us all day. But our safety, Bubba McDowell, knocked the ball away this time and the conversion failed. We won the closest game of the year, 26–25.

Then we mowed through six lesser opponents to go 9–0, and then came the week that half of Christendom had waited for.

When Lou Holtz got the Arkansas job in 1976 that I wanted, we had a good, honest talk and I left without any bad feeling between us whatsoever. Through his tenure at Arkansas, Minnesota, and Notre Dame, I've gotten along fine with Lou. (Although now, as an NFL coach, when I visit Notre Dame to look at players, Lou's secretary has been known to form a cross with her left and right forefingers and scream, "Aaaaaaaaaaaaaah!" when I walk through the door. She's just kidding. I think.)

Our guys at Miami loved playing Notre Dame. Rather than bitter, it was always a delightful time for us, and I enjoyed preparing the team. That week going into November 28, 1987, they couldn't wait to hear my little speech and I gave it to them as usual: "We're gonna kick their ass, and in fact, if that leprechaun tries to taunt me again, I'm gonna kick *his* ass." Everybody roared, and we went merrily but efficiently on with practice.

Notre Dame was the team on its way to war this time. Surely you've noticed how skinny Lou is. And that isn't from lack of eating. He's so intense he must have a metabolic rate of about a billion calories a second. And he prepares his teams with great intensity.

A little while before kickoff, we got a big kick out of their psychological preparation. Our assistant equipment man went into their locker room to lend them some equipment during pregame warmups. And he saw that in each locker was a T-shirt with "58-7" in big numerals. Underneath, the lettering proclaimed FROM THESE ASHES, NOTRE DAME WILL RISE AGAIN. They were 8–2 going into the game, and a win over us would just about make it official that Lou had turned the thing around in South Bend. So he was pulling out all stops to get them motivated. Every Notre Dame player wore one of those T-shirts under his pads during the game. Our players knew it before kickoff, and we were a little amused.

Irish emotion kept them in the game all of one quarter, and it wouldn't have been that long if Melvin Bratton hadn't fumbled at their one-yard line. After that, we were outstanding and put up ten points in the second quarter, seven in the third, and seven in the fourth to win 24–0. It was the first time Notre Dame had been shut out since 1983, when Gerry Faust lost 20–0 to Howard Schnellenberger's Miami Hurricanes. Except for Miami, no team had shut out the Notre Dame since 1978. And so Irish hearts went back to the ashes and continued to fester, and to count the days until October 15, 1988, at South Bend, Indiana.

We had a rougher time against a tougher opponent, No. 8–ranked South Carolina, to end our regular season. Their "Black Death" defense was as aggressive as ours, but their all-out rush left them in single coverage in the secondary and we picked on that enough to escape with a 20–16 win.

So we were 11–0 and ranked second in the nation as we headed into the Orange Bowl against Barry Switzer and No. 1 Oklahoma.

Linebacker George Mira, Jr., didn't give me as big a pain in the ass for this Orange Bowl as Brian Bosworth had given Switzer for the previous one, but he still caused some headaches. In NCAA-required urinalysis prior to the Orange Bowl, Mira had tested positive for a diuretic which was capable of masking steroid use. The NCAA ruled that he couldn't play against Oklahoma. The previous year, the campus police had intervened in a run-in between Mira and his girlfriend, and somehow during the incident, police had found a vial of what was believed to be steroids in his vehicle. He said the vial belonged to a friend, and the police dropped the charge. I had suspended him for half a game and let the matter drop—for then.

After the NCAA ruling on the Orange Bowl, Mira, son of a former great Miami quarterback, decided to take the matter to court, and sue for reinstatement. The testimony went on into the evening prior to the

Orange Bowl game, and half the national media kept hanging around the courtroom. I'd already told them he wasn't going to play, no matter what the court decreed, and I meant it. I'm the one who decides who plays for my team, and based on Mira's history, he was out.

That was the only unpleasantness in a delightful week for us. We were practicing at our own facilities, and we knew we had a virtual lock on the national championship. Throughout the week's functions and press conferences, Barry Switzer was in a particularly jocular mood. And through all his joking about that "little old squatty-body lineman" he'd first met back at Arkansas in 1961, I detected a man who knew he was about to get his ass kicked. Switzer was limping with a knee injury caused when some players had tumbled out of bounds and rolled up his leg on the sidelines during a regular-season game. He told an audience that he'd gotten some medical advice from Kenny Stabler, the old hell-raising Alabama and Oakland Raiders quarterback: "Stabler told me, 'Aw, hell, Switzer, just take eighteen aspirins and a fifth of scotch, and you'll be all right.'" Switzer is great in front of an audience. The guy could do anything from stand-up comedy to Shakespeare. I just sat there and gave my little low-key answers, knowing Switzer was going to need aspirin and scotch for a lot more than his knee.

We had beaten Oklahoma twice, soundly, in the regular seasons of 1985 and 1986. They were still running the wishbone. They were still struggling at times on pass defense. So we felt really good about the game.

And it was nice not to be the villains in a bowl, for a change. At least, we wore only one of *two* black hats in that showdown. I think it was our Brian Blades who dubbed this one "The Sweat Hogs' Bowl." (Although, as it would turn out, Oklahoma in the next eighteen months or so would end up with far, far more serious problems than we ever had at Miami.)

The outcome of the game was far more clear-cut, far earlier, than the final score of 20–14 indicates. We shut down their wishbone, and the player I had called on to step in at middle linebacker for George Mira Jr., sophomore Bernard Clark, ended up as the game's most valuable player. But with just over two minutes left in the game, Oklahoma scored with a fumblerooski, a play they'd developed after Nebraska had used it on them several years earlier. Oklahoma's quarterback, after taking the snap, laid the ball on the ground. Our defenders, not noticing this until it was too late, followed the flow of their offense while one of Oklahoma's guards picked up the ball and lumbered twenty-nine yards to score.

We ran the clock out, and even though I had expected to win, something completely new came over me as the digits clicked off that familiar old Orange Bowl scoreboard in the rainy night sky. It was the rush. The high. The feeling of winning it all, undisputed. Unlike the 1964 Arkansas Razorbacks, we would win every version of the national championship. There I was, lying on the shoulder pads of my players as they carried me off the field, kicking my feet and thrusting my arms in the air. This wasn't just a national championship. We had taken on a world of bullshit, and Florida, and Florida State, and Arkansas, and Notre Dame, and Oklahoma, and Edward Thaddeus Foote II. And we had kicked their collective ass.

On the afternoon of January 2, 1988, Malcolm Moran of the *New York Times* called on Edward Thaddeus Foote II, who was hosting a house party in celebration of the previous evening's Orange Bowl victory and the national championship. What Malcolm found was a rare appearance by Tad Foote, proponent of bigtime football. And a performance that was even rarer.

Foote called the victory "a glorious condensation of life. . . . It was a merging of the emotions that exist in all of us, in a game, an atmosphere of fun, at its best. And there's no question that it's a good thing for the university. This team has done it right."

Could you run that by us one more time, Tad?

"And there's no question that it's a good thing for the university. This team has done it right."

And Jimmy Johnson?

"He's a fine teacher," said Tad Foote, proponent of bigtime football.

Any chasms between you and Jimmy with regard to this football program, Tad?

"It's not a we-they thing at all," the *New York Times* quoted Tad as saying, "We're all teachers."

Since we were all teachers, Edward Thaddeus Foote II readily tagged along when the team went to the White House to be congratulated by President Reagan. The visit was scheduled for afternoon. That morning, we took a bus tour around Washington. When we parked near the Lincoln Memorial, Foote stood up in the front of the bus to make a little speech. I will never forget how ill at ease he appeared as he looked at all those black players and told them, patronizingly, that "I was here" when Dr. Martin Luther King made his "I Have a Dream" speech in 1963.

He was trying to imply to them, "I am one of you."

Our players looked at one another.

Our players looked at Foote.

And the looks on their faces said, "Shit! You're not one of us."

He hadn't been very supportive of them through some tough times. His public reactions had been that players would be disciplined for their actions, et cetera, when he hadn't taken the time to find out both sides of the stories. He had just automatically assumed they were wrong.

And now here he was, one of those holier-than-thou types who profess to understand what black people have been through. I didn't, and I don't, and I never will, because I have not been through it, and I admit it and go on and do the best I can. And I think black players have been a lot more comfortable with that than if I'd tried to bullshit them.

It just so happened that the contract of the "fine teacher" was to be reviewed that spring. Nick Christin, my friend and attorney, felt that it was time to talk about a new contract, since we'd just won the national championship with a 12–0 record and had gone 33–3 the past three years. Nick and I had found our time to deal with Edward Thaddeus Foote II.

And Tad Foote, advocate of bigtime football, that "glorious condensation of life," was ready to negotiate. I told Paul Dee, the school attorney, that the only way I would sign a new contract with President Foote was without the buyout clause—by that I mean a clause in my previous contract which stipulated that if I left before the contract ran out, I would have to pay a settlement of about $100,000. I doubted that I could coexist with Foote much longer. I could have cared less whether I signed a new contract, and I wanted it purged of a buyout clause so that I could leave anytime I wanted to.

Well, Paul came to my office with a new contract with a buyout clause in it, and with another sheet of paper, the likes of which I had not seen before. It was a separate written agreement. I was supposed to sign it, stating that I would never say publicly that Edward Thaddeus Foote II had reneged on his promise of a new contract the previous year. In essence, I was not ever to tell the story of how he lied to me.

I looked at Paul Dee.

I laughed.

I said, "Listen: I'll sign the new contract without a buyout clause. But you take this paper here, and you tell Foote to stick it up his ass."

Paul came back with a new contract, without the buyout clause, and without that extra sheet of paper. What Foote did with it, I'll never know. I can only hope.

SATELLITES AND
TUNNEL BRAWLS

I never have been the type to send out spies to opponents' practices, although that sort of thing happens. Supposed joggers, curiosity seekers, and even derelicts rifling through garbage have turned out to be paid agents of the opposition. During Bear Bryant's time at Alabama, university maintenance people were once startled, just as they were firing up the campus incinerator, to see a man come tumbling out. He turned out to be a spy for the upcoming opponents, and had been going through thousands of scraps of paper looking for sheets with Alabama plays drawn on them.

Nowadays, most major programs are very careful about what they discard and where. And most have tall, thick hedges or high, canvas-covered fences around their practice facilities. For example, Florida State's practice facilities are extremely secure, blocked from the view of the outside world, and there is only one way in and out of the practice area, a small walk tunnel underneath a street. I know this now because sportswriters have told me. Bobby Bowden allows writers at practice, but his trainers are pretty familiar with all faces who belong in there, and it doesn't take much to police the mouth of one tunnel. I also know because I have, as an NFL coach, been there myself to look at players.

It would have been foolish to try to penetrate FSU's security when I was at Miami, and even if it had been possible I wouldn't have tried, for ethical reasons and especially my feelings for Bobby. He loves to design innovative custom plays for a particular opponent and spring them at the least expected times. And I always figured, hey, either we've got the mental and physical firepower to stop it, or we don't.

That said, I must admit that in 1988, I wasn't above a little high-tech satellite snooping.

We had just won the national championship and been undefeated in 1987, but Florida State had a great team coming back, and they were ranked preseason No. 1 by consensus of the polls. That was understandable, because Bobby was bringing back, just about intact, that magnificent team we had escaped by a single point the previous fall. But we felt like we had a pretty good team ourselves.

And so the first big national showdown of 1988 was the season-opener: No. 1 Florida State at defending national champion Miami.

It's nearly five hundred miles from Tallahassee to Coral Gables. And the Florida Panhandle is a world apart from Greater Miami. And so outside those nice, secure practice facilities, the Seminoles can feel a false sense of security about things they say and do publicly, in a region where virtually every local resident falls into the category of "one of us."

I had heard that summer that Florida State was making a rap video featuring several star players. Then I heard they were going to air it on the Bobby Bowden Show on the Thursday night prior to the game. The FSU people probably thought, oh, what the heck, this thing was only going to be seen in the Panhandle initially; it was a great video and would get the FSU fans and players fired up; and way down there in Miami, we wouldn't even know about it; so, not to worry about giving the Hurricanes anything to tee off on. They were, however, going to put the feed up on the satellite, so outlying stations around the Southeast could tape it for showing at a later date.

I had a satellite dish just outside my office and a TV set right next to my desk. I used to watch and tape coaches' shows and ball games, and I really enjoyed getting into all the pregame stuff that would be shown only in a local area. It was not only amusing, but you never knew when that stuff would come in handy. That Thursday night, I had my satellite settings all ready, and I called all of our starting players into my office. Showtime, guys.

It was great. Deion Sanders, FSU's All-Everything cornerback, was the star. Deion's mouth already had a history of getting our players worked up. Deion and his teammates were rapping about how they were No. 1, and about all they were going to do to their opponents, et cetera, et cetera.

I clicked off the TV set and said, "Well, guys, they're coming to our home turf, to the Orange Bowl, where we don't lose, and they think they're Number One. We're the national champions, and we've got an opportunity to show them who *is* Number One."

I didn't need to say another motivational word to our guys going into the game. Deion and Co. walked into a buzzsaw. Our guys started kicking ass from the opening whistle, and the Seminoles spent sixty minutes like dazed and disoriented boxers. We totally dominated the game and won 31–0. And Bobby Bowden, being an absolutely class act, whined not once. Instead of trying to imply that Jimmy Johnson was an asshole for routing him, Bobby Bowden said, "Jimmy Johnson is a defensive genius." That statement indicates a helluva lot more about Bobby than about me.

The next week, we played as exciting a game as we ever played while I was at Miami. We went up to Ann Arbor, Michigan, in front of 105,000 people. In the fourth quarter we were down 30–14 to Michigan, but we rallied to score seventeen points, including a field goal with no time left on the clock. We won 31–30.

Two weeks later we beat Missouri 55–0, to go 4-0 on the season, and then got ready to go to South Bend. Notre Dame was ready.

CATHOLICS VS. CONVICTS—thus read the T-shirts worn all over Notre Dame Stadium on Saturday, October 15, 1988. Notre Dame was really psyched for the game, and so were our guys. The tensions were running high.

Even before the national telecast began, some of the networks broke into their earlier games and other programming to report that the Miami and Notre Dame players were fighting in the tunnel before they even got onto the field.

I sometimes wonder if Notre Dame hasn't configurated that tunnel, which leads from both dressing rooms onto the field, the way it is on purpose all these years. It's old, it's tight, it's crowded, and there's a lot of pushing and shoving, and, especially if words are being thrown back and forth as teams go on and off the field, the tunnel lends itself to altercation. Notre Dame has gotten into fights in that tunnel with Southern Cal, Michigan, and others.

But we were Miami. That made it a news bulletin. And, I admit, our players weren't the type to take any crap off anybody, especially Notre Dame. Some teams, like Florida State and Miami, have been pretty overt with their talking and therefore have a reputation for it. What most people don't know is that year-in, year-out, the Irish, though they usually conceal it beneath those classic gold helmets, can talk trash with the best of 'em. Many a college player, in his first outing against Notre Dame, has been at first shocked and then infuriated by the mouths on some of those strapping darlings of American sport, right there on the field where Rockne's ghost is said to roam.

So here both teams came through the tunnel at once, and words flew, and both teams' egos were such that nobody was going to let the other team go one-up on intimidation. Mainly it was just pushing and shoving, but the TV cameras caught it and it made for great last-minute promotion of the game, as if any more promotion were needed.

The game lived up to every bit of the billing. It was a heavyweight championship, toe-to-toe, blow for blow. Steve Walsh threw for more yards, 424 with four touchdowns, than any other visiting quarterback had ever amassed at Notre Dame Stadium.

Midway through the fourth quarter we were trailing 31–24 but were at the brink of scoring another touchdown. Cleveland Gary, our fullback, went down at the Notre Dame one-yard line. The ball hit the ground and the ground caused the ball to come loose, which of course meant no fumble. Even casual watchers of football on television know the rule that, put in layman's terminology, states that "the ground cannot cause a fumble." But the official called this one a fumble.

It was a classic case of a running back holding the ball with one hand, reaching out to try to put the ball across the goal line, hitting the ground with the ball, and losing control of the ball with the one hand. But the ground could not cause the fumble. But that's not the way the official saw it.

We got the ball back and scored again, went for a two-point conversion and missed, and lost the game, 31–30. After the game I told our team what I've told all my teams, including the Cowboys to this day, in such situations: "We have to be good enough to overcome a call that goes against us occasionally. One official's call never decides a football game."

Notre Dame went on to a 12–0 national championship season, including an easy win over West Virginia in the Fiesta Bowl. We didn't lose another game all season and wound up 11–1, including an easy win over Nebraska in the Orange Bowl.

In talking with Lou Holtz since then, I've learned that the '88 game probably is what caused the break in the series between Miami and Notre Dame. After that, they played twice with Dennis Erickson coaching Miami, but those were the only two remaining games scheduled. Lou said Notre Dame's administration decided not to renew the contract because emotions on both sides were running too rampant. I can understand the reasoning, but I think it's a shame, because that was one of the classic rivalries in all of college football. We wanted the series to continue, but Notre Dame was against it. In my opinion, the series should be reinstituted.

In our Orange Bowl game, we dominated Nebraska, but the final score was only 23–3. And yet because of my black hat, Bob Trumpy of NBC decided to say that I was running up the score on Nebraska.

Twenty-three to three? I did take offense at that. Everybody talked about us throwing late in the game. But Nebraska continued to blitz late in the game. And we've always had the philosophy that if the other defense is going to blitz us, we're going to throw the football, regardless of the score. We were always going to deal with the blitz by picking it up with our blockers and then taking advantage of the vulnerability of a blitzing defense: its cornerbacks are left in man-to-man coverage. Beat that coverage and you can have an easy score. That's the way our offense operates, and you can't turn it off and on, and you can't play it half-speed or half-ass.

Trumpy was just another supposed expert who left the realm of expertise to play to the grandstand. Show biz. Melodrama. Villains. Victims. Poor little old Big Eight champion Nebraska, being mugged by bad, bad Miami and the gangleader Jimmy Johnson.

My national notoriety as a college coach had begun in 1985 with Ara Parseghian's lament, and was ending now with the same old tune from Bob Trumpy. I didn't know it was ending that night. The previous week, I'd again sloughed off Jerry Jones's remark on the phone that he was "still working on this other thing." I was still head over heels in love with Miami, for a thousand good reasons, with but one little burr under my saddle, one little pain in the ass by the name of Edward Thaddeus Foote II. He was not a big enough reason, per se, to leave Miami. But he was enough to add to the attraction of the NFL, where you're judged by how many you win and how many you lose, without all the trappings and baggage and bullshit.

XIV

MIAMI, MYSELF

When President Clinton received and congratulated the University of Alabama football team at the White House early in 1993 for winning the 1992 national championship, Senator Phil Gramm of Texas was on hand to make a few choice remarks. Why a Republican from Texas would show up at a reception thrown by a Democrat from Arkansas for a bunch of young men raised mostly in Alabama, and then use that forum to criticize the University of Miami's football team, I don't know. The senator is a former economics professor, and I do have some experience with educators playing politics by making hip-shot public statements on subjects they don't understand and haven't bothered to explore.

The good professor turned politician—Senator Gramm, I mean— allowed as how "old-fashioned commitment" to American values and the American work ethic were being displaced in college football by "superstars and hotdogging" as personified by the likes of the University of Miami Hurricanes.

Art Kehoe, an assistant to current Miami head coach Dennis Erickson, wrote Senator Gramm a letter in response. Art sent copies of the letter to friends of his who are voters in the state of Texas. One copy was addressed to Jimmy Johnson, One Cowboys Parkway, Irving, Tex. Art correctly informed the senator that "we (Miami) have . . . the 17th best graduation rate for athletes out of 107 Division I institutions, back to back 100 percent graduation of our last two (football) senior classes, two first-team Academic All-Americans, four fifth-year seniors enrolled in our MBA program, and some of the classiest young men in college athletics."

That letter meant a lot to me. Four years gone from Miami, I could have said, "Well, the image is Erickson's problem now." But Miami football doesn't work that way. We may leave the enrollment or the employ of the University, but we never leave the team. At any Miami game, you'll see several former Hurricanes, who have gone on to the NFL or other endeavors, on the sidelines, encouraging the present-day players. In 1992, when Jerome Brown of the Philadelphia Eagles was killed in an automobile accident, and Shane Curry of the Indianapolis Colts was killed in a senseless shooting in Cincinnati, the shock and grief hit hard in Dallas, among the Cowboys who are former Miami players, and me.

One of the strongest attributes of the Miami teams for the past ten years has been the closeness and the bond that the players have with one another. A lot of it is due to the success of the team on the field. But a lot of it is also due to the amount of time they spend together off the field.

Because a lot of my Miami players came from disadvantaged situations and financially disadvantaged homes, during the summertime there really wasn't a lot for them to go back to. Because of that, I kept them on scholarship all summer, and they continued to go to school all summer. This has become a tradition at Miami, and it has gone on and on. The benefits I saw were twofold: First, it allowed them to graduate on time, and second, it formed a unity when they were in school together all summer and were able to work out together, not in an organized practice, but in an informal conditioning situation.

As a gauge for graduation percentages, remember that among the general American college student population, the average incoming freshman's chances of graduating are 50 to 55 percent. When I got to Miami, the graduation rate among football players was just above 30 percent. When I left Miami, the graduation rate for football players was more than 75 percent—better than the general student population. And the past two years, Miami's graduation rate has been 100 percent, thanks largely, I like to think, to a system we instituted.

While I was there we added two academic counselors and a full academic support system. We had a mandatory study hall. We had disciplinary action. If players missed classes or had academic problems we would get them up at 6 o'clock in the morning and run them. I did that personally sometimes. We had mandatory curfews after study hall. We put in some monitoring processes and some controls that really forced the players to be students, and at least got them started off on the right track. And after a year or two a player would be interested enough and could see the light at the end of the tunnel and he would do it on his own from there. To Foote's credit, he was trying to make Miami—how did he put it?—"this generation's Stanford." And every year, the academic standards were raised. And we in the football program stayed in step with those standards. And our graduation rate went steadily upward, while the University of Miami's general student population graduation rate was hovering just about 50 percent and, as I recall, slipped a bit in some years before adjusting to the tougher standards.

But when I was there, and I would go out and publicly talk about the graduation rate and the quality of the individuals, it almost went in one ear and out the other in my audiences, because people had it set in their minds that our guys were loud, boisterous, cocky (which was sometimes true), renegade (which was not true) players.

At times I have been asked, "Weren't you a Barry Switzer waiting to happen at Miami, before making your getaway to the NFL?" The question referred to the fact that Switzer had been forced out at Oklahoma in the summer of 1989, after his program had fallen into a world of trouble—one of his quarterbacks, Charles Thompson (who played against us in the national championship Orange Bowl showdown), had been arrested for selling cocaine to an undercover agent; Oklahoma had had a rape and a shooting in their football dorm; they'd gone on three years' NCAA probation for recruiting violations.

My reply was, simply, "No. I knew my players."

I didn't take bad citizens, or even questionable citizens, at Miami. I didn't take players who didn't belong in college. I didn't even take Proposition 48 players, after the first year the NCAA instituted the policy. ("Prop 48," for those who are unfamiliar, was an NCAA ruling that academically unqualified players could be signed to athletic grants-in-aid, on the condition that they not participate in practice their first year, in order to concentrate on academics and attempt to make themselves academically eligible to play by their sophomore years.) Most major programs loaded up on "Prop 48s." And the University of Miami would have allowed me to take them. But I didn't. I had taken three that first year the proposition was in force, 1986. One, Dale Dawkins, did extremely well and graduated. The other two were lost. They felt uncomfortable in the environment of a rich-kids' private school, and they couldn't even practice football. I had them in my office lots of times, because they had lots of problems. They didn't belong in school. After that, I told my coaches, "No more."

Oh, there were times with our football program that I wondered what would be next, that is, when might some smart-ass law student finish a chapter on pedestrian rights and decide to test his new knowledge by standing in front of one of my players' cars? Or when might some reporter decide that a black football player driving a nice car was automatically suspicious, and start digging through records until he found that the guy's parents bought the car with hard-earned, hard-saved money? Or when might some player seek to buy himself a physiological edge with biochemical substances on the edge of, or beyond, NCAA rules?

But wonder who would shoot whom? Or who would rape whom?

Or buy or sell cocaine? Or whether the NCAA investigators were on campus, ready to come down hard?

Never. Ever. I knew my players. I knew my coaches.

In 1989, as I left Miami for Dallas, Larry Guest of the Orlando *Sentinel* wrote, "I suspect that Johnson as the head coach of an NFL team with his own bobo as the owner will become an insufferable self-styled deity, and any problem will become the fault of the dastardly media. Much in the same order as Barry Switzer at Oklahoma. In fact, Jimmy and Barry not only are former staffmates and still late-night party pals, but philosophical clones."

Yes, I've known Barry Switzer a long time, since 1961. We were staffmates under Chuck Fairbanks at Oklahoma in the early seventies. And we've done some partying together, though not much late at night (I'm a happy-hour and early-to-bed man, myself), and none in recent years. On the surface we may at times have appeared to be "philosophical clones" in that we both believed in giving a kid a chance even if he didn't come from a *Father Knows Best* or *Leave It to Beaver* environment. I can't speak for Barry, but I always carefully evaluated my recruits, and did my best to guide them when they got to Miami.

Ever since our national championship Orange Bowl matchup, Switzer and I have somehow been portrayed as closer than we really were. I mean, we've been buddies in the past and have had a good relationship. But after he left Oklahoma in 1989, as if I didn't have enough worries ongoing in Dallas, people sort of assumed I would give him haven on the Cowboys staff. Reporters rushed to ask me about the Switzer situation. I told them as plainly as I knew how, in one sentence:

"He's not coming here."

Not many people really knew our Miami team or individual players. But we knew ourselves, and we knew each other, and we were very, very close. To this day, you don't speak ill of Miami in Valley Ranch, Texas. You'll have guys like Mike Irvin (who graduated in four years) and Russell Maryland (who graduated in three and a half years) and me to deal with. And from what I hear, you don't speak ill of the Dallas Cowboys at the University of Miami.

Maybe someday, with enough 100 percent graduation years and enough class acts coming out into society, America will finally let that ill-fitting black hat fall into the dumpster. I hope so. Even now, the University of Miami is my school. And the city of Miami is me.

LET ME OUT OF HERE

T here's an old saying around the NFL that in order to win, you must first hate to lose. This cliché is no longer fashionable, and no longer felt deeply or widely. I daresay there has never been a rookie coach who was more fanatic about following that particular dusty advice. I absolutely, positively, despise losing, no matter when or why, to a degree that I can only put into inadequate phrases such as "sick to my stomach." I *want* to feel that way.

Even to this day, writers talk about how I take losses so hard. They don't know how long I can survive in this game because losing wears on me too much. In midseason of 1989, we were losing at a rate I hadn't known since Picayune, Mississippi. Even when I expect to lose, and can see the dividends down the road, I am no less miserable after a loss.

Throughout regular season, the Cowboys' roster was a revolving door, and every day was tryout camp. At times we would work out a player on Tuesday, sign him Wednesday, play him Sunday, and cut him Monday. It was my biggest, longest scramble for players in precisely a decade since I had my two hundred walkons in Stillwater. But at Oklahoma State, we won seven games in 1979 and had a lot of fun. But this—this was like going to the dentist every day of the week, eighteen hours a day.

We were bringing in free-agent players who were adrift in the NFL and who in many cases were accustomed to losing. We would make do as best we could with those guys on a week-to-week basis. But from a Cowboys' veteran, a star, I would not tolerate a tolerance for losing.

Everson Walls was a helluva cornerback in his time. But in the fall of 1989 he was past his prime. According to our plan of going with younger players, we were not going to pay him the $700,000 he was scheduled to make in 1990. We would not renew his contract. He would, however, serve the Dallas Cowboys well one more time. When we hit rock bottom, in our tenth game, I blew the bedrock to bits. We might go into free-fall, but we weren't going to languish on the bottom any longer. I blew up. And Everson Walls was the detonator.

Going into our game at Phoenix, we were 1–8. We'd managed to scrape together a win at archrival Washington the week before, with their quarterback, Doug Williams, playing hurt.

At Phoenix we had the game won and blew it late in the fourth quarter. Troy Aikman had an absolutely fantastic game, but got knocked cold while throwing a 79-yard touchdown pass that put us in the lead. He had to be carried off the field, and after that, our defense gave up two long touchdown bombs at the end of the game, and we lost, 24–20.

As a lot of professional players do, some of our guys were getting together with their buddies from the other team as they walked off the field. I happened to walk by Everson and he was with a couple of Cardinal receivers, and for all I knew they might have been the receivers who caught the touchdown passes. They were laughing and cutting up, as friends do. The only thing was, it was just a couple of minutes after we'd got our ass beat.

I really blew off and said, "Everson, get your ass in the locker room! What the hell's going on?"

Everson came back at me and said, "Coach, what's the big deal? We've already lost eight of 'em. So why are you so hot after this one?"

And that just caused my blood to boil. I was so mad I couldn't even talk to him at that point.

I always meet with the team the day after a game and go through things from that game, and talk about what we're going to do the next week. This time, I told the team:

"Hey, if we ever get to the point where we can laugh and cut up after we get our ass beat, then something's gone wrong. I don't care how much money you're making. I don't care if it's professional ball or peewee ball. If you don't get sick to your stomach every time you lose a ball game, then you're really losing part of yourself. You're losing your pride, and it's time to get out of this game. It doesn't make any difference if we'd lost one, or eight, or one *hundred* and eight. You don't *ever* get to the point that losing doesn't hurt you."

Actually, I could understand Everson's feelings. We were 1–8 and the year before the team had gone 3–13. So he was used to losing and the whole group around here was used to losing. So it was no big deal to them. I made it a big deal. From that point on, not a single player with the Dallas Cowboys Football Club, Irving, Texas, felt a comfort zone. I mean, anybody crazy enough to trade Herschel Walker and chew out Everson Walls was likely to do anything.

I'd been accustomed to having a shoulder to lean on, all the time—Linda Kay's. And now, through my doing, I no longer had that shoulder. In fact, the divorce dragged on through the fall, doubling my misery as the Cowboys lost and lost and lost and lost. I gave Linda Kay virtually everything we'd accumulated in twenty-six years, except for a few things, such as my cabin at Crystal Beach, Texas. I actually borrowed money to enhance the cash settlement so I could keep personally meaningful things.

There were ongoing phone conversations with my lawyer as she talked with Linda Kay's lawyer. At times I even had direct phone conversations with Linda Kay herself—conversations which were very emotional on both parts. I wanted to do what was fair. I wanted to give her enough that she would never have to work. Her whole life had revolved around my coaching career, and now her whole life was changing. That was the part I felt, and feel, the worst about.

The maturity, intelligence, and independence of my two sons had not been lost on me before the divorce. In fact, the maturity of Brent and Chad was probably the major reason I felt free to seek my freedom. But it was during the divorce, when I was so down, that I was overwhelmed by just how mature and bright and wise my sons are. They were wonderful. Not only were they prepared to deal with the divorce themselves, but they both did an awful lot to help both Linda Kay and me deal with it better.

There are times when I think Brent, the oldest, knows me better than I know myself. He looks more like Linda Kay, and like his mother is softspoken, very sophisticated, very sensitive. He is a lawyer by education, but he hated law practice. He is independent and introspective, and is a budding writer. Everybody thinks they've got good-looking kids, but I can prove it: To support his writing, Brent has been able to find work as a male model virtually at will. Now, he is modeling while pursuing teaching and writing.

Chad has a hard and fast rule that he never, ever drops his father's name as a selling tool with his clients. He doesn't have to. There is no way you could walk into the PaineWebber offices in Dallas for a meeting with broker Chadwick Johnson and not say immediately to yourself, "That's Jimmy Johnson's son." If he looked a little older, he could probably walk out onto the Cowboys' practice field, blow a whistle, and everybody on the team would hustle up around him. Every time I set eyes on him, I look into a mirror and even see my bountiful head of hair. He loves to wheel and deal in the stock market the way I love to wheel and deal in the NFL draft. I drive a Corvette, and he drives a Porsche.

Both sons are very intelligent and very emotional. Chad shows it quicker, but Brent feels it deeper. Brent got married in 1992 and settled down, but Chad still dates someone different just about every night. Where Brent reserves his words, Chad tends to chatter on. The summer after Brent's freshman year in college, he stayed out late one night, and I questioned his coming in at that hour. He blurted at me, "Dad, why should you question what hour I come in, when all those hours I wanted to talk to you while I was growing up, you weren't there." We both teared up, and talked, and stood there sobbing and hugging for a while, and we've been very close ever since. Brent loves traditions, such as gift-giving at Christmas, and all those years of a father whose Christmases were distracted with bowl games or recruiting weighed on him, but we worked it out. Chad just hurries happily on through life, sometimes right past family birthdays and anniversaries and holidays, like me. They are different, but they are as close as any parent could hope for brothers to be. I don't think they've ever had a serious argument.

In the fall of 1989, nothing that was going on escaped Brent and Chad. They saw a father who, all their lives, had been upbeat, the life of the party, now seriously down. They saw a mother suddenly at a loss for what to do with herself. They reassured me that these things happen, that Linda Kay and I just realized that it wasn't what it used to be, that it had probably been building for some time, and that Dallas wasn't the cause, just the place. They told Linda Kay that she no longer had any restrictions on her life, that now she could do anything and everything she'd ever wanted to do, that there were other worlds than football society for her to travel and explore.

Our father-and-son talks were past. Now we were all three men. I'd fulfilled the major need of most men's lives, raising happy, healthy, handsome, successful children. Now, not only could I sit back and admire them, but I had two close and grownup friends and confidants.

And, while I was going through the divorce, I had started dating Rhonda Rookmaaker, one of the most upbeat, positive, bright, and witty women I'd ever met. California-born, Rhonda was a hairdresser whom I'd met—you guessed it—when I was getting my hair cut. More than a girlfriend, she's my buddy. She prefers to live by herself too. But she's a great companion for everything from happy hours (usually with my crew) to vacations in the Bahamas or Las Vegas (also with my crew).

Some people say we ought to levy a cover charge for putting our act on at happy hour, when we're one-lining each other. Now you take those cult members who sometimes drift into bars selling flowers. One afternoon at one of our favorite local establishments, in the improved year of 1992, the conversation went something like this:

CULT FLOWER LADY: Roses for your lady, sir?
ME (shrugging): If she wants to pay for 'em. She just got her income tax refund today.
(Cult flower lady is silent.)
RHONDA: He buys my beers. That's enough for me.
(Others at our table snicker.)
RHONDA: Geez, I sound like some motorcycle mama.
ME: I guess I'm going to have to take her home and slap her around some more.
RHONDA (laughing): He knows I love that.
(Cult flower lady exits, dumbstruck, for parts unknown. Others at our table howl.)

But in the fall of 1989, such conversations were few and far between. Rhonda is an artist at knowing when to leave me alone. One Sunday, Mother and Daddy had come to a game, which we lost, of course, and were waiting for me in the Sam Houston room, the sort of inner sanctum of Texas Stadium where the coaching staff and their families and close friends unwind after games. The Dallas crowds were so hostile toward me that I was worried about Mother and Daddy being harassed in their seats. I asked Daddy if we could go and talk privately. He got up without a word, and we went outside.

I said, "Daddy, it's so bad that I don't want you and Mother to have to go through this. I think it's best that you don't come to any more games until we start winning. Let me go through this alone."

"I understand," he said.

I really didn't need the patronizing, condescending little man-in-the-street remarks like, "Hang in there; you'll be fine." I wanted to say,

"Hey, I appreciate your comments, but I *know* I'm going to be fine, and I *know* we're going to win." They meant well, but I'd rather not hear it.

It was different coming from one of my fellow coaches, especially Bill Parcells, for whom I have tremendous respect. That October, when he brought his New York Giants team into Dallas and they were so much better than us and they just kicked our ass, 30–13, he came up to me after the game and said, "Just hang in there; keep your chin up." Still, I just didn't want to hear those comments, even from someone I held in such high regard.

I mean, hell, yes, it was the hardest time of my life, personally and professionally. And hell, yes, I was miserable. But one thing I never lost was the confidence that I knew enough about what I was doing that it would get better. Jerry Jones would say later that, awful as the 1989 season was, it allowed him to see something in me that he would not otherwise have seen. We never lost sight of what lay down the road for us, and what Jerry saw in 1989, he would say later, was that "I'd made the right choice."

Not even the two prime draft choices I had brought to the team were very thrilled with me in 1989. In addition to taking Troy Aikman in the regular draft, I had taken my winning quarterback from back at the University of Miami, Steve Walsh, in the supplemental draft that summer. The media took that as further grounds to declare me certifiably stupid—what the hell was I going to do with *two* first-round quarterbacks? There was long-range method to that madness too, but explaining it to the media at the time would not have helped at all, and probably would have hurt a lot.

And so for the time being, in the midst of everything else, we had that most precious, darling story for the media, a "quarterback controversy." From New York to San Francisco, and all points in between, there's nothing that can quite strike a local public's fancy like debating which of two, or occasionally three, quarterbacks ought to be starting for a team. Look at the Joe Montana versus Steve Young situation in San Francisco for several years. Look at Phil Simms versus (fill in the blank with any of several) in New York over the years. Look at the Jim Kelly versus Frank Reich controversy in Buffalo, going right into the Super Bowl against us in 1993. Because we weren't winning in 1989, we didn't have anything nearly as intriguing as all these examples. The point is, the public and media can get preoccupied with such situations.

Our little quarterback controversy would extend on through preseason of 1990. Since then, I have been accused of creating the controversy for ulterior motives. I did not actively create controversy. I do plead guilty to seeing both the opportunity and the need to rope-a-dope.

With the two men involved, I exercised caution, probably to a fault. Troy had been the top pick in the entire NFL draft, and under other circumstances probably would have gotten special attention from the head coach. Steve had won the national championship for me at Miami. I didn't want to give special attention or consideration to one over the other, so as a result I wound up not giving either quarterback the attention he probably felt he deserved.

That, plus my continuing policy in 1989 of refusing to be a phony by preaching team and unity to players in a revolving door, added to my image as a cold operator.

On Christmas Eve, we lost our final game of 1989 at home, 20–10 to the Green Bay Packers. It was horribly and atypically cold in Dallas. The pipes in the stadium were frozen. I went through all the postgame interviews and went up to the Sam Houston Room for a few minutes before heading home. Brenda Bushell, my TV liaison person from Florida, came in and asked if I'd step outside and do one more live standup interview for one more TV station.

I almost broke down. I told Brenda I just couldn't take anymore. I didn't want this season to last one more minute, one more second. She went out and declined the interview and I headed home.

When I walked into my house, all the pipes were frozen. My only thought was Let me out of here. The phone was working, and I called Rhonda, who lived a few blocks away, and asked her to come over and bring a bag packed for someplace warm. Then I called an airline and booked the next flight for Miami. We were at a Miami airport hotel late that night, and flew to the Caribbean the next day.

For a few days I would both thaw out and chill out, and then I would come back and introduce the Dallas Cowboys to my kind of football season, which lasts about 360 days a year.

XVI

THE FOUNDATIONS
OF WINNING

Michael Irvin had been drafted by the Landry regime in 1988 after playing for me at Miami. When I took the Dallas job, the resident Cowboys asked him what to expect. He'd been the only guy with an earring on the entire roster, and they asked him if they could all have fun under me. "You can have all the fun you want as long as we're winning," he told them. They liked that part. Apparently they didn't absorb the second part of what he said as well: "The key thing with him is, you'd better get in shape. Right now."

In response to all the perceptions of me as a coach lax on discipline, Michael once put it this way: "Discipline is a lot more than saying,

'Don't throw your hands up in the air when you score a touchdown.' Discipline is when it's 110 degrees in the Orange Bowl, no breeze, fourth quarter, a minute and a half left to play, fourth and three for the other team, you're dead tired, they come to the line and that opposing quarterback gives you a hard count: 'Hut-*HUT!'* And you don't jump offside. Because you're disciplined mentally and physically. *That's* Jimmy's discipline."

Because they were together year round, my Miami players were bonded and they were in superb physical condition. A lot of people don't think that stuff translates well from college to the NFL. Some coaches believe in letting professional players stoically go about their jobs and determine their own needs with regard to conditioning. Some coaches also let players take losses in stride, figuring, well, if they go 9–7 and make the playoffs, that's fine, that's a good year. Not me.

Because of the old Dallas regime and the way they'd done things in the past, the players really didn't work out much in the 1989 off-season. Their definition of "in shape" was different from mine. Some players didn't heed Mike Irvin's warning. And those players are gone.

After my few days in the warm weather in December 1989, I came back to work and so did everybody else in this organization. We remodeled the weight room and brought in a new strength and conditioning coach, Mike Woicik. Tony Wise, our offensive-line coach, and Dave Campo, our defensive-backs coach, had both worked with Mike at Syracuse. They both recommended him highly. (That's how my crew continues to regenerate: Tony Wise had worked with me at Oklahoma State, and had worked with Campo at Syracuse, and they both came to Miami and then to Dallas with me. Loyalty. Trust. Chemistry. Then when we wanted to improve our conditioning program at Dallas, they had a recommendation, and I knew them well enough to trust their judgment fully, and it worked.)

We instituted a conditioning pay period so that players were paid to work out and get in shape. We demanded that players attend off-season programs, quarterback schools and minicamps, and we started building some unity on this team, which I feel is an even bigger benefit than the strength and conditioning itself. Hard work together builds a bond that is vital to the team concept.

There were other teams paying their players for conditioning programs, but I don't think anybody had the attendance and the off-season practices like we had. With what they'd gone through the year before, the players knew if they didn't voluntarily show up for a workout they might be sent packing. So we had 100 percent participation, and in essence, we practiced the full off-season leading up to training camp. This gave us a determination to win even though we were facing some pretty stiff odds.

Via the draft, we began to lessen those odds.

Wheeling and dealing for draft choices doesn't do a bit of good unless you know precisely what you're doing with each of those picks. We at Dallas go about the player evaluation process somewhat differently than any other team in the league. If I had gone to any other NFL team to coach, I don't know that I could have had as much success, as fast, because it is very unlikely I would have gotten the kind of control over personnel that Jerry Jones gave me.

Most NFL franchises still rely on large scouting departments. Ours is one of the smallest in the league. Jerry wants it that way and I want it that way, because I want to pick the players I'm going to coach. If that sounds entirely logical to the point of "so what?" to the layman, you'd be surprised at how most of the league works. Coaches don't always get full say-so as to the players selected. You'd be surprised how many coaches in the past have been given players and told, "Here, coach them." In fact, when the Cowboys hit the skids in the last years of the Landry regime, many observers claimed it wasn't so much a matter of Landry's coaching as of his staff being given poor talent by Gil Brandt's scouting staff.

The two best-known success stories of coaches who have had total control over personnel are Don Shula at Miami and Bill Walsh during his tenure at San Francisco. But Shula and Walsh exercised that control based on opinions they'd formed mainly from scouting reports and film. In other words, they still relied on scouting departments for their information. They didn't get on the plane and go see the players as often as I do.

Doing homework isn't nearly enough for me in preparing for the draft. At Dallas, we do our road work. We as a staff go personally to the Florida States and the Michigans and the Notre Dames and the Southern Cals and the Ohio States and on and on and on, looking at players personally. And we evaluate a helluva lot more than vertical leap and forty-yard dash times. If I'm talking with a group of prospective draftees and one kid's sitting there flipping ice at his teammate or kidding around, he'll be hard-pressed to stay on my list for more than about five more minutes. I have formal training in the psychology of learning, but none of that does any good on an unwilling or uncaring pupil.

About half the NFL head coaches go to the big scouting combine workouts where large groups of players are brought in at once, but I almost never see other NFL head coaches on the college campuses where I go. Two other head coaches, David Shula of the Cincinnati Bengals and Dave Wannstedt of the Chicago Bears, are on the road a lot—Shula was in Dallas with us for two years and Wannstedt was with us for four years, and they understand the benefits. Shula's other reason is that Cincinnati has the smallest scouting department in the league. That's the way the Bengals' owners structure it, for financial reasons as much as anything else. We do it purely for effectiveness in making the right draft choices. My assistant coaches and I are responsible for picking the personnel we will coach, although Jerry Jones makes the final decision about whether a player is worth the money he's asking. (And, as tight with company money as I am, Jerry rarely accuses me of overvaluing a player.)

Deep inside the NFL, there have been horror stories about power struggles between personnel departments and coaching staffs. There have been cases where scouts and coaches spent so much time undermining each other with the owner that neither side could do its real job thoroughly. General managers and player personnel directors have gotten coaches fired, and vice versa. Jerry is his own general manager, so there's no one over whose head I ever have to go. Larry Lacewell now runs our college scouting operation, but Larry and I have communicated so well, for so long, that Jerry never has to mediate between rival opinions. Larry and four scouts have the coaching staff up to speed on talent nationwide; as soon as we finish coaching the season we get ready to hit the road.

I've had discussions with others around the league about our system. The old guard is reluctant to adopt it, because it's just not the way it's been done in the past. And they are critical of our system because it cuts out some jobs. Anybody who is in pure personnel, pure scouting, doesn't like this system for the simple reason that if any club's coaching staff starts doing the scouting, there's no longer a need for ten or eleven scouts.

The other thing is some people have tried giving personnel control to the coaches and been unsuccessful. Ray Perkins had control of the scouting and personnel departments at Tampa Bay and it didn't work.

We've probably been successful at making the most of our picks for the very reason we were criticized when we came into the league: We were a college staff. Colleges don't have scouting departments. Coaches work and travel their asses off scouting and recruiting. We were not only used to the work, but we had excellent firsthand knowledge of players coming up in the draft, because we'd either played against them or recruited them ourselves, or at least tried to recruit them.

While Emmitt Smith was rushing for 8,804 yards and 106 touchdowns at Escambia High School in Pensacola, Florida, I didn't need *Parade* magazine and *USA Today* to tell me he was the top prep running back in the country. Our staff at Miami had broken out of Howard Schnellenberger's "State of Miami" recruiting boundaries and didn't mind going into Florida and Florida State recruiting areas in the northern parts of the state. We tried to recruit Emmitt, just as we'd tried to recruit Troy Aikman at Oklahoma State. As with Troy, when we didn't get Emmitt, we kept him firmly in mind for the future.

In the spring of 1990, Emmitt took advantage of new NFL policies which allowed underclassmen to declare themselves eligible for the draft. At the University of Florida, Emmitt was All-America, and had been All-Southeastern Conference in each of his three years with the Gators. I didn't need to see his résumé. I knew that he was what Herschel Walker wasn't: a nifty runner. Emmitt also has a solid-as-a-rock personality and background. His parents are teachers. Emmitt is the kind of guy you can yell at on the practice field without worrying that you're going to crush him. He's too secure for that. He came out of college early, but he was plenty mature.

As the worst team in the league again in 1989, we would have gotten the first pick in the entire draft of 1990, except that we'd used that pick to take Steve Walsh in the supplemental draft in the summer of 1989 (and that little chess move had yet to be completed). But we moved up high enough in the first round to take Emmitt by trading the first-round pick we'd acquired from Minnesota in the Walker trade, plus a third-round pick we'd acquired from San Francisco, to Pittsburgh in exchange for their spot in the first round. Emmitt would go on to be NFL Rookie of the Year.

In our rush for young receivers, we took Alexander Wright of Auburn in the second round. He would play for us through 1991, the year Alvin Harper arrived from that gold mine of receivers, Johnny Majors's Tennessee Volunteers, and established himself as our other starting receiver with Mike Irvin.

Our regular third-round pick was gone as part of the Walker trade. But by dealing in a flurry that involved Denver, the Miami Dolphins, and New England, we came up with the third-round pick that allowed us to take defensive tackle Jimmie Jones, one of my former University of Miami players who remains with the Cowboys.

The great challenge in any draft is using lower-round picks to find players who can help you. In the ninth round, we took defensive back Kenneth Gant out of little Albany State in south Georgia. There's some scouting work and research I'm proud of. Walt Yowarsky, one of our key scouts, first saw Kenny, and we sent one of our coaches to work him out. We saw that Kenny was very aggressive and had the speed we were looking for, and that he was a playmaker. Kenny Gant would go with us all the way to the Super Bowl.

Also, we became extremely active in Plan B, the new NFL rule where players whose contracts were up, and who were left unprotected by their teams in the new free-agency plan, could be signed by other teams. Many such players, whom other teams didn't feel the need to protect, were better than what we had at several positions. We signed sixteen Plan B players in a seine-net approach—place a large enough net vertically in the water and pull it through to catch virtually everything that swims in its path, and the law of averages says you're going to catch at least a few big fish. We were so devoid of talent in some areas that we might as well take a lot of Plan B players. Since there was no limit on these guys, we were seining through and taking a bunch, realizing that only a few would pan out. Three who panned out were linebacker Vinson Smith and safety James Washington, who also were destined for the Super Bowl with us, and, most importantly, tight end Jay Novacek, who would become a Pro Bowl starter.

I didn't simply want our special teams play to improve. I wanted us to have the best special teams in football. In my first days as a head coach, at Oklahoma State, we were able to win games against teams that had more talent, because of our efforts on special teams. That carried over to Miami, where we made excellent teams even better with special-teams play, and the philosophy continues in Dallas.

I had known Joe Avezzano since the Iowa State days with Johnny Majors. Avezzano had gone with Majors to Pitt and then Tennessee, where they ought to build a special-teams hall of fame—General Bob Neyland was the first great and thoroughly demanding proponent of the kicking game as a weapon. Avezzano had been a head coach for five years at Oregon State, and then offensive line coach and offensive coordinator for Jackie Sherrill at Texas A&M, where the Aggies' "Twelfth Man" special teams, made up mostly of nonscholarship students, became local legend.

We hired Joe Avezzano, and by 1991, after he'd been with us two seasons, he was voted NFL Special Teams Coach of the Year by the widest margin in the history of the award. The vote was taken among his peers, the twenty-eight special teams coaches in the league. During that two-year period, our punter, Mike Saxon, didn't have a single punt blocked, while we blocked six opposing punts.

Still, we had adjusting left to do on the coaching staff. Jerry Rhome, who'd coached quarterbacks, left after the 1989 season and I put David Shula, then our offensive coordinator, in charge of quarterbacks. David had been a wide receiver as a player, and I prefer to have a quarterbacks coach who has been a quarterback. As it was, the departure of Rhome, with whom Troy Aikman had worked well, extended Troy's less than comfortable feelings, even after we'd resolved our shortlived "quarterback controversy."

During summer camp of 1990, we played the quarterback cards we'd been holding. The New Orleans Saints were an excellent team with an acute problem that summer: Their starting quarterback, Bobby Hebert, was holding out in a bitter contract dispute with Saints' general manager Jim Finks. Hebert would sit out the entire season. Coach Jim Mora had to do something fast. We happened to have what they needed: Steve Walsh.

We traded Walsh to New Orleans for three picks: a one and a three in 1991 and a two in 1992. By parlaying those picks, we would obtain eight players, six of which would contribute and three of which, offensive tackle Erik Williams, linebacker Dixon Edwards, and wide receiver Jimmy Smith, would remain with our Super Bowl championship team.

During the 1990 season, it was said at times that I'd pulled some more wool over another franchise's eyes. It was also said that I'd built up Steve Walsh in the media to increase his trade value. If we have thoughts of trading any player, we're going to be really conscious of how he is presented. So there's no question that a lot of the comments made about Steve were for trade value. But I truly believed that Steve could be a winning quarterback in the NFL. I still do.

I think the public reaction to the Walsh trade was due to my, uh, previous notoriety for the Great Minnesota Train Robbery, and to the fact that nobody could step into a crash learning program of the Saints' offense, start immediately, and do as well as Hebert could have. Hebert's experience in their scheme simply couldn't be replaced. As it turned out, Walsh played well enough to get them to the playoffs, but as soon as Hebert returned the next year, he stepped right back into his old starting role.

Besides, I paid dearly for not having an adequate backup quarterback in 1990. If I'd had one, we probably would have gone from 1–15 in 1989 to the playoffs in 1990, and our turnaround would have come even faster and more obviously than it did.

Without the determination we'd developed through all the off-season work, I think our guys would have pulled back when we found ourselves 3–7 after suffering three straight losses in the middle of the 1990 season. But we'd put in too much effort to fold and make it all for nothing. We were so bound and determined to win that we were able to turn it around. At 3–7, we went to Anaheim and beat the Rams, came home and beat the Redskins on Thanksgiving Day, and then beat New Orleans and Phoenix at home. We won four straight, improved our record to 7–7, and knew that all we had to do was go to Philadelphia and win, and we were in the playoffs. If the Walker trade had been our big-picture turning point, then this should have been our on-field turning point, in the won-lost column.

But the real catastrophe of the season happened at Philadelphia. Troy Aikman suffered a separated shoulder in the first quarter, and we lost 17–3. Babe Laufenberg was our backup quarterback, and we just couldn't do anything offensively against Philadelphia and Atlanta those last two games. No playoffs for us. Our last game was on December 30, and we got wiped out by Jerry Glanville's Atlanta kamikazes, 26–7.

Even with a 7–9 record, I was named NFL Coach of the Year by the Associated Press. (In fact, perhaps the one point on my résumé that I'm proudest of is that in every year since that 1–15 season of 1989, I have been named coach of the year by one organization or another.)

And even after losing the final two games, we came out of 1990 with a lot of positive feelings, because we'd won four games in a row and felt that without the injury to Troy we'd have made the playoffs.

That said, losing the last game of the season to Jerry Glanville was a unique irritation. I don't hold the kind of simmering grudge against him that former Bengals' coach Sam Wyche or former Steelers' coach Chuck Noll did. But Glanville is the only NFL coach who rubs me a little raw, for the simple reason that most of the things he does, all that hotdogging, driving in stock car races, riding motorcycles, appearing in videos, strutting around in his black cowboy hat and dark glasses, detract from the performance of his football team.

My first experience with Glanville came while I was coaching at Miami and went as a guest of the Cowboys to the Super Bowl played in Miami in 1988. Tex Schramm invited me to an owners' luncheon, given by Dolphins' owner Joe Robbie, the day before the game. It was a select group of forty or fifty people. There were a few NFL coaches there, including Glanville, who was then head coach of the Houston Oilers. I'd never met Glanville, but I'd seen him on television and was aware of him.

He came up to me and kind of nudged me and said, "Jimmy, I like your style. You and I, we're two of a kind."

I looked at him and smiled, but I was thinking the whole time, bull*shit*. We're not two of a kind. Don't put me in your category, and for that matter, don't put me in anybody's category.

I will tell you this about Glanville: He drives you crazy and he drives me crazy, but I'm glad I'm not in the same division with him. He can get people to play. That team is dangerous—they may not be consistently good, but they can blindside you with that roller-coaster emotion of theirs.

I think he's a good coach. But all those things he does detract not only from his team, but from his own coaching ability. And all his hotdogging would, in 1991, net the Dallas Cowboys and me a helluva defensive tackle named Tony Casillas, who wanted to be traded by the Falcons mainly because he couldn't put up with being part of the cast of extras in the Jerry Glanville Show any longer. I got Tony for two draft choices, a two and an eight. Talk about a steal of a deal. And it wasn't so much because we outsmarted Atlanta as because Glanville is stubborn, and will put a player in his doghouse and never let him out.

Glanville, Tony has said, "has sort of a narcissistic personality. There's no room for other egos. It's him or you're out. And to appease Glanville, you have to get down and basically kiss his butt."

Tony was another guy we'd known from way back. We'd tried to recruit him at Oklahoma State. He liked my crew a lot while we were recruiting him, but chose Switzer's Oklahoma for the higher profile and tradition. When we got to Dallas and Tony got into Glanville's doghouse, Tony came to our staff and said, "Hey, if there's any way I could get an opportunity to play for you guys . . ."

An opportunity? Hell, the guy would start all sixteen games for us in '91. He was, and remains, an enormous force in making us consistently one of the best defenses against the run in the league.

Tony Casillas came to us because he knew and liked the way we treat people. A former Lombardi Trophy winner, he had been miserable in Atlanta, and his production hadn't been up to par, because of the way he was treated. Tony came to us at precisely the right time. In 1990 I'd gone back to doing things I'd always done—meeting with the players on a regular basis and talking to them about being a team. In 1991, as our turnaround became obvious to the football-watching nation, I would be able, truly and completely, to treat players the way I believe in, and the way I know best. You can have the greatest eye in the world for physical talent, and fill a roster with the finest players in America, and be the smartest Xs and Os coach in America, and you can still watch a team fall flat on its face. Why? Because human beings haven't been made to feel the best that they can possibly feel about themselves. Seeing people as the best that they can be, and getting them to see it too, is my job. And I am pretty good at it.

XVII

SINCERELY POSITIVE, AND POSITIVELY SINCERE

I never tell a running back, "Don't fumble." I never tell a place-kicker, "Don't miss." I say to the running back, "Protect the ball." I say to the placekicker, "Make this." You'd be surprised how few coaches understand the simple psychology I'm using here. But in my opinion, it is vital psychology.

The human mind, upon receiving the message, "Don't fumble," will record the word "fumble" and, consciously or not, worry over it. The "Don't" doesn't help. If anything it hurts, because it's a negative. And so the running back told, "Don't fumble," is more likely to fumble than if the coach had said nothing at all. So I try never to plant a negative seed. I try to make every comment a positive comment.

In recent years, specialists called sports psychologists have been collecting some nice fees from some professional athletes. For these fees, all they are doing is teaching the athletes to turn their thinking around—to think, "protect the ball" or "make this," or in the case of baseball pitchers, "throw strikes." We have even seen psychologists sitting behind home plate so their clients could see them from the mound. Why? Well, because they're doing part of the job which, in my opinion, any coach or manager should be doing, which is to make the player feel as good about himself as he can possibly feel, all the time. You'd think every coach, manager and CEO in America would understand this by now. Certainly, any CEO who might have hired James W. Johnson as an industrial psychologist would have had it made abundantly clear to him. There's just too much scientific evidence to support positive management.

Many a football coach, to start the season off, will really poor-mouth his team. Then, when the team exceeds what the coach has predicted, the coach comes out looking like he did a great job because they played better than what people perceived them to be. We take an opposite approach.

In 1990 I came out publicly, before the season, and said, "I expect us to win as many as we lose." That was a bold statement considering that we'd only won one game the year before. But our players knew from Day One what I expected of them, and they lived up to it, and if Troy Aikman had stayed healthy, I think we would have won at least as many as we lost.

In 1991 my bold public statement before the season was "Not only will we make the playoffs, but we will have success in the playoffs." We indeed made the playoffs, and won the first playoff game.

In 1992 I said, "We will exceed what we did a year ago."

And all three times, the media looked at me like "This guy's nuts." But all three times, our players got a message that was strong and positive about high expectations, and all three times they lived up to the expectations.

There is a saying: "Treat a person as he is, and he will remain as he is. Treat a person as if he were what he could be and should be, and he will become what he could be and should be."

There have been numerous psychological studies to support this type of approach. It's called the Pygmalion Effect, or the psychology of self-fulfilling prophecy. A Dr. King at Tulane University did a study with unskilled laborers taking a welding course. To the welding instructor, Dr. King named certain individuals in the class who, Dr. King said, had special talents to be outstanding welders. Dr. King also named certain individuals in the class who, he said, had no aptitude for welding, did not have the eye-hand coordination, did not have the intelligence. The welding instructor did not know that Dr. King was lying. Dr. King had picked all those individuals at random, and really had no information about their abilities to become welders. But because the instructor treated the students in the class as he expected them to be, that's how they turned out to be. The ones he was told could be outstanding welders got his individual attention and were talked to in a very positive way. And they scored highest on their final exams. The ones he didn't expect to be good got only a token amount of individual time, were treated in a negative way, and at the end of the class scored very low on their exams.

Whether I'm treating the individual player as a true winner, or treating the team as if they're going to win, or treating the assistant coach as if he is in my opinion the brightest, hardest working coach in the league, I do it with the scientific knowledge that if you treat people that way, long enough and sincerely enough, then more times than not, that's what you'll get from the person. Even if you don't attain the final goal, at least the treatment will have such a positive influence that he'll come closer to attaining the goal than he would have otherwise.

Some coaches bring their rookies into camp and, though they might know their first- and second-round picks by name, take the approach with the lower-round picks and free agents in camp that "Oh, I'll learn his name *if* he makes the team." What some don't understand is that *whether* a player makes the team might hinge on something as subtle as *whether* you know his name, and *whether* you treat him as an individual that you care about, with talent you believe in. You should sit with me some afternoon on the bench in the breezeway leading to our locker room at the complex, during our April minicamp, when we bring the rookies in. You should see those disoriented, uncertain, anxious faces filing in. And you should see them light up over something as simple from me, as "Hey, (first name), I saw you doing some really good things out there today. We think you can play here. We like you."

And you know what? We *do* like them, and we *do* think they can play here. Sincerity is the most important part of positive treatment. The only thing worse than a coach or a CEO who doesn't care about his people is one who pretends to care. People can spot a phony every time. They know he doesn't really care about them, and, worse, his act insults their intelligence.

The critical factor in proving sincerity is consistency. You can't say, "This person I'm going to treat positively, and this person negatively, and this person I'm not going to pay attention to." And that applies to everyone in an organization, from star players to assistant coaches to equipment men to front-office secretaries to the janitor who comes in to clean my office.

You can't turn it off and on. I think you've got to treat everyone that way. You create an environment where everybody feels good about themselves, everybody is upbeat and positive, everybody feels like a winner. It's not only for them; it becomes second nature to you and it becomes part of your personality.

And yet I treat everyone as an individual. That may seem contradictory. Let me explain: I'm going to be consistent with my personality with everyone. I'm also going to give everyone individual attention. To get the same response from two individuals, you might have to go about it differently with each. But it's all done in a positive way, with adjustment of what is emphasized to which individual, according to his personality.

Ever since I was a kid I have been more interested in studying people than textbooks. I constantly wonder what the people with whom I come in contact are thinking. That's why I dislike small talk so much. I don't want to hear a joke that someone has memorized and is simply repeating, because the person isn't telling me anything about himself. If someone tells a true story that involves himself, then I'll listen, because he's telling me something about himself. I sincerely want to know what people are thinking.

As head coach, or CEO, it's my job to put everybody who is in the organization in an environment that allows them to be the best that they can be. The best way to go about that is, 1) give them the responsibility for their various roles so that they know that if they don't do it, the job won't get done, and the feeling that when they accomplish something they will share in the accolades, and, 2) have enough personal involvement with each one of them in a positive way that they know I'm interested in them individually, and that I am extremely supportive and loyal, and, 3) in my own way give them enough guidance to make, in essence, a decision that I want them to make.

And so, you see, I am not telling them what to do. But I am getting them to think the way I want them to. Tony Wise, my longtime friend and offensive line coach, used to tell people that "Jimmy's into all that psychology baloney." Then Tony would turn right around and, in effect, acknowledge how the "baloney" worked on him. He would tell people that "Jimmy will come by and say, 'Tony, what if we did such-and-such?' And then he'll let it go for a couple of weeks, and then I'll get the picture and go by and say, 'Jimmy, I think we ought to do such-and-such.' And Jimmy will say, 'Tony, that's a helluvan idea.' "

I mean, who *cares* who makes the decision, as long as it works? The important thing is to keep everybody feeling as positive about himself, as consistently, as possible. Here are examples of the results you can get: In 1990, Dave Wannstedt was NFL Assistant Coach of the Year; in 1991, Joe Avezzano was NFL Special Teams Coach of the Year; in 1992, Mike Woicik was NFL Strength Coach of the Year. They all saw themselves at the very best that they could be, and they became that.

Our teaching methods work in much the same way, except that they do include an element of punishment. It's been proven in the psychology of learning that the most effective way to teach is through a combination of positive reinforcement and punishment. We rely 90 percent of the time on positive reinforcement, but when we do have punishment for an inaccurate response, it really makes an impact on our football team and on the individual. I think at times the punishment can have a short-term negative effect but give you a long-term positive reaction in that it really reinforces the learning that you want to instill.

Here's a simplified example with, say, a receiver. Nine times out of ten when I'm talking to him, I'm saying "get off on the count . . . concentrate on the count . . . nice catch . . . great catch . . . super job of running your route . . . perfect release off the line . . . great attitude . . . excellent job of working in the weight room . . ." And then all of a sudden I come down hard because he jumps offside. I may scream at him and even use some foul language. The one time that I come down hard and embarrass him really stands out, and that reinforces the learning in an optimum way.

Coaches who constantly scream and cuss at their players don't get much reinforcement when they really do need to come down hard. How do their players know when they're really coming down hard? How can one tirade seem more serious than another? It all begins to go in one ear and out the other. On the occasions when I do scream and cuss, the player knows something is up. Something is wrong. Bad wrong.

Everybody says you have to coach according to your own personality. But I think you've got to take it one step further: You've got to be able to control your personality. In order to get the optimal response, you have to be strong enough mentally that you can govern how positive, and how sincere, and how negative you are. You can't be controlled by outside situations. For example, through the 1989 season, I never chewed out a player because I was in a bad frame of mind over my divorce or the reaction I was getting from the public. I did it when I got an inaccurate football response from the player. You've got to be able to block out situations, and regardless of whether you're winning or losing, have the response that you've programmed into your mind.

I didn't know the late Vince Lombardi, but I'm sometimes amused at how his life is perceived as one long tirade. It is clear to me, just from hearing a few classic Lombardi stories, that he was in control of himself and quite calculating.

On one end of the spectrum, the story goes that a stray dog once ran onto the practice field in Green Bay and the trainers and ball boys spent several futile minutes trying to get the dog off the field. The dog finally trotted up to Lombardi, and Lombardi bent over and screamed right in the dog's face: "Get outa here!" And the dog ran off the field and out of sight, never to return, and everybody laughed. Now what did Lombardi do there? He exerted his overwhelming authority, and everybody got the message, in a way that made no individual on his team feel negative.

On the other end of the spectrum is a story once told by Paul Hornung, Lombardi's great running back. Hornung was quite the party guy. Lombardi had a hard rule against players drinking during the season. One night Hornung had a dinner date in Milwaukee and figured he was out of Lombardi's scrutiny range, so he and his date had drinks at the restaurant's bar. And then out of nowhere, Lombardi appeared. "Those'll cost you $150 apiece," said Lombardi, who'd been counting the drinks from a distance. And he disappeared. In those days, that was quite a fine, roughly twenty times the price of the drinks at the bar. The Lombardi of legend would have made a scene with a tirade. The real Lombardi simply quoted the price of drinks with the Green Bay Packers in the fall of 1960, to a player too intelligent and sophisticated to respond to tirades. It's like I said: calculate, adjust to the individual and the situation. Then when you do occasionally jump a case, you really make an impact.

Now: How and where and when do you jump a player's case? That depends on the individual. And you have to know the individual well enough to determine how and where and when to punish.

For instance, to cuss at Michael Irvin publicly might draw such a negative reaction that it counteracts what I'm trying to accomplish. With his pride and his prestige, it might be best to call him in, one-on-one, and say, "Michael, you're doing this or that, and we can't have that." Once, I was hearing some off-field rumors about Michael being a little bit of a roustabout, a party guy, which I knew not to be true. It was more a matter of image, of Michael giving some people the party-guy impression because of some places he'd been seen. We had a private talk about it; he fully understood the need to avoid even appearances that might lead to an inaccurate roustabout image; he stopped going to those places; that was that.

Emmitt Smith, I might yell at on the practice field. And he wouldn't be devastated. We have such a good relationship that we can laugh and cut up and even needle each other with other players around, without feelings being hurt. There have been times, in practice following a game where Emmitt had carried the ball maybe thirty times, that I knew he was hurting. He would ask the trainers if he could go in early from practice, to get treatment for myriad bumps and bruises. And I would say, "Hey, Emmitt! You know better than that! The only stars around here are the blue ones on our helmets!" And he would return to practice, and we would both get a good laugh out of it—along with anyone else who might be listening.

With someone like Troy Aikman, there might be almost a silent treatment—not giving the positive response might bring out the reaction you want. When Troy's and my relationship was a little bit strained after we took Steve Walsh in the supplemental draft of 1989—and I was somewhat standoffish toward both quarterbacks that season—Troy needed the kind of trust that can only come with one-on-one conversations. We had them, and continue to have them. So any silent treatment, say, over lack of sharpness in practice, is departure from the 90 percent positive norm for Troy, and can be more punishing to him than yelling at him.

If a free-agent player making $60,000 a year misses a meeting, a $5,000 fine might have a great deal of impact on him. Fining Troy $5,000 out of his big salary might have little impact on him. It would be like a parking ticket.

And there are all kinds of ways to feed positive responses to people. With one individual, it might be bragging about him publicly in the newspapers. With another, it might be putting my arm around his shoulder walking off the practice field. With another, it might be saying something in a team meeting about his accomplishments. The important thing is to motivate every individual.

There seems to be a school of thought nowadays that some individuals may reach a status or an income level, whether in business or sports, where they no longer need pats on the back. The notion that all these highly paid athletes nowadays don't need stroking, can't be motivated, and won't perform as team players—that's all bull. *Everybody* needs positive reinforcement. And *everybody* wants to win. And no matter the salary, players can be bonded with one another, and care about one another as a team, if they're treated the right way.

Getting a team ready to win means not just telling them that we're going to win, but how we're going to win, before we even begin practice for a particular opponent. By 1991, every week it was "After we beat Philadelphia," or "When we beat Washington," immediately followed with "Here's how we're going to do it." We always have a plan mapped out by our Monday or Wednesday meetings, of how we're going to win. And we let it be realistic, having studied, as a coaching staff, the opponent well enough to know how we're going to do it.

Usually the meeting on Monday involves an evaluation of the previous game, and one thing I always try to do is have a scouting report on Monday of the upcoming opponent. That way we eliminate feelings from the previous Sunday, whether we've won or lost. Our players have Tuesdays off, and I don't want them celebrating for two days after a win or moping around for two days after a loss. So we plant seeds in their minds so that even on their day off they're thinking about the next opponent. By the time they actually begin to practice, they know precisely what we need to work on, and why.

If all this sounds overly optimistic, the concept has in fact been given credibility by success. Fortunately, beginning in 1991, we were able to pinpoint certain areas that allowed us to win, and our way of doing things just snowballed. Time and time again we've won games and could point right back to the plan.

A perfect example was the game at Philadelphia in 1991. In our first meeting with the Eagles that season, they'd crushed us 24–0 in Dallas. By December 15, Troy was hurt and Steve Beuerlein, for whom we'd traded in the offseason, was our quarterback. We were headed to Philadelphia for a game we had to have to make the playoffs, and Philadelphia was an outstanding team, a team that we had not beaten since I arrived in Dallas. After really studying Philadelphia early that week, we said, "The one thing we're going to do is avoid the bad play. We're going to win the game with defense and the kicking game, and not beating ourselves offensively." We were going to take a rope-a-dope approach. I told Steve, "I'm not really concerned about how many passes you complete. But I don't want any interceptions and I don't want a sack."

That Sunday, in the first half, Steve was 2-for-17 passing, but we had no turnovers and no sacks. Randall Cunningham, Philadelphia's highly mobile quarterback, was out with an injury and we sacked their backup, Jeff Kemp, seven times. We hung on by our fingernails and got an 85-yard punt return by Kelvin Martin (remember Joe Avezzano and the special-teams work I wanted?) and won the game and put our team in the playoffs. So when the plan works, it gives you credibility when you go back and talk about how you're going to win the next game.

When you have success, there is glory for all. With success and glory come great feelings for one another, and recognition of one another's contributions. If you keep harping on that time and time again with the players, and have credibility to back you up, you can somewhat prevent the "star system." You're not just throwing the word "team" around loosely. The term is real, and deeply felt. You have a team.

XVIII

ADJUSTING ON THE RISE

Establishing relationships with players isn't always simple or easy. The development of my relationship with Troy Aikman is a prime example. In 1989, because we had Steve Walsh and because of my attitude of not getting deeply into a team that I knew was in rapid transition, I was really standoffish. That caused a strained relationship with Troy. Even though we'd known each other since he was in tenth grade in Henryetta, Oklahoma, it got to the point in 1989 that he wasn't really sure he trusted me. But I think if you talked to Troy today, you'd find a completely different response. Getting there took some doing, and came about as part of other adjustments.

Even after we traded Steve in 1990, Troy was still somewhat uncomfortable because Jerry Rhome, a quarterback coach who had himself been a quarterback, was gone. In evaluating that season, I felt that we needed some more offensive input and I wanted another quarterback coach who had played quarterback. I felt we could be more productive with Troy, and help his progress. So I talked to our offensive coordinator, David Shula, who had been a receiver in his playing days, about coaching receivers and tight ends. I explained that it was nothing negative toward him, that it was just that I wanted a quarterback coach to work with Troy, and I wanted more offensive input. I was looking outside for a new offensive coordinator and quarterback coach.

I called David's father, the Dolphins' head coach Don Shula, and told him about it before I talked to David. Don was not happy about it, of course. Don has gone through lots of staff changes himself, but when you start dealing with relatives, sometimes that makes things a little uneasy. Don said, "You have to do what you think is right, but personally, I felt like you had an outstanding season considering the injury to Troy, and you came on strong and played well, and a lot of it had to do with David."

And I give David a lot of credit. He did a good job for me. But I wanted more. I really tried to get David to stay, but he didn't want it to be perceived as if he'd been demoted. David accepted a job with the Cincinnati Bengals to coach the receivers, the same job he would have had here, but changing teams eliminated the appearance of demotion. As it turned out, it was best for everybody, because David eventually got the head coaching job at Cincinnati.

But that wasn't all of the uneasy feelings between Dallas and Miami during the offseason in 1991. Gary Stevens, who'd been my offensive coordinator at the University of Miami, was now Don Shula's offensive coordinator with the Dolphins. In searching for a new quarterback coach/offensive coordinator, I first talked to Gary, who had been calling me on a regular basis and had indicated interest in coming to Dallas. Gary had worked specifically with quarterbacks, and had called our offensive plays at the University of Miami. But Xs and Os are not as important to me as chemistry among the staff. Gary was especially close to three members of my old University of Miami crew who now worked in Dallas, all on the offensive side—running-backs coach Joe Brodsky, receivers-coach Hubbard Alexander, and offensive-line coach Tony Wise. Because they'd all worked together in precisely the same roles previously, I knew what to expect if I made Gary our offensive coordinator.

After talking with Gary for a while, I offered him the job. He said he would give it some thought and that he would let me know at the Senior Bowl, a college all-star game in Mobile, Alabama, where most of the NFL coaches gather to evaluate players.

I'd had quite a few people express interest in the job and I had feelers out for various people. John Robinson at the Los Angeles Rams had given me permission to talk to Norv Turner, and I knew that Norv was very interested. Norv had more pro experience than Gary, but I didn't have firsthand knowledge of Norv's talent at the time. Gary was the first choice only because he would have made for the smoothest transition, or so I thought at the time.

During Senior Bowl week, Gary came to me one night and accepted the job. I told Jerry Jones he had accepted. Then Gary met with Don the next day and changed his mind. I don't know what happened. The thing that irritated me was that it was almost like the old Tad Foote thing. When someone gives me his word that he's going to do something, I take it.

When Gary came to me and told me he'd changed his mind, I was upset. And I told him so. I told him I didn't agree with the way he handled things. His reasoning was that Don could help him get a head coaching job. That may or may not have been a factor. I don't know. (I do know that in 1993 I helped my longtime defensive coordinator, Dave Wannstedt, get the head coaching job with the Chicago Bears, which he chose over the New York Giants, who were also very interested in him, and that Gary Stevens is still an assistant coach in Miami.)

That was the end of my relationship with Gary Stevens. I responded as I do with anybody who breaks his word. I have had minimal conversation with him since that day, and that's the way it will always be.

I hired Norv Turner, and that ended up being one of the best staff moves I've ever made. I'd known going into the 1991 season that we would be steady on defense, and now we were going to make real progress on offense. Norv came in and I had him visit with Troy, and they hit it off right away. (And now, I really believe the relationship between Troy and me is as good as you'd ever want it to be between a coach and his quarterback.)

In the 1991 draft, we used another first-round pick from the Walker trade with Minnesota to take defensive tackle Russell Maryland, a very intelligent overachiever who'd played for me at the University of Miami. With our own first-round pick we took a prime receiver, Alvin Harper of Tennessee. With the second-round pick acquired from New Orleans in the Walsh trade, we took linebacker Dixon Edwards of Michigan State. Our lower-round jackpots that year were Leon Lett, defensive tackle out of little Emporia State in Kansas in the seventh round, and cornerback Larry Brown of TCU in the twelfth, and last, round. Larry Brown started for us in the Super Bowl. All of these guys played in Super Bowl XXVII, though Leon's most remembered play, as we shall see, was a somewhat dubious distinction.

Our offensive collapse at the end of the 1990 season had more than adequately impressed upon me the need for a solid backup quarterback. We traded a fourth-round pick to the L.A. Raiders for veteran Steve Beuerlein (the ironies of background never cease in this game—Beuerlein had been Gerry Faust's starting quarterback at Notre Dame). Before we traded for him, we made it very clear that he would come in and be the backup. Troy was far and away our guy. Steve handled it as well as you'd ever want anybody to handle it. And he proved to be as valuable a trade as we've made since I've been in Dallas.

We came to a stretch in the season where we had to play three crucial games on the road, at Houston, at the New York Giants, and at Washington. We knew that to get into the playoffs, we had to win one of the three, and that it was going to be difficult to win any of the three.

The Houston game went right down to the wire and into overtime, and we were in field goal range and decided we were going to get it a little closer, when Emmitt, who's one of the best in the NFL at protecting the football, lost a fumble. And Warren Moon took the Oilers down the field and they kicked a field goal to win 26–23. In our quest for one of three, we were 0–1.

The game we felt best about winning, because we'd beaten them earlier in the season, was against the Giants. I guess it was just one of those days, because in all the years that I've been in football, it was as big an off day as I've ever seen officials have.

The two key bad calls, upon review at the end of the season, were reversed by the league—our 22–9 loss, of course, was not. The first big one was when the officials ruled a catch and fumble by Emmitt Smith, when in fact Emmitt never had possession of the ball so it should have been ruled an incomplete pass. As it was, the Giants took over at about our thirty yard line and went in for a touchdown from there. But the crowning blow, and the one where I really lost it, came when Jeff Hostetler, the Giants' quarterback, came rolling out, attempting to pass toward our end zone. Maurice Carthon, the New York fullback, was downfield, blocking one of our linebackers, Dixon Edwards. Hostetler couldn't find a receiver and scrambled. The officials called Dixon for defensive holding on the running play. But because the play had begun to develop as a pass, even Carthon admitted after the game that he initially thought the flag was against him for offensive pass interference, which is how it should have been called. The Giants took advantage of the break, and scored.

And twice the Giants fumbled and we recovered, only to have the officials rule that the plays were dead before the fumbles. I strongly felt that both plays were whistled dead prematurely.

I always do my best not to use officiating as an excuse for losing. But with the pressure of knowing we had to win one of the three games, and with my prediction on the line that we were going to make the playoffs, I just about had it in that game. Knowing I would be reprimanded by the league, I decided I just couldn't let this kind of officiating affect our players. I had to speak out. If nothing else, for our guys, who had to understand that they were good enough to win that game. In the postgame press conference, I said, "Never, since the day my Daddy said, 'Look, this is what you call a football,' have I seen officiating like this."

Since it was my first reprimand, and since I had not been any kind of a problem in that way before, and for one other reason—NFL Commissioner Paul Tagliabue had been at the game and had seen it all with his own eyes—the league didn't fine me. They just gave me a warning and said don't do it again. But in our quest for one of three, we were 0–2 with the toughest opponent yet to come.

For the biggest game of the year, on November 24, we went to RFK Stadium to play the undefeated Washington Redskins, who would go on to win that season's Super Bowl. But first, at our Wednesday meeting, we explained to our players not only that we were going to give the Redskins their first beating of the season, but how we were going to do it.

I told the team: "In studying Washington, we find that every team that has played them this year has gone with a normal game plan and come up short. My feeling is that if you're going to hit a big old gorilla, you don't tap him and run; you hit him with all your might. We're going to take a lot of chances. We're going to go for it on fourth down; we're going for onside kicks; we're going for Hail Marys. We have an opportunity to beat a team that is undefeated."

Dave Wannstedt, our defensive coordinator, felt that to smack the Redskin gorilla, we had to disrupt their offense. That meant completely disrupting and disorienting their quarterback, Mark Rypien. Dave felt we should blitz. A lot. Inordinately. Out of character for us. Dave had been with me most of the time since I was defensive coordinator at the University of Pittsburgh in 1977. I trusted his judgment thoroughly, trusted him to adjust his defensive scheme and get his players to execute well, all on a few days' notice. I said, "Let's do it." We would blitz in the sense of the literal translation from the German: lightning. Rypien had only been sacked five or six times previously that season. He was not used to constant pressure. It was up to Wannstedt's unit to surprise him, disrupt him, and keep disrupting him.

That Sunday at RFK, the Redskins scored first, but on an interception return, and led 7–0 after one quarter. Then we began executing our gambles. Driving downfield just after they had scored, we went for it on a short fourth-down situation at about their 40 and made it, but on the next series they put us in what appeared to be a certain passing situation—third-and-15 from the Washington 32. We ran it. On the draw play, Emmitt Smith not only made the first down but kept on going to the end zone. We tied the game 7–7 and immediately tried something completely out of character for any team early in the second quarter of any game: We tried an onside kick, and we recovered it. We did not score with the ensuing possession, but we did make a statement of our style of play for the day: The Washington gorilla, so accustomed to being tapped-at bashfully with standard game plans, knew now that he would spend the day ducking all-out punches.

We landed another premeditated punch before halftime: the Hail Mary. Troy hit Alvin Harper for a 34-yard touchdown, and we led 14–7 at intermission. After throwing the Hail Mary touchdown, Troy went down with a knee injury, and it would be up to Beuerlein to help us finish the job.

On defense, we continued to blitz Rypien throughout the game, and we completely broke the rhythm of the Redskin offense that way. We ended up sacking Rypien five times, matching the total he'd suffered all season going into the game.

And Beuerlein filled the bill as a backup to Troy, putting us up 21–7 in the fourth quarter with a 23-yard touchdown pass to Michael Irvin. Washington recovered for another touchdown to get within seven, but we added a field goal to go up 24–14 in the waning minutes. They scored a desperation touchdown as the clock ran out, so the final score, 24–21, made the game sound closer than it was.

What had we told the team the previous week and what had we accomplished on Sunday? We would go on fourth down—accomplished; we would go for the onside kick—accomplished; we would throw the Hail Mary—accomplished; we would blitz Rypien unmercifully—accomplished.

In the immediate aftermath, John Madden, who was CBS color commentator for the game, said this was one of the best coaching jobs he'd ever seen. You think my chest wasn't puffed out the next week? But three other chests on my crew deserved to expand too. Dave Wannstedt, my closest friend and defensive general, had directed the rattling of Rypien; Norv Turner, my ideal hire at offensive coordinator, even if it had resulted from the Gary Stevens problem, had directed the go-for-broke offense; and Joe Avezzano, whom I'd known and trusted since the 1960s at Iowa State, had gotten the job done on special teams.

In the category of turning points, beating our archrivals, who just happened to be the best team in the league at that point, on their turf, right in the face of their band blaring "Hail to the Redskins" every five minutes, had to be the psychological turning point for our fans. Beuerlein not only helped us do that, but helped us win five more games to get us into the playoffs and win the first playoff game against Chicago.

We came home from Washington and beat Pittsburgh on Thanksgiving Day; then we beat New Orleans; then we went to Philadelphia for the rope-a-dope game that locked us into the playoffs. After Steve's performance that year, there were rumblings of the old public lust for a quarterback controversy, but there really wasn't one, and Steve knew it and Troy knew it.

We ended up 11–5 in regular season and some of our premier players had absolutely outstanding years. Emmitt Smith led the league in rushing, Michael Irvin led the league in receiving yardage, and Jay Novacek led all NFL tight ends in receptions, with fifty-nine. And we stayed fairly healthy, with the exception of Troy's knee injury.

In the first round of the playoffs, we played a really good game at Chicago and knocked off Mike Ditka's Bears, 17–13. We set the tempo of the game by blocking a punt right off the bat. Again: Special teams play can be a magnificent weapon. We had a field goal and a touchdown, a 10–0 lead, before the Bears knew what hit them. Our defense played so well that through three quarters, all Chicago had to show on offense was a pair of field goals, and we led 17–6. They scored once in the fourth quarter and threatened again, but our defense came up with its best effort of the day, a goal line stand to keep the Bears from taking the lead. Then on Chicago's last-gasp possession, safety Bill Bates got an interception to seal the win.

But the next week, we got blown out by Detroit, 38–6. That wasn't exactly a shock. The Lions had beaten us 34–10 in regular season. We had a difficult time against a team that spread us out on defense, and isolated our defensive backs one-on-one. We simply had trouble against any form of run-and-shoot offense. Houston and Detroit had beaten us, and Atlanta, where Glanville's "Red Gun" is a version of the run-and-shoot, had scored 27 points on us, although we'd gotten out of that year's game against the kamikaze pilots with a 31–27 win.

To compound our problems against Detroit in the playoffs, we turned the ball over to the Lions four times, twice on fumbles and twice on interceptions. We were down at halftime 17–6, and they kept isolating our defensive backs in one-on-one coverage, and kept hitting passes, and kept scoring. There simply wasn't anything we could do about it, that day. They were up 31–6 after three quarters. With our defense spread and struggling to deal with their passing game, the Lions' spectacular running back, Barry Sanders, completed our humiliation with a 47-yard touchdown run in the fourth quarter.

Our vulnerability to the run-and-shoot pointed out the last area we needed to strengthen to become a championship team. Even in the press conference after the Detroit playoff game, I said we would have to shore up our pass defense and we'd have to get some players who could play one-on-one coverage. Our run defense had been solid since we'd traded for Tony Casillas and drafted Russell Maryland and Leon Lett. The last piece of the puzzle was pass defense.

In the 1992 off-season, I adjusted the staff again, hiring Bob Slowik from East Carolina. I gave him the responsibility for working with our nickel package—our five-defensive-back coverage on third-down situations. We drafted Darren Woodson, who would start for us in the nickel, and also inserted Kenny Gant, who'd been with us, but as a special teams player, in our nickel. With our first-round pick we took cornerback Kevin Smith out of Texas A&M, who could play man-to-man coverage.

In the defensive line, we got our second windfall of a talented veteran player in as many years. As Tony Casillas had been unhappy in Atlanta, defensive end Charles Haley had been having problems with the coaching staff and administration in San Francisco. John McVay, one of the 49ers' vice presidents, called me just at the end of the 1992 training camp, and we were actually talking about trading other players. John mentioned Haley. I said there was an interest there. (Talk about trying to keep a poker voice in a phone conversation! Charles Haley was the premier pass-rusher in the league. We'd been busy shoring up our secondary, but if we could get Haley in the defensive front for passing situations, that would be a leap in our pass defense that we hadn't anticipated.) John and I talked about it initially, and then Jerry Jones and Carmen Policy, the 49ers' president, finalized the trade.

Just after the 1992 season began, we acquired strong safety Thomas Everett in a trade with Pittsburgh. The year before we'd had the top special teams in the league; offensively, we were on top with our running back leading the league, and one of our receivers leading the league; our quarterback was now healthy, and we had a solid backup; defensively, I felt good about the consistency, and I felt good about the run defense; and now we had bolstered our secondary and pass rush. Haley and Everett were the last two pieces of the puzzle, to make a run at the whole deal.

XIX

CUTTIN' UP

B y the end of May 1992, I felt caught up. Not satisfied, but caught up. We had completed the draft and gone through the spring minicamps. Except for the process of summer camp and the Haley and Everett trades, the hay was in the barn, as the farmers and ranchers would say, to make the Dallas Cowboys the class of the NFL, in the manner to which the state of Texas had become accustomed so many years before.

And in my life, the hay was in the barn: I would turn forty-nine that summer, and I wouldn't have traded it for any other age. It's great to be forty-nine and have the storms and uphill roads behind you, and to realize that your life has come to just exactly what you want: living alone in a big house with no other living creatures except for six big aquarium tanks full of tropical fish; my girlfriend and buddy, Rhonda, a few blocks away, always there when I needed cheerful companionship; my sons in Dallas, successful, independent, but likely to drop by and help me eat, oh, say, a hundred-dollar takeout order of barbecue ribs from Tony Roma's; my big screen TV and my monster sound system and my satellite dish and my stacks of laser-disk movies; my two Corvettes and a Nissan 300ZX that Rhonda and I drive; happy hours and rollicking vacations with my crew; coaching the most popular team in the most popular sport in America; and knowing it was about to become one of the most successful teams of its time.

My obsession with the tropical fish was a fairly new one, and Dave Wannstedt, knowing my history with little obsessions, predicted that, "As soon as training camp starts, somebody is going to get some really nice fish and tanks and supplies, *real* cheap." But I have yet to get over my fascination with the fish. When I wake up at 4 a.m. and it isn't nearly time to go to work, I can sit for hours watching the fish interact. It's both relaxing and amazing to watch their behavior, some aggressive, some skittish, some cooperating. Rhonda gets onto me about not letting the anemone move about naturally, and people kid me about coaching my collection. But the damned anemone keep going where I don't want them to go, so I pick them up and move them.

I like things a certain way in my house, which is to say, neat. Chad once considered moving in with me for a little while, but my reaction to finding a hamburger wrapper lying around made us realize being roommates wouldn't work, even for a few weeks. Chad couldn't take my housekeeping habits, and vice versa. My mother tells people that "Jimmy's as particular as any woman I've ever seen, about his house." Once, when my family was up from Port Arthur, Daddy and Wayne were standing outside, smoking. (I can't stand the smell of smoke and don't let anyone smoke in my house.) When I realized they were out there smoking, I asked Mother, "They're not throwing the cigarette butts on my lawn, are they?" She said, "No, Jimmy, they're throwing them in the swimming pool." They weren't, of course. But she knows how to get me going.

My eating habits make perfect sense to me, but not to many other people. Out on a happy hour with my crew, if we're at a Mexican restaurant, I might order a dozen complete dinners to go. I'll take them home and put them in the freezer and microwave them as I want them. When I get tired of Mexican food I might order a similar amount of Cajun food, go through the same cycle, and then bring home a lot of barbecue. Sometimes I get the crew to do it too. At a place called On the Border in North Dallas, there is a railing about waist-high that we all lean on while we're standing there drinking. One night I told the waitresses, "Start bringing entrees to go, and keep stacking 'em until they're this [railing] high." They didn't believe me at first. They asked which entrees and I said, "Some of all of them, and stack 'em this high." All of us had plenty of Mexican food for a while.

As for my den, John Blake, a young, bright, aggressive defensive line coach I hired from Oklahoma in 1993, said it best when I invited him over, put a laser-disk action movie on the big screen, and turned up the sound system so that the walls were reverberating. John sank into a chair, put his hands behind his head, and said, "Coach, I could *chill out* in here." Which is precisely what I do.

And so here I was in the spring of 1992: In my life, I was doing just exactly what the hell I wanted to do. At last.

That Memorial Day weekend, Rhonda and I got into the Nissan and headed three hundred miles down I-45, turned left on Galveston Island and took the ferry to the Bolivar Peninsula. I was going home to the Gulf of Mexico. Home to see my mother and daddy and brother and sister, and my piece-of-work of an uncle, Billy Sharp, and his Japanese wife Miyoko, all together for the last time before the monumental football season of 1992 began.

Crystal Beach, between Galveston and Port Arthur, was the logical meeting place because Uncle Billy, my sister Lynda Johnson Hodges, and I all have houses there—well, they have full-fledged houses and I have my cabin. It's not worth much money. But somehow it means security to me. When I sit on my porch, drinking beer, looking at the Gulf, not even the offshore oil rigs spoil my view. They have been on the horizon so long that they too seem like part of home. At night, when they're all lit up, you can see a lot more of them and they're actually kind of pretty.

My stretch of the Bolivar Peninsula is a long way from anywhere. Some days you kind of feel like saying "To hell with all you people. Leave me alone. I'm gonna go to the beach and watch the waves roll in." Not that they're bad people. They're great people. Great fans. But everybody talks about "putting pressure on yourself." It's the public that puts pressure on *you*. You spend your entire life, your entire personality, to make people feel good. Make people feel happy. And there are just times when you say, "Geez, I don't want to make 'em feel happy anymore. Just leave me alone. I want to go to the beach."

(All through the years, even back when I was an assistant coach, especially then, Larry Lacewell and Barry Switzer and Galen Hall and all the crew used to come down to the beach and stay with us. We'd get into the water and fish with a long net and then come out and sit on the beach and drink beer. One time there were twenty-three people staying in the cabin, so Barry and Larry came out on the porch to sleep one night. Then in the middle of the night the breeze stopped and they came screaming back inside: The mosquitoes were just eating them up.)

That Memorial Day weekend of 1992, we did most of the partying at Uncle Billy Sharp's house. Lynda came from next door, Wayne drove an hour and a half from Baytown, the Houston suburb where he lives, and Mother and Daddy drove an hour from Port Arthur.

To look at Uncle Billy's face, weathered and calm beneath his old straw Stetson, is almost to hear the East Texas twin fiddles playing in the winds crashing in from the Gulf. He is my mother's brother, and spent a naval career traveling the world. After he retired, he came to the Gulf to stay. He is near his family and near the sea he learned to love in so many places other than Port Arthur. Miyoko has adapted so well that you could say she is unquestionably the best Cajun cook ever to come out of Yokohama.

With Miyoko and Lynda in charge, we boiled a few mountains of crawfish and a few mountains of shrimp, and made a few huge pots of gumbo and several pans of boudin. Throw in several cases of beer, brands selected by my brother Wayne, Uncle Billy, and me, and we were ready to cut up.

When my family gets together—well, there is a right way to hold a family reunion, and it isn't half-speed or half-ass. It is not a one-day party; it is not a two-day party; it is at least a three-day party. That is the ancient Cajun tradition of Louisiana and Southeast Texas.

This would be the most widely publicized reunion in our family's history. Guys from *Sports Illustrated* kept drifting in and out, day by day, working on a major story about me for their NFL Preview issue of 1992. They'd sensed what was about to happen in Dallas and wanted to be the first media outlet to call the shot. Funny, how the magazine that had once ripped my Miami program was now working on such a positive story. Oh, well. That's transition from college to the NFL—from being nit-picked to death, to being judged by your bottom line.

In the NFL, it's okay to be me—no fund-raisers, no silly-ass alumni sitdown dinners listening to people's small talk, no image-conscious pretenses. Funny how my divorce in Dallas had been little more than noted in the newspapers during a time when everything else I did made headlines; if I'd gotten the divorce in Miami, it would have made big headlines for days on end.

Even as teetotalers, Mother and Daddy stay right in the middle of the party. To this day, they allow their kids to be themselves, even when we do and say things they wish we wouldn't.

By Memorial Day itself, I was pretty well loosened up. I was telling the *Sports Illustrated* guys, "You ought to see my bust. I got a bust, right there with Janis Joplin, in the public library in Port Arthur."

Rhonda tried to keep a straight face as she said, "They've even got a display case with Beat Weeds' panties in it."

"Beat Weeds' panties," I said. "She never wore any panties." Now that drew some amused looks and raised eyebrows, until I said, "From what I understand."

(Later, after the *Sports Illustrated* story appeared with that quote in it, Rich Dalrymple, whom I'd brought to Dallas from Miami as our public relations director, reflected kiddingly on the changing times for the Dallas Cowboys. "Tom Landry held this job for twenty-nine years,"

Rich said, "and he probably had twenty-nine thousand stories written about him. And not once was he ever quoted as using the word 'panties.' ")

Mother and Daddy had a tiny dog named Little Bit that was seventeen years old. I got to ribbing them about how that little old dog's days were numbered, teetering and tottering as it was.

"Well," Mother said, "the little thing's about blind, and she can't hear good."

"She's having a tough time," I said.

Mother calculated the ratio of dog years to human years and came up with one of her zingers: "And, Jimmy, when you get to be a hundred and nineteen, you'll probably teeter and totter a little bit too."

"Mama," I said, "if I get to be fifty, I'm gonna be extremely happy. And if I get to be fifty-two or fifty-three, I'm going to be ecstatic!" I laughed, but I noticed that nobody else did. I guess they worry sometimes about my intensity and the hours I put in.

Uncle Billy, amused at his sister's family, said, "You can't kill these Johnsons. His blood line will take him to a hundred and ten. Then you have to take a twenty-pound hammer and beat their livers to death."

"Aw, Jimmy, I turned fifty-two just recently," Wayne said.

"Congratulations," I said. "When?"

"May fifteenth."

"May fifteenth, huh?" I said.

"A while back," Mother said, "my birthday had been past for three or four days, but finally a big box appeared on my doorstep. It was from Dallas. I said, 'Oh, Jimmy's remembered my birthday—late, but he has remembered.' It was so heavy I couldn't even lift it. I was excited. I pulled it to the garage, and opened it up. And there they were: power tools. Circle saws, electric drills . . . power tools."

(My TV show in Dallas was sponsored by a hardware store chain, and I got several gift certificates for sets of tools. I decided to send out a set to everybody I knew who I thought could use them. I mean, I was just sending Mother and Daddy some tools for their household. It hadn't even dawned on me that it was time for Mother's birthday.)

"I called Jimmy," Mother said, "and thanked him for my 'birthday present.' Later, I got a diamond cluster ring, with a note that said, 'Thought you'd like this better than tools.' "

"I get gifts out of the blue too," said Rhonda. "And I appreciate that more." (Yeah, and I can tell when Rhonda is setting me up.) "See? It all works out," she said. "Daddy's got all the tools, Mama's wearing diamonds, and I've got a couple of sports cars."

"You keep talking," I said, "and your little ass'll be in a Pinto!" Everybody laughed.

"It's like I always say," said Rhonda. "It takes a special person to travel with a hero."

And then somehow, in spite of myself, I got a little serious. "If there is one thing that is the most important thing in your life," I told them, "and you have to block out everything else, family, friends, everything, and say, 'This is the one thing I want to achieve in my life,' it will happen. I've told Brent and Chad, 'Hey, I'm sorry for the way I am, but that's the way I am.' And they understand."

And over the crawfish and boudin and beer, I told my mother and daddy and brother and sister, as all our eyes teared up, "I don't mean to be a bad guy, and I don't mean to be cold. But you know, there's some things I've got to do. And then the day will come when I won't do them anymore."

"That'll be next year," said Uncle Billy, "when you get to the Super Bowl."

TOTAL CHEMISTRY

When a season starts, 50 percent of the teams in the NFL have the ingredients to win the Super Bowl. That's right: Fourteen teams began the 1992 season, as any season, capable of winning it all. If you don't believe that, I can understand. I never would have believed it either, before I came into the NFL. There is a fine line between the best and the worst in this league, where there are only 28 teams, as opposed to NCAA Division I, where there are 107 teams.

Now, what are the variables when so many teams have the ingredients? The way they're blended, of course. It's that worn yet little-understood cliché, "chemistry." Chemistry means a lot more than a quarterback and a receiver butting helmets, congratulating each other at a moment of success, when they've just combined on an 80-yard touchdown. Chemistry is more than getting along on the surface; chemistry is detailed, minute, indeed molecular. The second variable is also a cliché, "attitude." But we take it far beyond the rah-rah, gung-ho stages, high into the realm of the psychology of the self-fulfilling prophecy.

At the outset of the 1992 season, four of the five teams in the NFC East division were capable not only of winning our division, but of winning it all—Dallas, Washington, Philadelphia, and maybe New York. I qualify the Giants with a maybe, because in the previous season, something had changed about the team that had won Super Bowl XXV in January 1991. They still had the ingredients—the talent hadn't changed at New York. Maybe they'd gotten a couple of years older, but they also added a couple of young guys. They added Rodney Hampton, who's a great running back. So what changed?

The Giants had some great players who weren't playing great. They had some good players who weren't playing well. Their chemistry and attitude had changed. The New York Giants' head had been lopped off, following their Super Bowl win. Their CEO, their leader, their chief chemist, Bill Parcells, had resigned in May 1991. Nothing meant here against Ray Handley, who replaced Parcells under tough circumstances. May is in fact late in a football year to take over as head coach, and Ray had to fill the shoes of a guy who'd just won a championship and then quit in his prime. (I could relate, remember? I had taken the Miami job in June, and in the wake of Howard Schnellenberger, who'd just won a national championship.)

There's a helluva lot of difference in knowing Xs and Os and being a head coach, or being the CEO, or the leader, or the president, or the manager. There's a helluva lot of difference in knowing the technical part and knowing the organization. Running an organization is more a matter of knowing people than knowing the mechanics of how the game is played or how the product is manufactured. If you can't get the best out of the people in your organization, it doesn't really make any difference what you know.

Could Vince Lombardi have been successful in the NFL in the

1990s? Yes. Could I have been successful in the NFL in the 1960s? Yes. If a person has talent, there may be a transition period and there may be an adjustment. But Bear Bryant was good coaching at Alabama, and he would have been good coaching the Dallas Cowboys, and he would have been good as the CEO at IBM.

If I had to predict an individual's level of success, I would look at two things. One would be hard work. The other would be dealing with people. In most NFL franchises, they work hard. The difference in the group at the top is dealing with people. And when I say people, that means players, strength coaches, trainers, secretaries, the media—all the people you come in contact with on a daily basis.

After Parcells left, the New York media started to rock and roll in their own unique way, and Ray took it hard. Getting into standup arguments, or stomping out of press conferences (as Ray did in New York and Mike Ditka did in Chicago) can only set off the kind of fight a coach cannot win. And even if he could win, the overall effect on him and his team would be terribly negative.

Even though I've had my moments—at times I have been short with reporters immediately following tough losses—you can't neglect the media because they can create such a negative environment as to make it difficult for your players to play to the best of their ability. I think the media are vitally important to the success of our operation. I don't mean to say that I manipulate the media. But I do believe that you work with the media so that at times you can send a message to your players or to whatever group of people the message is directed to, and make sure the right message gets to them. If you work with the media with a level head, and explain your reasoning carefully enough, they'll usually print it or air it accurately. But if you don't work with the media, don't reason with them, and don't make your point clear, you could very well have the wrong message sent, and it would make your job that much harder.

On a professional football team, we're dealing with a lot of high-profile and very egotistical individuals. And anybody who says they don't pay attention to the media is either lying or not very intelligent. So I've got to make sure the right messages are sent through the media to the people I'm working with.

When I told the media, "We're not only going to make the playoffs, we're going to have success in the playoffs," or "We're going to exceed what we did a year ago," how many times do you think our players read and heard that, and were asked about that? Many, many, many times. So all the media people were doing was reinforcing what I'd told players in team meetings. A lot of things I tell the media are simply repeats of what I just got through telling the players a few hours earlier, and I keep the reinforcement cycle going.

At the outset of 1992, I made a statement to the players and the media which, if you think about it, is a sort of riddle put in the form of a statement rather than a question. I said, "The best game we will play will be the last game of the year." The media didn't read much further into that, but they did keep printing it and saying it. Which had, precisely, the optimal effect.

As elements have their valences—measures of atoms' ability to combine with one another to form molecules—so the chemistry of human personalities, which I call bonding, has loyalty: the force which enables human beings to cooperate and reciprocate. There is no such thing as a team without loyalty. There is such a thing as the word "team" being thrown around loosely as a mask for one-sided loyalty (and there we go back to the worst possible kind of CEO, the phony). Loyalty must be reciprocal, and it must be initiated from the top. Demanding loyalty from your people, without first showing your loyalty to them, is disastrously phony.

Michael Irvin once put it this way: "He'll sit there and listen. I mean, really listen. He's in our corner. That takes the load off. Then when you go on the football field and the man says, 'Look, I want you to run down there, catch that ball and run into that wall,' then who are you to say no? You catch that ball and you run into that wall. You say, 'Okay, Coach, you were there for me; now I'm gonna give it up for you.' That's crucial."

And do you know what else is just as crucial? For the Gloria Alexanders and Joyce Brodskys and Kay Campos, all the wives of my assistant coaches, to be able to say, honestly, as the season goes on and the husbands are away from home for hours on end, days on end, weeks on end, months on end, "We too are willing to sacrifice, because we too feel bonded with this team, we too feel important to this team, and we too will reap the benefits."

I told the *Sports Illustrated* guys on Memorial Day weekend, "We *will* win. Everybody in this league knows we're going to win. That's the way it is." When their NFL Preview issue came out, they called us the Team of the Nineties and ran various articles explaining why, from the youth on our team to my focused personality. They left out one major element I told them about.

I told them, "One of the big reasons we're going to win is that my crew and I are all going down to the Bahamas for a few days together."

Bonding. At two o'clock in the morning in the middle of November, when they've been home with the kids alone for days, the wives don't think of me as some asshole boss who's wringing every ounce of life out of the husbands. I'm just Jimmy, the guy who was cutting up with them at the bar, or around the casino in Nassau, and who during the season is not asking a single minute of his crew that he doesn't put in himself.

I took the whole staff and their wives and girlfriends down to Nassau in June of 1992. This wasn't any sort of thinly disguised "retreat," with any ulterior motive of brainstorming about business. We spent three or four days just having a good time.

In the casinos, I'd put, say, a hundred dollars in front of everybody at the blackjack table—not company money; my own money. Then one night, in front of Bruce Mays, my administrative assistant, I put a five-thousand-dollar chip. I said, "Okay, Bruce, if you win, half of it goes to Woicik." So now: Woicik is over playing the slot machines. Mays wins. Ten thousand dollars. He starts yelling, "Mike! Mike!" Bruce is looking for Mike to give him his five grand, and in the meantime Bruce has forgotten about his chip in front of him on the blackjack table, and they're starting to deal the cards again.

I said, "Bruce, that's your five thousand. Do you want to play five thousand or not?"

He grabbed that five-thousand-dollar chip and said, "Nope." He put a five-dollar chip on the table, and five thousand in his pocket. Now if either Mays or Woicik, or both, had wanted to bet his five grand, and it had all gone from my pocket to the dealer in thirty seconds, fine. They're my guys and I wanted them to have a good time.

It was one of those occasions that Joe Brodsky lumps under the heading of "When Jimmy Gets on a Roll." That can mean picking up a five-hundred-dollar bar tab, or stacking Mexican dinners waist-high, and sometimes the crew thinks I go a little nuts. But hey: They're my crew. They're a part of why I make a nice salary, and they're going to share in the fun I have with what I make.

The Philadelphia Eagles of 1992 set out as the most ferocious team in football—at times. They would have a roller-coaster season. They had a different kind of bond, highly emotional, detonated by a tragedy. Their field leader on defense, tackle Jerome Brown, had been killed in an automobile accident during the off-season. I too had been to war alongside Jerome Brown, as had several of my current Dallas players, back when we were all at Miami. The loss of Jerome hit us hard in Dallas, but it both devastated and inspired the Eagles. When they peaked in 1992, we would just have to steer straight into the storm and face the fury. There was no rope-a-doping them this time. But we also knew that after peaks come valleys.

In preseason camp of 1992, I knew we were good enough to win it all, if we could make steady progress through regular season and avoid the highs and lows that some teams go through, and then get on a roll in the playoffs. In 1992 I wanted to make sure we didn't get too excited about a win or too devastated by a loss. In our division, with the Eagles emotional, the Giants troubled, and the Phoenix Cardinals just not as talented as the rest, there clearly would be one team likely to follow precisely the same kind of course we wanted to follow.

Out at Redskins Park, near Dulles Airport in northern Virginia, our most serious threat of 1992 was in camp. Washington was coming off a Super Bowl win, and for coaches other than Joe Gibbs, that might create problems. After enormous success, teams tend to absorb a lot of what is said and written about them, and bask in the glory. But nobody was better at bonding and focusing a team than Gibbs. He had kept the Redskins uniquely reticent in the limelight—almost to a man, they shied away from personal glory and media attention.

We were to play the Redskins in Dallas in the opening Monday Night Football game of the season. We really pointed hard for that game, all through off-season, and I mean, all the way through the spring minicamps and quarterback schools. Every time I talked to the team, I would finish with just a little seed to plant in their minds, about how we needed to do this or that in order to be ready for that first Monday night game against the Redskins.

Other than having our team completely psyched, we as a staff had to find an element of surprise for Gibbs and his staff. A lot of times I say, "To hell with the Xs and Os—if everyone in our organization is performing at maximum level, we'll win." This time, we also had to out-X-and-O the opponent. Surprising Gibbs, himself a master of surprises, would take some doing. But we would surprise him.

BATTLES AND THE WAR

W e had seen the Redskins use the no-huddle offense some in the Super Bowl. So we expected to see it in the Monday night game. The no-huddle can be quite rattling to a defense accustomed to using the opposing offense's huddle time to huddle on defense and call alignments and coverages. The Redskins' no-huddle offense could take away ten or twelve precious seconds from a defense. Historically, our way of dealing with the no-huddle had been to lock into one coverage and one front and take our chances.

At least that's the way we let it look, all through preseason of 1992. In a preseason game against Miami, Dan Marino on their opening possession ran the no-huddle—the Dolphins had been running it as long as anybody—and we stayed in the same front and the same coverage, and Marino picked us apart. We could have played better defense than we did. But we didn't want to show what we could do. Not yet.

We talked it up in the press. We shook our heads and said, "Hey, we're locked into one coverage and one front against the no-huddle." And we could just hear teams around the league licking their chops. In fact, we had been practicing hard against the no-huddle since the spring.

We had worked really hard on being able to call our whole defensive package without a huddle—being able to signal it in from the sidelines. Talk about confidence—we would have our defensive package considered, called, aligned, ready, and certain, a step ahead of the Redskins' hurry-up. Washington was going to come barreling in and—*hel*-lo.

Again our players were told, and they believed—no, they knew—not just that we were going to beat the Redskins, but *how* we were going to beat them. When you talk to a team, there is a world of difference between pep-talking and stating facts.

When we went onto the field at Texas Stadium that Monday night, before the Washington game even started, I told Norv Turner and Dave Wannstedt, our offensive and defensive coordinators, "We'll beat Washington. The game that concerns me is the Giants." I was already setting up my postgame talk to the team.

The Redskins started right off the bat with the no-huddle, and we went completely out of character on the very first play, blitzed an outside linebacker, and Vinson Smith tackled Mark Rypien for a big loss. Next no-huddle play, next shock: Jimmie Jones nailed their running back, Earnest Byner, for a three-yard loss. Next: Rypien threw incomplete. We stopped the series and blocked their first punt for a safety. They had come out hoping to knock our defense off balance and keep us off balance. The opposite happened. We surprised the surprisers with thoroughly unexpected defense, and stuffed them with special teams play. With the entire Redskin psyche reeling after the safety, our offense drove 84 yards for a touchdown to give us a 9–0 lead.

They did score on us in the second quarter with a 30-yard pass from Rypien to Gary Clark, but we countered with another touchdown and led them 16–7 at the half. We went on to win, 23–10. We manhandled the Super Bowl champions. From then on, the media said of us, "They're playing the best football in the league." That is, from Day One of the 1992 season, we had everybody joining in the self-fulfilling prophecy. Our work against the no-huddle paid immediate dividends, and would pay them much, much later, against a team we would not face during all of regular season—the Buffalo Bills.

Usually, I try to eliminate thoughts of the just-past opponents from the players' minds on Monday morning. Now, late on a Monday night, and after months of buildup to the Washington game, I had to bring the players off a high immediately. I said, "Hey, all we've done is win one game, so put this completely behind you. We've got to make sure we're ready for the Giants—in fact, Norv, you and Dave, what'd I tell you before the game?"

They said, "You're concerned about the Giants, not the Redskins."

And that was the truth. The Redskins were better, but we'd had all summer to zero in on them. We had a "short week" as they're called between Monday night games and regular Sunday games, to prepare for New York. And we had to play up there. It was a Sunday of good news and bad news and good news.

We played a flawless first half and were up 27–0 at halftime. Our offense was clicking, Troy was playing well, and the receivers were making plays. My concerns about a letdown after the Redskin game were lessening. But in the second half, after we scored another touchdown and went up 34–0, there transpired before our eyes a series of events we simply couldn't control.

Phil Simms came in at quarterback for the Giants. He began drilling desperation passes and his receivers were making catches which belonged in a highlight film. For once, we'd gone a bit conservative in the second half, because of our big lead, and I reeducated myself about what can happen when you do that. By the fourth quarter we were holding on by our fingernails, 34–28. But we did hold on: James Washington got an interception to stop the Giants' final possession, and then Troy completed a crucial pass to Michael Irvin for the first down that allowed us to maintain possession and run out the clock.

We came home and beat the Phoenix Cardinals 31–20, and then the NFC East had an open date, like each division has now, to ponder the coming storm, along with the rest of the NFL and anyone who knew and/or cared anything about football. Two teams were playing the best football in the world, at that point: the Dallas Cowboys and the Philadelphia Eagles.

This was a time for me to differentiate, as the generals say, between the tactical and the strategic, or, in layman's language, the matter of losing battles but winning wars. We and the Eagles were both 3–0. There was a national buildup for an early season game that you see often in college football, but rarely in professional football. The difference was that in college you have to win virtually every battle, even early, to win the war. Not so in the NFL. My concern going into the Monday night game against the Eagles was that we'd had a fast start and were undefeated, and they'd had a fast start and were undefeated. This game was going to take the wind out of somebody's sails, and that wouldn't necessarily be predicated on who won and who lost.

We were at a severe disadvantage playing on the road in a Monday night game. Playing at home in such a game is, I think, as big an advantage for any team as there is in football. We'd enjoyed it against Washington; now we faced it at Philadelphia. Not only is it prime time TV; not only is the home crowd in such a frenzy by the time the game starts that it's like home court advantage in basketball; but the visiting team knows in its collective mind that it faces a long flight home into a short week, while the home team will sleep in its own beds following the game, and so the short week is not nearly as taxing.

Further, we were playing a team that had given us more problems than any team we'd played since I'd been with the Cowboys. My biggest concern was that in average age we had the youngest team in the NFL, and if we were to put too much stock in that one game and come up short, it might have an inordinately negative effect on us for the majority of the season to come.

And so, going in, I tried to downplay the game to our team. All over the city of Philadelphia, they were treating it like Super Bowl week. In the Dallas–Fort Worth Metroplex, there wasn't nearly the hoopla.

I didn't write the game off as a loss going in, but I knew it would be awfully difficult to win up there. Their defense, led by guys like Reggie White and Seth Joyner and riding the memory of Jerome Brown, was playing on a whole other psychological plane from the rest of the league. On offense, Randall Cunningham, their every-kind-of-threat quarterback, was healthy.

And the Eagles had acquired a running back who doesn't normally hold grudges but who, this time, was being told by the world that we'd made him look like a goat: a guy by the name of Herschel Walker. The *Sports Illustrated* article on me in September had quoted Tony Wise as observing that at the time we traded Herschel, I hadn't felt like his "heart was in it" for the long haul. True, I wondered at times whether he might retire, and I knew he carried all that baggage about becoming an FBI agent or competing in the Olympics. But as I've explained, I questioned his talent more than his heart. Well, later in September, *Sports Illustrated* ran another story indicating that Herschel was all worked up over people questioning his heart, and that he treated it as a personal insult. Going into the game, I wasn't so much concerned that Herschel might go into some sort of vengeful rushing frenzy on us, so much as that he provided another element of the overall Philadelphia frenzy.

By Monday night we were hyped up for the game, we were enthusiastic, we were prepared. But on the very first snap of the game, Troy Aikman was called for intentional grounding, which cost us 12 yards and a loss of down. The Philadelphia buzzsaw was on and screaming. Mike Golic stopped Emmitt Smith for no gain, and then Troy was intercepted by John Booty, who returned 22 yards to our 14-yard line. Cunningham darted immediately to our 3-yard line and then scored from the 2. Veterans Stadium was rocking. But we kept our composure and countered with a nice 84-yard touchdown drive immediately, with Troy throwing 7 yards to Kelvin Martin for the touchdown.

Philadelphia kicked a field goal late in the first quarter and the second quarter was a scoreless standoff. All things considered, we were in pretty good shape, trailing only 10–7 at halftime. And then Herschel Walker gave the writers a story. His touchdown runs of 9 yards in the third quarter and 16 yards early in the fourth broke the game open. But both of those touchdowns had been set up when we'd turned the ball over and given the Eagles good field position. Herschel wound up with 86 yards rushing that night—not bad, but not exactly rubbing our noses in payback. Keith Byars scored again with just over three minutes left, and, on paper, it appeared that the Eagles had blown us out, 31–7.

However, not only were we not devastated by the loss, but we actually came out of the game with a confident feeling that the next time we played Philadelphia, we would be successful. On offense, we had moved the ball better than we ever had against the Eagles. That fact alone kept us on an even keel going into the next week. We had simply been pressing at Philadelphia and making mistakes, and then in the second half we took some chances trying to get back into the game and made even more mistakes. Mistakes can be corrected. Despite a loss that sounded bad, we were fine.

I told the team in the locker room, "Hey, it's just one game, it's early in the season, we've got a lot of football left to be played, and really, we did some good things. We did some excellent things in all phases of the game, and it'll pay some dividends the next time we line up against them, back at Texas Stadium."

Remember I mentioned Philadelphia's roller-coaster emotion? And how this game was going to take the wind out of somebody's sails? I still look at the effect of that game on the two teams. The Eagles lost their next two games, and three of their next four. That third loss was to us, 20–10, in Dallas. We, on the other hand, went on from the Monday night game in Philadelphia to win our next five in a row, and remained on an even keel for the remainder of the season.

On November 1, against the Eagles in Texas Stadium, we had 22 total first downs to their 9. We had 389 yards to their 190. Emmitt Smith rushed for 163 yards to Herschel Walker's 44. There wasn't any trickery involved. We simply knew, based on what we had seen in the first meeting, that if you took away their emotion and our mistakes— that is, if you took away the Monday night circus—we could beat them.

On Sunday, October 11, six days after the Monday night game at Philadelphia, the Seattle Seahawks came to Dallas. The game itself is of little note—we won, 27–0. The important occasion of that weekend, I still have written in an old pocket appointments book. In the block for Friday, October 9, it reads, "Dinner with Bill Parcells." Bill was out of coaching at the time, and came in as a color commentator for NBC. Now you know me about dinner—I've usually had my beer, and am headed for the exit with a takeout order, by the time the others sit down. But at this dinner there was no small talk. At the table, at one of my favorite local establishments, Humperdink's, were Bill, Rich Dalrymple and his wife Roz, Dave and Jan Wannstedt, Rhonda and me. And Bill and I were the last ones to leave the table. The subject, for four hours, was how Bill Parcells had gotten ready for the Super Bowls the Giants had won. By getting ready, I mean all the logistics during the two-week stretch following the NFC Championship game. I needed to know.

From Day One of training camp I had preached the message by which we could win it all: "We want to make steady progress, we want to get better every week, and we should get better every week, because we're a young team." And I always concluded, "and the best game that we play will be the last game of the year."

And each time we played an excellent game during regular season, I would repeat, "Hey, this was a great ball game. But remember: The best game that we play will be the last game of the year."

It became the overriding theme for our guys. If you hear it enough times, and you think about it enough times, you realize you're going to win the last game of the year, and if you continue to win in a playoff system, that means you've won it all. I was setting them up from Day One to win the Super Bowl. I never said "Super Bowl," and in fact, through the season, I never said "win it all." I use the expression now, but throughout 1992 I avoided even saying Super Bowl to myself. (I used the term with Bill Parcells at dinner, but only as part of questions relating to what he had done.) Sometimes if you deal in subtleties rather than cold hard fact, it has more of a message and it seeps in and it grows in a positive way, more so than if you slap somebody in the face.

If I'd said Super Bowl on Day One, or Super Bowl in the middle of the season, or Super Bowl once we got into the playoffs, that might have been a little scary. The players might have tightened up. The public would have had a reaction to it. The media would have said, "Hey! Here this guy is, talking about winning the Super Bowl!" But if you say, "The best game that we will play will be the last game of the year," nobody directly identifies that with the Super Bowl. If you really think about it, it means you're going to continue to play until it's all over with. But nobody projected it on out and stated it blatantly.

And so I was able to use the Pygmalion Effect, the psychology of the self-fulfilling prophecy, and present a very lofty goal, a high expectation, without saying Super Bowl. At times media people would try to press me on this: "Do you think you have a chance to go all the way?" And I would respond, "There's no question we have a chance to go all the way." But I don't think you could go back and research all the newspaper articles and videotape and ever find me using the words, "Super Bowl." A moderator might have used the term. But I don't recall ever saying the words myself.

I don't know that any loss ever actually helps you, even in the long run. You get through some with less damage than others. And some are real attention getters. In 1988, the Dallas Cowboys had been the most penalized team in the league. By 1992, in the nearly four years I'd been there, we had become consistently one of the least penalized teams in the league. The real danger in success is that when you get on a roll, people pat you on the back and you begin to believe what you hear about yourselves, and sometimes you don't work as hard as you worked to get where you are. And there's a dropoff.

Going into our home game of November 15 against the Los Angeles Rams, we were 8–1 with a five-game winning streak; we were on a roll; we were solid favorites over the Rams. They upset us, 27–23. We didn't play well. How didn't we play well? Mainly, we were penalized seven times for 60 yards, while the Rams were penalized only twice for 10 yards.

How did that hurt us? Let me count the ways: In the second quarter, we got an offensive holding penalty that pushed us back from the L.A. 17-yard line to the 27, and on that possession we ended up having to settle for a field goal rather than a touchdown. That's four points, the final difference in the game, right there. On the Rams' next possession in the second quarter, the Rams threw incomplete on third and 14 and would have had to punt, but we were penalized 5 yards for jumping offside. That gave them another chance, and on third and 9 they completed a 13-yard pass, kept their drive alive, and went on to score a touchdown. That made an 11-point swing based on penalties against us, on back-to-back possessions for us and the Rams. Still, at that point, we only trailed 14–13. In the third quarter, we were leading 23–21. As they punted, we caught a 5-yard defensive holding call, just enough to let them retain possession. They went on to kick a field goal and led 24–23. On their very next possession, we got a 15-yard facemask penalty and a 5-yarder for offside to help them sustain a drive to another field goal for their final margin of victory, 27–23. Take away our penalties, and we very likely would have won the game, at least 27–14. But our penalties cost us 4 points and gave them 13, for a total 17-point swing.

We'd been on a roll, and then we had let our discipline lapse in every phase: offense, defense, and special teams. You see, to me, there is no more important indicator of discipline than *not* getting penalized. You don't have to come down on a team after a game like that. The players know what has happened, even as they walk off the field. In fact, they know it as it's unfolding. What we'd done that day was curable.

And then there are times when you have to be a bit of an asshole. We went into RFK Stadium on December 13 with a chance for a slam dunk on the season. Beat the Redskins at their place, and we would be 14–2; we could clinch the NFC East title that day. And what a statement it would have made, to do it on the home field of the archrivals and Super Bowl champions.

With 3:14 left in the game, even though we had fumbled three times and lost the ball twice, we were clinging to a 17–13 lead. On a second-and-7 from our own 5-yard line, Troy dropped back to our own end zone to pass. (Now you ask, "Why were you throwing from so deep in your own territory?" Because that's our style. We weren't about to go into a shell. Later, in a playoff game against San Francisco, we would look like geniuses and heroes in a similar situation.) Troy was hit by Washington's Jason Buck, and the ball popped loose. Television replays would show clearly that Troy's arm was moving forward when the ball came loose. According to the rules, that meant there was no fumble, just an incomplete pass. But the officials didn't see it that way on the spot. They ruled fumble. Emmitt Smith, whose instinct was get the ball and ask questions later, recovered, but in the melee was unable to get enough control of the ball to protect it. So then the Redskins' Andre Collins worked the ball loose from Emmitt in the end zone, and Washington's Danny Copeland recovered in the end zone for a touchdown. Washington led for the first time all day, 20–17. And that would be the final score.

The next week, the league would give us a ruling that when Troy was hit at the goal line, it was in fact an incomplete pass and not a fumble. That didn't do us any good; we already knew that; and we knew that the score would remain in the record books: Washington 20, Dallas 17.

On the charter flight home, from somewhere over my shoulder I might have heard a chuckle, or thought I heard a chuckle. I got up and went back there, and they knew what was coming. I gave them that look. I saw a young offensive lineman, Frank Cornish, kind of smiling and laughing.

I said, "What the hell are you smiling about?" He started to try to explain why he'd been smiling. I said, "Don't mess with me! Just sit your ass down and shut up!"

Again he tried to explain. Kevin O'Neill, our trainer, told him, "Hey, don't talk to the man right now. Just sit down and shut up and talk to him later."

I wasn't finished. I continued down the aisle, getting on anybody who moved. Assistant coaches. Even flight attendants. I'm not sure exactly how I looked, but Larry Lacewell would say much later, "I've known the man for twenty-six years and he was the best man in my wedding. And there I was, trying to find a way to hide under my seat when he came walking through. Put it this way: There was no doubt who was in command."

I told one of the assistant coaches standing in the aisle, "Look, I can't be this hard on the players if I'm not this hard on y'all. You better go ahead and sit down." And to the flight attendants, I said, "Hey, dinner service is done; y'all just—let's everybody sit down until this trip is over."

Well, maybe I didn't talk to them as nicely as I'm putting it here.

Dave Wannstedt talked to me about it the next day. Out of all the guys on the team and the staff, all of whom were probably pretty gun-shy toward me at the time, Dave, as my longtime righthand man, my defensive coordinator, my best friend, was the one who could and would come to me and make the first reply to my tirade, after I'd simmered down.

He said, "Jimmy, you were really hard on everybody last night."

I said, "I know. I wanted to be hard on 'em."

He said, "You even told the flight attendants to sit their asses down."

I said, "Yeah."

I got to thinking about it, and I called the head flight attendant— the same American Airlines crew always travels with us—and I said, "Hey, I hope you understand, I didn't mean anything personal against y'all. It was just that I didn't want anybody to take that loss too lightly. That's just the way I always want it to be."

I didn't want our players to say "Well, we actually won that game, so everything's okay." Because we *didn't* win it. The scoreboard said Washington won, and that's what counted. And it all went back to my idea that you can't use one mishap by the officials as an excuse. We shouldn't have turned the ball over the first two times and we shouldn't have been backed up to our own goal line leading by only 4 points with three minutes left to play.

I didn't want anybody in a festive mood for any reason. We'd just got our ass kicked—well, in a way.

Our guys took that loss hard. I mean, they were sick. But I wanted them to be sicker. I wasn't angry at them. But I wanted to intensify the pain and frustration. I wanted everybody to experience the pain and sorrow to the maximum because that could become a driving force.

I'm glad I've been able to experience the severe pain and frustration of a loss like that. I'd much rather have suffered through it, and almost accelerated and intensified the pain and sorrow, so that I could enjoy the absolute ecstasy at the other end. I would hate to be one of those individuals who goes through life and never experiences that pain or that ecstasy. And so I have appreciated the times that I've been able to enjoy that kind of pain and sorrow. Because it makes the positive that much more positive.

We would not lose again in the 1992 season, or the playoffs. But not all of us who were on that flight home from Washington would get to the Super Bowl.

Eight days after the Washington game, we beat Atlanta 41–17 on Monday night and locked up the division championship. There wasn't much celebration. Even though we'd beaten the Falcons soundly, I was in a somber mood at Atlanta. I told the team simply, "We were sloppy, but we won."

An "easy game" can hurt your progress. If you have the mental ingredients to be a championship team, you're not concerned about the opponent, you're concerned about yourselves. After a win like the one in Atlanta, I'm sure some players were thinking, Why doesn't Coach let up? But at times I have to be the bad guy just to keep things in check. After the Atlanta game, I would issue no more warnings. I was through *talking* about sloppiness.

For the last game of the season we came home to play the Chicago Bears. We had the division title wrapped up, and on paper we had nothing to lose. Early in the third quarter we went up 17–0 and began putting substitutes in. Curvin Richards scored the touchdown that put us up 24–0, and toward the end of the third quarter Lin Elliott added a field goal to make it 27–0, so we began pouring in substitutions.

Curvin Richards was finishing his second season with us. He'd been our fourth-round draft pick in 1991 out of Pitt. He was our backup running back, behind only Emmitt Smith. But with 14:25 left in the game, he fumbled at our 30-yard line and Chicago recovered. We intercepted them to get the ball back at our 29, but then Steve Beuerlein, in for Troy Aikman, threw an interception which the Bears' Donnell Woolford returned for a touchdown. It was 27–7.

On our next possession, Curvin fumbled again. Chicago's Chris Zorich picked up the ball and returned it 42 yards for a touchdown. Now all of a sudden it was 27–14. Of course, the game was over with; it was late in the fourth quarter. But I was just fuming.

The next day, I cut Curvin Richards.

People couldn't understand. It was the final game of the season; we had won; he was our backup running back; we were headed into the playoffs, and going strong. Even the league office didn't understand. One of their guys called and said, "Coach, why did you cut Curvin Richards yesterday? You know, of course, that you're going to have to pay him the total playoff money and everything. He gets a full share, for as far as you go in the playoffs, because he completed regular season with you. It's not like you're saving money."

"I know all of that."

"So why?"

"Because I couldn't depend on him. Why are you asking me?"

"Well, it's just something that has never been done. I don't think anybody has ever cut somebody after the last game of the year, when they had the playoffs sewn up."

It had no bearing on anything that was going to happen, other than that it was the right thing to do. I talked to the players. "When we get into the playoffs, you get no second chances. If it's early in regular season and a guy fumbles the ball, even if we lose the game, we've got other games to play to situate ourselves. But I didn't want to go into the playoffs with a guy I couldn't depend on and you couldn't depend on."

That made an impact. Ninety percent of the time I'm saying, "Protect the ball; protect the ball." Then all of a sudden a player drops it on the ground twice, and he's cut. That one time made more of an impact than all the times I'd said "Protect the ball." It would do Curvin Richards no good, but for forty-six other individuals it was the guarantee that they had optimum retention of learning. And they would respond in the optimum way thereafter when I said, "Protect the ball." (Throughout the playoffs, we would have only one turnover until the final quarter of the Super Bowl, when we had the game locked up and had a couple of fumbles by substitutes, most notably, of course, Leon Lett's embarrassing freak turnover.)

For the Dallas Cowboys, there was a profound new meaning when I told them what all coaches tell all teams as they go into the playoffs: "You get no second chances."

XXII

THE BATTLE OF THE BEST

T he San Francisco 49ers, with their 14–2 regular season record to our 13–3, were assured of home-field advantage for as long as they could remain in the playoffs. Only if the 49ers were knocked off could we hope to play the NFC championship game in Dallas. And with the playoffs starting, monsoon rains swept the San Francisco Bay Area. We figured we were bound there, and we knew it would be a mess.

Our record and division championship got us a bye in the first round of the playoffs, and on January 10, 1993, there was a playoff game in Dallas for the first time in more than nine years, since December 26,

1983. And for the first time in more than eleven years, the Cowboys won a home playoff game. We beat the Philadelphia Eagles 34–10. The 24-point margin was an exact turnaround of their 31–7 win over us in the early season Monday night game. Playing at home was an edge, but going in, we'd proved to ourselves that we could now play the Eagles well in all three phases of the game. So our team played with a tremendous amount of confidence that day. It wasn't the Eagles who worried us. It was the 49ers.

The same weekend we beat the Eagles, the Washington Redskins, who'd slugged their way past the wild-card round of the playoffs, fought a war in the rain in San Francisco. Had the Redskins won it, as they nearly did, Washington would have had to come to Dallas for the NFC championship game. But a key Mark Rypien fumble in the wet turned the tide of the game against Joe Gibbs's team.

So we were indeed going to San Francisco for the NFC championship game. It was, I firmly believed, a stronger pairing than the Super Bowl could possibly be. Ours were the best two teams in football. Whoever won this one, very likely, could overwhelm either of the teams that might emerge from the AFC championship game, the Miami Dolphins or the Buffalo Bills, in the Super Bowl.

All week on the West Coast, it continued to rain. And rain. And rain. The natural turf at Candlestick Park was such a mess that it became a daily story on the nation's sports pages. The NFL sent in its own groundskeeping experts to help the resident crew at Candlestick. We were what the oddsmakers call a "turf team." Texas Stadium has artificial turf, and our team was somewhat geared to it. We would have to do what we could with what we found there.

We prepared extremely well for San Francisco. We felt like we had a plan. As bad as the footing promised to be, most football fans figured we would run the ball. But the 49ers had an excellent run defense. In our Wednesday meeting, I told the team, "We're going to come out throwing the ball all over the field. And don't get frustrated because we're not handing it to the guy who has carried us to this point (meaning Emmitt Smith). We're gonna be wide open, and once we do that, we'll loosen up their run defense and start handing it to Emmitt in the second half, and he's going to break some, and we'll be able to control the game with our running game at the end."

It was an exact reversal of the conventional wisdom of game plans, which is of course that you must establish the run before you can pass effectively. We planned to establish the pass so that we could run effectively. San Francisco was one of the best defenses in the league against the run, but they'd had problems on pass defense.

Defensively, we had our hands full because they really had a great offensive football team. At quarterback they were as good and as deep as anybody had ever been in the history of the league: 1992 NFL MVP Steve Young, backed up by Joe Montana, backed up by Steve Bono. Jerry Rice (who has been called the greatest receiver ever to play the game) was one wideout. John Taylor was the other, giving them as good a tandem as there is in the league. Their top running back was a spinning power runner, one of Lou Holtz's stars of the 1988 national championship team at Notre Dame, Ricky Watters. He was backed up by the darting, slicing Amp Lee, one of Bobby Bowden's former stars at Florida State. Their fullback was a blood-and-guts guy made for the mud and slop, Tom Rathman out of Nebraska. They had a veteran offensive line.

What were we to do about all that? Well, we had an excellent run defense ourselves, and our pass defense had shown the improvement we'd hoped for since preseason. But we had not played San Francisco in regular season. We decided we had to be somewhat conservative on defense, because if you blitz the 49ers you're going to have major problems. You're chasing a quarterback, Steve Young, who is so mobile he can kill you scrambling, and you're leaving Jerry Rice and John Taylor in single coverage. We had to worry Young, hurry him, and force him to throw into coverage. And that pressure must come in a manner long dear to Jimmy Johnson's heart: upfield pressure from the defensive line. We had the guys to do it: Tony Tolbert, Tony Casillas, Russell Maryland, and a Mr. Haley. Charles Haley. An old weapon of the 49ers, turned against them. We were counting a bunch on Haley harassing his old teammates so that we could hold up with a three- and four-man rush. And that would happen.

We had a good plan, but this game was by no means the kind of lock to which we'd become accustomed. San Francisco had a helluva team, and we were going to let everything fly.

When we got to San Francisco, the rain finally subsided to a mere intermittent drizzle. Still, the earth was saturated. We went out to check the field, and had a walkthrough. George Toma, the league field supervisor, had put in new turf in various parts of the field, and had given us a map of where the new turf was and where the old turf was. Jockeys about to compete in the Kentucky Derby will often ride in an earlier race that day at Churchill Downs, to "find the good ground" on the track. Military commanders' first priority, with any battle imminent, is to check the terrain and find the good ground. We studied the map and walked the field. On the old turf, there was going to be some slippage.

I normally sleep really, really well the night before a game. The night before the San Francisco game, I didn't. I got up about four o'clock in the morning, and got out the map of the turf, and went through our game plan. I wanted to see if there was some edge we might get, some adjustment we might make for various parts of the field. For instance, at one end of the field we had good footing from sideline to sideline. At the other end of the field, the good footing was only between the hashmarks.

I made a bunch of notes and called a staff meeting for seven o'clock that morning, six hours before kickoff. We went through our entire game plan, offensively, defensively, and in the kicking game, every phase, making adjustments according to where we were on the field. That made it two or three times as complex as a normal game plan.

For instance, in the kicking game if we were on the receiving end of the field where we had good footing all the way across, we could have a middle or sideline kickoff return. If we were where the footing was only good in the middle, we had two choices: Play it safe and go for the middle return or take a chance on a big play where a defender might slip, and go for the sideline return. We made such adjustments and introduced such variables all through every phase of the game plan.

We even made asterisks regarding the footing for Emmitt specifically. If it was a critical down, we were going to run the ball inside, where we had good footing, rather than out to the sidelines where Emmitt might slip. I had the hotel send in a blackboard and we made a chart, fitting our entire game plan to the groundskeepers' map.

Funny, how after the game, so many media stories ended up indicating that the footing didn't have much effect on the outcome. *Sports Illustrated*'s game story even stated flatly, "No slips." They were almost right. There was only one. By one 49er defensive back. And all it did was win the game for us.

By halftime it was 10–10 and most categories were pretty even, and the game was going the way we'd planned. Haley was harassing them and they were concentrating on him so much that Casillas was getting good pressure from the inside—he'd sacked Young once in the first half, and would end up with three sacks for the day.

In the third quarter we began to turn the game. We opened the half with a 78-yard drive keyed on a 38-yard pass from Troy to Alvin Harper at the San Francisco 7. Emmitt gained 4 around the right side, and then our own version of a blood-and-guts fullback made for the mud and rain, Daryl Johnston, scored from the 3 to give us a 17–10 lead.

Casillas got his second, and perhaps most important, sack on San Francisco's next possession, helping to stifle their drive. They settled for a field goal and we held onto the lead, 17–13.

We traded touchdowns in the fourth quarter and with 4:22 left to play, we took possession on our 21-yard line. Okay, with a four-point lead late in the game, surely we were going to run on first down, right? Look at what had happened to us at Washington when we tried to throw from back in our own territory with a 4-point lead in the final minutes.

On the headset, up to the coaches' booth in the press box, I said, "Norv, let's go ahead and open it up. Do what you gotta do to pick up another first down."

Since 7 a.m. we'd been so familiar with the groundskeepers' map of the turf that we didn't even have to talk about the area we were in. Norv said, "The slant would be safe."

I said, "Okay, let's throw the slant."

We were on the end of the field where there was slippage at the yard numbers marked on the field. On any other route that would have done us any good, our receiver on the play, Alvin Harper, would have had to make a cut and could have slipped on that part of the field. On the slant, the defensive back covering him had to make a quick cut, but Alvin didn't.

Alvin caught the ball about six yards beyond the line of scrimmage. The defender slipped down and Alvin angled across the field and went 70 yards to set up our clinching touchdown. That was the key play of the game. And it happened because we'd adjusted our game plan according to the footing in the various areas.

Very few people picked up on what had happened. They were so busy watching Alvin run, they didn't notice the 49er defender back there on the ground. Alvin got to the San Francisco 9. Then Emmitt carried to the 6, and Troy threw to Kelvin Martin for the touchdown that iced the game.

We won, 30–20. The CBS crew must have been impressed with my jumping up and down on the sidelines with the knowledge that we were going to Pasadena, because they replayed it a lot in slow motion. Maybe I was a candidate for the All-Madden team with my vertical leap.

In the locker room, the CBS cameras stayed on me for my post-game talk to the team. You may have heard that talk. You might remember that the term "Super Bowl" was conspicuous by its absence, and what I did say.

I said: "We do have one more game left to play."

And for positive reinforcement, I said, "How 'bout them Cowboys!"

The season-long message need not be repeated. It was firmly implanted in every Cowboy mind: "The best game that we play will be the last." And we were on our way to play it.

XXIII

PREPARATION FOR
PREPARATION

We had two weeks to prepare for that one remaining game. I had spent, oh, the better part of the past decade preparing to prepare for it. We didn't have our strategy meeting until Thursday, January 21, ten days before the game. I wanted to give us, the staff, three days to study Buffalo. I also didn't want to drag this thing out too far from our standard practice routines. And, because negative seeds were going to be showered on this team from now through January 31 from the outside, I had to try to immunize the players from the hoopla before it hit.

When we met, I told the team: "You've got to understand this:

The game can be as big in your mind as you want it to be. If you take Buffalo's team—and we have studied them thoroughly—and our team, and we all go right out here on this practice field, we'll kick their ass.

"With no anxiety, no distractions, nobody watching, we win. That's the approach you've got to have for the game. You focus in your mind that you're playing Buffalo on the practice field at Valley Ranch.

"Now if we take a two-by-four and lay it on its broad side across this room, nearly everybody in this room can walk this two-by-four, right across the room, and never flinch." I kind of laughed and pointed to a couple of the assistant coaches and said, "Well, some don't have the athletic ability." Everybody laughed. I said, "But everybody else in this room does." I paused for a moment. "Now you take this same two-by-four, and you put it ten stories up. It would be a difficult time for anybody to walk between two buildings ten stories up. Because the focus of your mind now is not about walking the two-by-four. Ten stories up, you're thinking, 'I don't want to fall.' Your entire concentration is, 'I don't want to fall, I don't want to fall, I don't want to fall.' So what do you do? You stumble and you grab hold of the two-by-four, and you hang on.

"And so your focus playing Buffalo will be, We're on the practice field, we're the best team, and we are going to win. Now if you go out there [to Pasadena] and your focus is, This is going to be the most watched television program of all time. A billion people or so are going to watch this game. It's the most televised sporting event in the world. It's the most important game of the year. If your focus is on that, you're going to be so uptight you're going to make mistakes."

(Here, I should explain the media logistics of a Super Bowl week. There are several thousand accredited media people, working every day, all week. They come in by the busloads to a team's hotel or some other designated site, at a set time each day. Usually in a ballroom, there are dozens of tables set up, just like at a huge formal dinner. Each table has a player's name and number on a large center card on a stand much the way you'd find your table number at a banquet. Each card will read, "8—Troy Aikman" or "22—Emmitt Smith." Your players walk in at a given time and sit down at their tables, and chances are there are already a few dozen reporters swarming around any individual table. At Troy's or Emmitt's table, there might be, say, two familiar Dallas or Fort Worth writers; three radio guys, from San Francisco, New Orleans, and Minneapolis; a *New York Times* columnist; two writers from Boston; two from Milwaukee; one from the Chicago *Sun-Times* who's trying to slip his questions and answers past the guy from the Chicago *Tribune* who's standing nearby; some guy from the Miami *Herald* who's really working on a feature on Michael Irvin or me, but needs to ask Emmitt or Troy about us; and about eight more writers who never identify themselves or their purpose, and who are going to have to check their media guides to find out how to spell "Emmitt" or "Aikman" correctly. And that's just the start. Throughout the session, it's like an enormous buffet. Reporters roam from table to table. A player may be asked the same question twenty or thirty times in the span of one hour. Some of the questions can be uneducated and irritating, but relatively harmless, such as, "Troy, why did you transfer from Oklahoma to UCLA?" Others can fall under the heading of The Standard NFL Writers' Question of the Week, and can really weigh on a team almost to the point of brainwashing if you're not careful. Back to my speech to the team now, and I'll give you an example.)

I told the team, "Everybody's going to be saying to you, 'Well, you've never been to a Super Bowl before. What about all these distractions? Aren't they going to affect you guys?' Hey: There aren't gonna be any distractions. We're gonna go through all those interviews, we're gonna be loose, we're gonna enjoy it, we're gonna have a good time.

"And we're gonna work our ass off in practice. We've got everything programmed to work out just like a game week during the regular season. Nothing's going to change. Everything is going to be down to the minute of our regular practice schedule. Because if we do it like that, we're the best team. If we take Buffalo out here on this practice field, we're gonna win.

"We're going to go through all that stuff, people talking to you about distractions. You just say, 'Hey, we're fine. We're enjoying it. We're gonna take care of business. And we're gonna go out there and play the best game we've played all year long. That was our approach from Day One.' "

Then I told the players how we were going to win, and, as always, I put some meat on it.

"Everybody talks about us being a wide-open football team. We *are* a wide-open team. But there's a flaw in Buffalo's team: They turn the ball over. So don't anybody get uptight and say, 'Oh, Jimmy's pulling back,' when we start off the game a little conservative, to let them turn it over and get in a hole. Once they start turning it over, then we're gonna turn it loose.

"Defensively it's the same way: We're gonna hold back on the blitzes until they start turning it over, and then we're gonna blitz 'em more than we have some of the other teams.

"Here's how we're going to practice: We're going to have two scout teams to simulate their no-huddle offense, which will really give them some problems, because we'll be prepared for that tempo. We have studied it. In practice, we're going to run plays every 15 seconds to give you that tempo. It's actually about 18 or 19 seconds between plays that Buffalo runs.

"And because they call so many plays at the line of scrimmage, we're really going to concentrate on disguising our coverages to give 'em some problems.

"Offensively we're going to run the ball to get 'em in three-deep coverage." (Three-deep is when you get one of their safeties to rotate up to play the run, as opposed to four-deep, where all four defensive backs play pass coverage. Three-deep coverage means they've got to leave at least one of your receivers in single coverage, because the safety who would normally be helping the cornerback on that receiver has gone up to play the run. If you run the ball effectively enough, and throw the ball underneath their linebackers effectively, then you pretty well force them to bring up that safety to help, and leave the others in three-deep.)

"We're going to play some ball-control but we feel like we can get 'em on an out and up [receiver pattern], we can get 'em on some deep passes, with our receivers isolated in one-on-one coverage."

We talked about individual players. For example, Buffalo had a great pass rusher in Bruce Smith. We were going to use some schemes to double up on blocking Smith, and have one-on-one protection with some of the other defenders, to give Troy time to throw the football.

Okay: We had addressed the elements of the game itself, and we could begin practice. Meanwhile, I had to work out ways to head off just about every kind of distraction imaginable, once we got to Pasadena. I was prepared.

What made me such an expert on getting ready for a Super Bowl, when the only way I'd ever been to Super Bowls was as a guest in a skybox? Well, years ago, while I was coaching at the University of Miami, I used to visit Don Shula at the Dolphins, and I would ask him all about how he got ready for a Super Bowl. At the time, I was trying to take some of his logistics and combine them with things I already knew to prepare for national championship college games. Then, once while I was at Miami and once after I got to the Cowboys, I talked to Joe Gibbs of the Redskins about the same subject. Then I had that long conversation with Bill Parcells. So I had done quite a bit of research on how some of the successful coaches had prepared. All across America, everybody was making a big deal about, "Buffalo has already been to the Super Bowl twice in a row and Dallas (this group of players) has never been, and that's going to be an advantage to Buffalo." Well, Buffalo had been twice and lost twice. I researched the coaches and the teams that had *won* the Super Bowl.

One of the things stressed by all the successful coaches I talked to was to have the bulk of your game plan done before you ever got to the site of the Super Bowl. So we did that in Valley Ranch.

Parcells in October mostly reiterated logistics others had mentioned, but he did give me two new ideas. One was that, during the NFC playoffs, we might want to send a couple of scouts to see teams which we might face in the playoffs but which we hadn't played in regular season. We did that with San Francisco and it gave us extra, faster information. It wasn't necessary against AFC teams, because whomever that conference sent to the Super Bowl, we were going to have two weeks to prepare for them.

Also, a lot of my experience at taking teams to national championship bowl games applied to Super Bowl logistics, right down to changing hotels the night before the game, to get ourselves in a road game atmosphere similar to a regular season game, and away from some of the hoopla.

But Parcells also talked about one very important area, which was different from the way we'd done it in college. He said, "The biggest thing you need to do is have a meeting right away with the players about their tickets, their merchandise endorsements that sometimes hound you during the Super Bowl, and their family arrangements for going to the game. That will be the biggest headache of all: worrying about their families and friends getting hotel rooms, getting [side] event tickets, getting game tickets. You need to make sure not only that they take care of that early, but also that you assign some people in the organization that the players can go to to get it done."

So at our very first meeting after winning at San Francisco, I assigned four guys from our operations department—Bruce Mays, Steve Carichoff, Craig Glieber, and Carmen Grosso—to the players. They would handle all the family arrangements. Any questions or any problems could be taken straight to those people, people the players knew.

A college bowl game, because it's in a festive atmosphere, is more relaxed. Guys have time to take care of their friends and families. Because of the significance of the Super Bowl, it's not nearly as relaxed for the players or the coaches. It's truly a business trip. Still, players are concerned that their families enjoy it. So we had somebody, all the way through, that players could tell, "Hey, make sure you take care of my girlfriend," or "Take care of my wife, my mother and daddy, make sure they get over to this place and get some tickets for that." The players didn't have to worry about it.

And I gave Bruce Mays one more assignment: "For the night of January 30, book us into a different hotel. Somewhere in the Pasadena area. Find one, book it, and don't tell *anybody* else. Not even me. I don't want to know."

Game elements were set, and Pasadena logistics were set. Now I had to deal with the biggest distraction of all, an enormous and bittersweet one which, if I wasn't careful, was going to distract even me.

XXIV

MY GOOD RIGHT ARM

W hen I first met Dave Wannstedt, in 1977, he was a graduate assistant under Jackie Sherrill at Pitt. Dave had just got through playing college ball as an offensive lineman. One afternoon we went to play racquetball in downtown Pittsburgh, and when we got through, we had a couple of beers. He was contemplating whether he ought to go into coaching as a profession. I really had an instant affection for Dave. I liked the way he dealt with players, I liked his commitment, and so I told him, "Hey, you hang in the coaching profession and I give you my word, I'll take care of you."

Then when I went to Oklahoma State, I took him with me as

defensive line coach, and later promoted him to defensive coordinator. He left for a couple of years and went to Southern Cal, and then I hired him back with me at Miami and made him defensive coordinator and linebacker coach. Toward the end of the 1988 season, before I began to take Jerry Jones seriously about his buying the Cowboys, Dave indicated he wanted to go into professional football. So I talked to Don Shula, and Don hired Dave as linebacker coach with the Dolphins. But no sooner had I taken the Cowboys job than Dave packed up his family and came to Dallas with us. He has not only been an outstanding coach for me, but he is probably the person I was closest to, day in, day out, especially through the tough times in Dallas. I really don't have a lot of contact with anybody other than assistant coaches.

I had known for several years that Dave was well qualified to be a head coach in the NFL. After the 1991 season he had the opportunity to interview for the Pittsburgh Steelers job, and we all felt like he was going to get it. And we were all disappointed that he didn't get it, because he's from Pittsburgh and I knew his feelings for the area. And even though it would have been a loss for me both personally and professionally, I really wanted him to get the job. Then his alma mater, the University of Pittsburgh, called, and Dave and I talked, and I told him, "If you go to Pitt, you'll probably triple your salary." But I knew he really wasn't going to be satisfied unless he could be a head coach at the professional level. So he withdrew his name from consideration at Pitt.

And then as the 1992 regular season ended and we headed into the playoffs and toward the Super Bowl, Mike Ditka was fired at Chicago and Ray Handley was fired at the New York Giants.

The Giants called first, and George Young, their general manager, visited with Dave about the possibility of going there. Dave was really excited, and really liked George. Then we had an inquiry from Chicago. Mike McCaskey, president of the Bears, had talked to Jerry Jones about the possibility of hiring Dave. But it was our understanding that they were in no hurry to make a decision.

Dave and I sat down on a couple of occasions and had heart-to-heart talks about what he wanted. We talked about the Giants and we talked about the Bears, and by hearing all of Dave's various reasons, I got the feeling that if he had the opportunity at both places, he would probably prefer to go to Chicago. We just tried to see where he would be most successful. I think in the back of his mind he preferred not to be in the same division as Dallas, so that worked against the Giants. Also, Chicago offered him much more of the kind of Pittsburgh atmosphere that he's used to.

I talked to Jerry about it, and we called Mike McCaskey and, I guess you might say, lit a fire. We told Mike that they had permission to talk to Dave, and that in fact if they were going to be doing anything with Dave, they'd better get on the stick, because this thing with the Giants could be finalized in the near future.

So Mike McCaskey came down to Valley Ranch, and visited with Dave at length. Mike and I sat and talked in my office and I really had a good feeling about him. Knowing I had strong feelings for Dave, Mike said, "If this thing comes about, I want you to work with me and help me to help Dave to be the very best head coach he can be." Which of course hit precisely the right chords with me. He sincerely wanted to work with Dave and make Dave successful.

All this was going on, just beneath the surface, the weeks of the Philadelphia and San Francisco playoff games. Just before our trip to San Francisco, we got it all taken care of, and I said, "Why don't we put things on hold until Monday after the San Francisco game?" Dave and Mike agreed, and we went to San Francisco and Dave coached a helluva game, thoroughly focused.

Then Dave went to Chicago, was announced as head coach, and had his press conference. He was readily accepted in Chicago because there are a lot of similarities between Dave and Mike Ditka. Both are from western Pennsylvania, both played at Pitt, both are big, tall guys with mustaches, and they both came from the Cowboys.

After his press conference, Dave came back to Valley Ranch, and for the entire time of preparation for Buffalo, Dave never let his new job distract him from his remaining job with the Cowboys.

He did ask my advice: Should he address the matter with the Dallas players? I sat in on one of his final meetings with the defensive players.

He talked about things, but never addressed the job change head-on. I told him after that meeting that I thought he'd done it the best way by far, because everybody knew how he felt. And he knew how they felt. Dave was extremely close to our players, and it wasn't something that needed to be said in words because it would have taken away from the focus of our game.

We also knew that Tony Wise, my offensive line coach, was going with Dave. I'd also known Tony since Pitt in 1977, and he had been with me everywhere I'd been a head coach. Over the years, I hadn't talked strategy with Tony the way I had with Dave, but Tony had run what must be the most unselfish unit of a football team. Offensive linemen have to have a special, highly stable mindset. As the old saying goes, the only time an offensive lineman's name is mentioned in accounts of a game is when he is called for holding. Through Oklahoma State, Miami, and Dallas, Tony had kept the same sort of low-key, loyal, but in his own way highly aggressive, mindset.

Most of all, it was their friendship I would miss—around the blackjack tables of Vegas, and the beaches of Nassau, and happy hours at Humperdink's or On the Border—so much more than the Xs and Os.

In order for me not to be emotional, I have to block things out. So I tended to block both Dave and Tony out during the weeks leading up to the Super Bowl. I had a lot of affection for Dave and Tony, and was happy they were moving up, but terribly sorry to lose them. I'm a lot more emotional than I usually show. As I said earlier, whether it's my personal life or my job, I focus on what I'm doing with blinders on. And a lot of times that may seem cold to other people. But the feeling is there.

I think I have an obligation to help the people who give it their all when they're with me. I want to reward people who have done a good job. And certainly the greatest reward, for any assistant coach who wants it, is to be a head coach. When I left Oklahoma State, I spent considerable time calling the board of regents and visiting with them, to make sure Pat Jones would get the head coaching job there. And I visited with Mike McCaskey on Dave Wannstedt's behalf, and I will do what I can for anyone on our staff who is pursuing a head coaching job in the future.

In my opinion, we've got several candidates. For example, I've made Norv Turner my assistant head coach, and I think that might be a step in a logical progression to a head coaching job. Butch Davis has now replaced Dave Wannstedt as defensive coordinator, and Butch has now been with me longer than anyone else on the staff—fifteen years. (Butch says a lot of families don't stay together that long.) Joe Avezzano is coordinator of my special teams and has had head coaching experience at Oregon State. So we have candidates, and when their times come, I will help them. If you reward your people who give their all, then you assure yourself of bringing in more bright people willing to give their all, knowing that they too will be rewarded.

When I hired my longtime friend Larry Lacewell to run our scouting department in 1992, I hired him because I felt Larry would do a good job in that role. I wouldn't ever want to hire someone because he was a friend. Because we have a job to do. And, as I told Larry, I'm not the same guy I was in 1970 at Oklahoma. There's no doubt in my mind that I'm a lot more focused and committed, and a lot simpler. Nowadays I live a very simple life, with very few people. But that's the way I want it.

And in this simple life, those closest to me are my assistant coaches. And so to block out losing Dave and Tony going into the biggest game of all our lives was a monumental task for me. Robert E. Lee called Stonewall Jackson "my good right arm." Jackson could be counted upon, all the time, to pursue his assignment with relentless and indefatigable energy and sacrifice and focus. And by those measures, Dave Wannstedt had been my good right arm. Take Jackson and Longstreet from Lee; take Sherman and Sheridan from Grant; take Patton and Bradley from Eisenhower . . . and that is how I could have let myself feel about losing Dave Wannstedt and Tony Wise. But I couldn't let myself. Not if we were to win in our last and greatest hours together.

Early in the evening of January 30, Bruce Mays had the buses waiting outside the Loew's Santa Monica Hotel, where we'd been staying since we'd arrived for the Super Bowl. We boarded and rode for a while, and then pulled up at the Beverly Garland Hotel, not too far from the Rose Bowl where the game would be played the next day. There were a few Cowboys' and Bills' fans in the lobby, and they seemed shocked to see our buses pull up. Bruce had kept a total secret. (And not until weeks later would I learn that the Beverly Garland was the same hotel to which Joe Gibbs had moved the Redskins the night before their Super Bowl XVII victory in Pasadena in 1983, and to which Bill Parcells had moved the Giants the night before their Super Bowl XXI win in Pasadena in 1987.)

We had an extremely quiet night. All the phones were shut off. Nobody knew where we were. People couldn't call in or call out. We were sequestered out there, and we prepared ourselves mentally for the game.

The last meeting I had with the team, the night before the game, was emotional because of Dave and Tony, and how close they were to the players. Bobby Slowik was going with them to Chicago, and would be missed, but Bobby had only been with the Cowboys for this one season and so the attachments weren't quite as deep.

I didn't want the players to get so caught up in the emotion and the personalities that it distracted them from their focus. First, I talked to the players about technical things. I reminded them that everybody who had had two weeks to prepare for the Buffalo offense had given them problems. I talked again about the turnover situation—how we would start off conservative and then open it up once we started getting the turnovers. We talked about our substitution package, how we were going to move a lot of players in and out of the game and keep them fresh. We were going to keep our defensive line fresh with backups against a hurry-up offense.

And then I teared up, and my voice cracked. I said, "I know that your thoughts are that you'd like to do this for certain individuals. The best way to honor those individuals is to go out there and play your ass off for yourself. Because this is something that all of us will have with us for the rest of our lives. The best way for those people to remember you and remember this game is with a Super Bowl ring on their finger, remembering the feeling of the win."

I left the meeting room and went to bed. I slept really good that night. We had done everything possible to have the team ready to play. Technically we were ready to play, physically we were ready to play, and emotionally we were ready to play.

I was 100 percent sure we were going to win that game. It was just a matter of how much. I had as much confidence in winning that game as any game that I have coached. We held a royal flush. It was just a matter of dropping the cards.

XXV

PLAYING OUT THE HAND

S everal of us left the Beverly Garland at about seven o'clock on the morning of January 31 to have ourselves a thirty-minute jog: Dave, Tony, Bruce Mays, Kevin O'Neill, Joe Avezzano, Steve Carichoff. Ben Nix, the league security guy and a former FBI agent, went with us. I'd been blocking out Dave and Tony for the past couple of weeks, but not today. This was our day. We laughed and talked about the game a little bit. It was a very relaxing jog. As near the Rose Bowl as we were, we didn't get within sight of the stadium and there wasn't much traffic. Not many people were out that early, even on Super Bowl Sunday. We went in, had our pregame meal, had our meetings, and turned it loose.

We always run two team buses to a stadium. I took the early bus, two hours before the second one. I walked into the Rose Bowl locker room, got dressed, and went out to walk the field. As usual, I walked down the center of the field. The closer to the sidelines you walk, the more you're likely to run into people who want to stop and make small talk. I'd just as soon meditate. So I walked for quite a while alone, except for shaking the hands of an occasional media person or assistant coach from my staff.

It might be more colorful to tell you that I was consumed with tense, suspenseful thoughts. But there were none. Oh, I was excited and happy, and anxious to get started. But as for the sort of feeling a commander has as a great battle looms—no, that had come two weeks earlier, at San Francisco. Now, the Rose Bowl was beginning to fill with people who would total 98,374. Around the world, a billion people were preparing to watch the game on television. And we, the Dallas Cowboys, were getting ready to play the Buffalo Bills on our practice field at Valley Ranch, Texas, and kick their ass. With our minds thusly set, it would follow quite naturally that Buffalo's offense would turn the ball over; that we would run to draw their defense into three-deep coverage, isolate their defensive backs in one-on-one coverage, and complete passes; that we would turn up the blitz as the game went on, forcing more and more turnovers. Twenty-eight years of coaching told me that all of this would come to pass, about as surely as forty-nine years of life told me that the sun, now high in the southern California sky, would set at game's end. And so: No. I had no reservations or concerns whatsoever about our game plan.

As the time grew near for pregame warmups, I visited with some of the Buffalo players I knew. I'd known Jim Kelly since I was coaching at Miami and he was playing for the Houston Gamblers of the USFL. We'd been preparing to face some college version of the run-and-shoot back then, and Jim helped me understand it. He'd been quarterbacking it in the USFL under one of the run-and-shoot's pioneers, Mouse Davis. Buffalo's offense is not a run-and-shoot, but it does have some elements of it. I saw Jim on the field, and we talked a couple of minutes. I'd read in the newspapers that week that Thurman Thomas was still a little upset with me that I had promised him I was going to stay at Oklahoma State when I had recruited him back in 1984, and then had left and gone to Miami. He'd said kind of jokingly that he was going to have to talk to me about that. I saw him right before the game and shook his hand and we said a friendly hello, but that was the extent of our conversation. It must have been a more tense time for the Bills than for us, because they'd been to two straight Super Bowls without a win. It would be three when this day was done. I knew that.

It seemed like the pregame show lasted forever. Garth Brooks sang the National Anthem. Garth had been at Oklahoma State my last year there, though he'd been a baseball player and I hadn't known him. He came over and we had a pleasant talk, though I must admit that country music and Stillwater were a million miles away in my mind at the moment. Again, it wasn't butterflies so much as anxiousness to lay that royal flush on the table and rake in all the chips.

Buffalo won the toss and elected to receive. That was fine. Let their offense handle the ball first. We chose to defend the goal that would put what little wind there was to our backs.

The Bills, quite naturally, had several early surprises planned for us. And initially, quite naturally, those surprises worked for them. On the first offensive snap, Jim Kelly probed a defensive miscalculation we had made. We'd gone in planning to double-cover Andre Reed, their star receiver, when he lined up in the slot. We had a linebacker, usually Kenny Norton, working inside coverage on Reed for the crossing route, and a defensive back, Kenny Gant, working outside coverage. But Reed was just so quick that he was able to work past the linebacker on the crossing route, putting Gant in the chase position. On that first play, Kelly hit Reed for 14 yards. But that was the only big play of Buffalo's first possession. On a third-and-one, Kelly scrambled out of the pocket and Thomas Everett came out of coverage to make the sack and force them to punt.

We didn't go anywhere with our first possession, but hadn't expected to. Remember: Patience. But then, we had a punt blocked for the first time since the 1989 season. Now that might have appeared, to all the world on television, to be a much more disconcerting problem than it really was. I saw immediately what had happened. Buffalo had done a good job scouting us. They knew that Dixon Edwards, who normally plays left tackle on our punt team, had a pulled hamstring and was questionable for the game. Sure enough, on our first punt, we substituted a rookie, Robert Jones, for Dixon. Buffalo spotted that and took advantage. They put their excellent special teams player, Steve Tasker, on Robert Jones. At the snap, Tasker slanted inside Robert and got in to block Mike Saxon's punt.

Immediately, I went over to Joe Avezzano and told him, "I don't care if Dixon's hurt or not. Put him back in the lineup." That would cure the problem for the afternoon, but for the moment, Buffalo had the ball at our 16-yard line.

We almost stopped that threat, or at least almost held them to a field goal. On a third-and-three from our 9, Charles Haley sacked Kelly. But Larry Brown was called for defensive holding, and Buffalo got a first-and-goal at our 5. Thurman Thomas ran the ball twice, and the second time, he scored. Buffalo was up 7–0.

I wasn't worried, but I was quite irritated that we had allowed Buffalo to get momentum that we were going to have to take back. And I was especially upset that we'd allowed it in an area we had so much pride in: our kicking game.

They surprised us with some of their linebacker blitzes and gave Troy pressure early in the game. We hadn't worked as much on their inside blitzes. They were bringing both inside linebackers and it really surprised us, because they hadn't done much of that in regular season. But once we adjusted, we were fine.

We didn't score with our second possession. Still we were patient. Still we felt fine about the game. Still it was a matter of playing it out.

On their next possession, the Buffalo turnover flaw began to show. Kelly, pressured by our blitz, was intercepted by James Washington, who returned 13 yards to the Buffalo 47. I can't say I was elated, because we'd felt all along that we'd get some turnovers. But little did we know, at that moment, that this was the first of a Super Bowl record nine turnovers we would collect from the Bills.

Our offensive game plan, in addition to throwing to our receivers in one-on-one coverage, had a contingency for when Buffalo played two deep, that is, had both safeties back, each covering half the field. We would throw to our tight end, Jay Novacek, across the middle. After the first Buffalo turnover, we converted a third-and-16 play when Michael Irvin found single coverage and caught a 20-yard pass from Troy at the Buffalo 33. Two plays later, we caught them in two-deep coverage and Novacek split the middle of the field, between the safeties, on a 23-yard catch and run for a touchdown. The game was tied, and beginning to unfold inevitably in our direction.

They had the ball back for one snap, and *we* scored off their snap. We set it up by adjusting our pass rush. Charles Haley normally lines up on the defensive right side. We moved him over to the left side. Haley sacked Kelly again, this time at the Bills' 2-yard line; Kelly fumbled, and our Jimmie Jones caught the ball in midair and went in for a touchdown. We led 14–7 as the first quarter ended, and we would not trail again.

On their next possession they hit Reed on the crossing route again, this time for 40 yards, to key their drive down to our one-yard line. I could see that we were going to have to adjust our coverage on him. But he was the only problem I was concerned about. I decided to wait until halftime to adjust, because when there's more than one player involved in coverage, I prefer to draw it on a blackboard. Reed was a problem but not a crisis. We confirmed that by stopping them at our goal line after Reed's 40-yard catch.

We made that goal-line stand with two of the biggest plays of the game. On third-and-one, Buffalo running back Kenneth Davis came left, and Kenny Norton made a great play to stop him for no gain. When we saw that Buffalo was going for the touchdown on fourth-and-one, we got out of our goal-line defense (in which two extra linemen are substituted for two defensive backs) and put our regular pass-defense unit back in. Buffalo had run at us twice consecutively for no gain, and we were virtually certain that Marv Levy and his staff weren't going to try it again on fourth down. Sure enough, they threw, and Thomas Everett intercepted Kelly in our end zone.

We continued to play ball control, attacking them with Emmitt's runs and with underneath passing, working them, working them, relentlessly pushing them toward three-deep coverage. We didn't score with our next possession, but on Buffalo's next possession, they lost Jim Kelly for the remainder of the game with a knee injury. Kenny Norton blitzed and hit him. Knowing Jim and liking him, I felt bad that he was injured. But football-wise, I knew we were going to have to adjust our defensive thinking. Frank Reich, their backup quarterback, had had a superb playoff season, so the Bills weren't exactly out of weapons. Reich isn't the riverboat gambler Jim is. Reich likes to control the passing game where Jim will take a few more chances down the field.

On Reich's second play of the game, he hit Andre Reed—the crossing route again—for 38 yards to our 22, but we were able to hold them to a field goal on that drive. It was 14–10, but we were fine.

On our next possession, Emmitt broke a 38-yard run down to their 19. It was a simple tailback off-tackle call that Emmitt just broke, as he does so well. After that, we knew immediately that Buffalo was going to start cheating their safety up to stop the run. So on the very next play, anticipating three-deep coverage—one-on-one against our receivers—Troy threw to Michael Irvin for a 19-yard touchdown, and we were up 21–10.

Now I'd love to be able to tell you I was just going bonkers on the sidelines. But frankly, it was the first time I had relaxed on the sidelines all season. I'm not sure "relaxed" is the exact word, because I'm always so into a game, but I had no feeling of tension or suspense. Why should I? We were just laying down the cards on the table, one-by-one: "Ten of hearts . . . jack of hearts . . . queen of hearts . . ." One billion people watching on television and another hundred thousand or so in the Rose Bowl weren't certain we held the rest of the cards. But we were.

The turnovers were becoming a deluge. Reich threw a screen to Thurman Thomas, Leon Lett came up and stripped the ball from Thurman, and Jimmie Jones recovered at the Buffalo 18. We work on stripping the ball year round, and we hadn't come into the Super Bowl with any plan of reaching for the ball more than normal. It was just paying off for us more than usual.

Our offense followed the Thomas turnover immediately with a touchdown on the first snap. It was—ho-hum—another Aikman-to-Irvin pass against man coverage to make it 28–10.

Larry Brown intercepted Reich on Buffalo's next series, and with only thirty seconds left until halftime, some teams would have run out the clock and gone in happily with an 18-point lead. But we wanted more, as always. We are always looking to score, whenever we have the ball, whatever the situation. Aikman-to-Irvin again got us 20 yards to the Buffalo 45, but the clock ran out as Emmitt got us to their 40.

At halftime, the first order of business was correcting the Reed-across-the-middle problem. We told Kenny Gant to start working inside leverage on Reed, because Kenny's speed matched up better with the receiver. Then we told Kenny Norton, or whoever else might be the linebacker on Reed, to work outside coverage. That took away the crossing route and eliminated what had been Buffalo's best weapon. Other than the Reed matter, we felt pretty good about the way we were playing. On offense, we were blocking Bruce Smith fine by doubling up on him, and we'd picked up the inside linebacker blitzes.

Because of the Michael Jackson halftime show running a bit long, I got a little fidgety in the locker room. I wanted to get back on the field and keep playing, so we wouldn't lose any momentum. At one point I stepped out the door and asked Todd Christensen, the former Raiders' tight end who was now a broadcast reporter for NBC, how much time remained until the Jackson show was over and we could get back at it. Todd said he didn't know. But as long as he had me out there, he wanted to do some reporting. He wanted to know if I'd talked to the team about the way Buffalo had come back against Houston in the AFC playoffs. In that first-round game, Reich had brought the Bills back from a 32-point deficit to win, the biggest comeback in league history. I blurted to Todd, "We're not Houston."

I wanted to cut off that topic immediately. I had not talked to the team about it. I did not want to plant negative seeds in our players' minds by saying, "Now remember, Buffalo came back against Houston." Instead, I said, "We're going to approach it like it's nothing to nothing. We're going to approach it as we always do: as a sixty-minute game."

And so we went out to drop the king and the ace on a billion-plus people.

We got a field goal with our first drive of the second half, and I just relaxed and enjoyed the game. It was in hand. The only irritation I had in the second half was on the last play of the third quarter. Reich scrambled and stepped across the line of scrimmage, but then threw a 40-yard touchdown pass to Don Beebe. Reich was obviously across the line of scrimmage when he threw, but the officials didn't call it. Upon review after the game, the league would confirm that we were right. Oh, well. It was 31–17 at the end of the third quarter, but we had control.

Now we would turn the storm loose. Alvin Harper found single coverage and Troy hit him for 45 yards and a touchdown. It was 38–17. Thomas Everett got his second interception, this time off Reich, and returned 22 yards to the Bills' 8. Three plays later Emmitt scored to make it 45–17. Now the game was out of hand, becoming one great merry blur. Next Buffalo possession, next Buffalo turnover, next Dallas touchdown: Reich fumbled, Kenny Norton recovered and returned it 9 yards into the end zone to make it 52–17, and we still had half a quarter left to play.

Because of substitutions and turnovers, the fourth quarter seemed to last forever. There was one other milestone we wanted to reach: The record for points scored by one team in the Super Bowl was held by the San Francisco 49ers, who beat Denver 55–10 in 1990. One more touchdown and we'd have the record, 59. But we were pouring in substitutions. There was a stretch where we and the Bills kept turning the ball over to each other. Leon Lett forced Steve Tasker to fumble and Clayton Holmes recovered at the Buffalo 44. But Steve Beuerlein, in for Aikman, fumbled it back to the Bills at the Buffalo 47.

And then came the play that everyone who watched that game remembers. This one, rather than all the good things Leon Lett did that day, would be his dubious distinction in Super Bowl history. Buffalo had driven down to our 31 when Jim Jeffcoat sacked Reich and forced a fumble. Leon, who is a six-foot-six, 287-pound defensive tackle, recovered the fumble at our 35 and began to thunder downfield for what, surely, would be the most memorable, if not the only, touchdown return of the big defensive lineman's career. Leon was so overjoyed that he held the ball out, just short of the goal line, in celebration. Don Beebe, the Bills' receiver who'd chased him down, reached out and slapped the ball from Leon's hands and out of the end zone, giving Buffalo possession and costing us the record for points scored in a Super Bowl.

Even without the record, even I was able to laugh a little when Leon came off the field, because the game had become such a romp. No need in chewing out Leon. He felt bad enough. Suffice it to say he would never celebrate prematurely again. (In weeks to come, I would feel bad for Leon as he got a tremendous amount of negative mail from people. Many came right out and stated that they'd been in office or tavern gambling pools and that his fumble had cost them the winning number, the "9" in the 59 we otherwise would have scored. One man even wrote that it cost him his son's education. That should teach 'em not to bet on football.)

In the locker room immediately after the game, I told the team, "The feeling you have at this very moment is one of the best things you will ever have in life, especially the feeling you have for one another, more than the event itself, the feeling of accomplishment with a teammate, more than the actual winning of the Super Bowl."

And, yes, I choked up. Which shouldn't surprise you at all by now. But when Michael Irvin went out of the locker room and "leaked" to the media that I had teared up, a lot of the writers dashed to their keyboards and sent out what, to them, was a bulletin: the iceman Jimmy Johnson, the cold calculator, the wheeling-dealing trader, the cold-hearted punisher who had cut Curvin Richards going into the playoffs, had choked up.

As the league representatives whisked me through the press conferences, I talked about all the people who had come so far with us. But

I suppose I still didn't seem very emotional, because all of this would not really hit me until more than a week later, at the parade they held for us in Dallas.

After the press conferences, I took a quick shower and got into the limo with Brent and his wife, Chad and his date, Nick Christin and his wife, and Rhonda. We did have a few Heinekens on the way back to Santa Monica. I got on the car phone with Mother and Daddy, back in Port Arthur, and talked about the game. And as much as anything, with that private group, the ones in the car and the ones on the phone, I was gloating. Relaxing, having a good time, and talking about how we truly kicked their ass.

We had the limo stop at a little hole-in-the-wall pizza place we found along the way, so that we could all go to the bathroom and replenish our Heineken. I signed a couple of autographs in the pizza parlor, and the people just couldn't believe I was the guy who'd just won the Super Bowl.

I went up to the postgame party in the hotel for about an hour. Dave Wannstedt was with his mother and father. I told them, "You know my feelings for Dave." We all hugged.

Still, the evening wasn't overwhelming to me. It all hadn't hit me yet. I guess it was because I'd programmed myself so thoroughly that it was just another game. If you're going to be the best that you can be at convincing people of something, you'd better believe it yourself. And I had believed that it was, in fact, simply "the last game of the year."

And it's almost magical, when you look at the score against Buffalo. That might indeed have been the best game that we played. Obviously the task against San Francisco was enormous, because of the quality of the 49ers. But when you take control of a Super Bowl in the third and fourth quarters the way we did, it was pretty impressive. But for a slap of Don Beebe's hand on an unprotected football, we would have scored the most points ever in that "last game of the year."

The 1960 expansion-franchise Dallas Cowboys finished 0–11–1, and it took them six seasons after that to make the playoffs—in those days there was only one step, the NFL championship game. And they lost in 1966 to Vince Lombardi's Green Bay Packers. Not until 1970 would the Cowboys reach a Super Bowl, and not until 1971 would they win one. It took eleven years to complete the turnaround off the bottom of the NFL.

Since 1960, seventeen NFL teams have finished a season with one win or none. Of those, the Dallas Cowboys turned around, from a 1–15 season in 1989 to the playoffs in 1991, faster than any other franchise.

Not since 1958–1961 had a team come so far, so fast. In 1958, the Green Bay Packers went 1–10–1; in 1959 Lombardi was hired and then they went 7–5, 8–4 and in 1961 went 11–3 and won the NFL championship. They went on to become the Team of the Sixties.

Taking note of that, *Sports Illustrated* found a pattern that has seemed to recur at the turn of every decade. In 1968, the Pittsburgh Steelers were 2–11–1; in 1969 Chuck Noll was hired and they went 1–13, 5–9, 6–8, 11–3, and then went on to become the Team of the Seventies, winning four Super Bowls. In 1978 the San Francisco 49ers went 2–14; in 1979 Bill Walsh was hired and they went 2–14, 6–10, 13–3 and went on to become the Team of the Eighties.

In 1988, the Cowboys were 3–13, worst in the league and mired there. In 1989, I was hired and we went 1–15, still worst in the league, but we knew we were turning the thing around, even then. We went 7–9, 11–5 and 13–3 with a Super Bowl win, and my proudest personal accomplishment was to be named NFL Coach of the Year in some form in each of those years. But if we are to be the Team of the Nineties— well, when I settled back into Valley Ranch in February 1993, I found one serious price of winning the Super Bowl: I was behind schedule on getting ready for the 1993 season and beyond.

EPILOGUE

I n February a lot of the coaches and personnel people at the scouting combine's mass workout in Indianapolis seemed astonished to see me sitting in the stands with a clipboard, watching college players and making notes, nine hours a day. People would come up and say, "Geez, didn't you take any time off after the Super Bowl?"

I said, "Oh, yeah. I went to the Bahamas for three days."

"All of three days?" they would say.

But, hey, we were behind on evaluating players for the 1993 draft.

Why have there been so few teams to win back-to-back Super Bowls? And none to win three in a row? Why has it become a hackneyed saying in sports that "the only thing harder than getting to the top is staying there"? The answer, in two words, is human nature. We all want satisfaction in life, and when we get it, we tend to relish it. It takes time to bask. And that means complacency. No sooner have you gotten the edge on the rest of the National Football League, or any other business arena, than you lose it, unless you can keep yourself just as mindful of, and focused on, exactly what the hell got you there in the first place.

During the first day of the 1993 NFL draft, April 25, ESPN commentators Chris Berman and Joe Theismann looked at their monitors, which showed me sitting silently by a silent telephone in our draft room in Valley Ranch. They said I looked like "the Maytag repairman" of the NFL, that is, lonely, because my product didn't need fixing. But I was sitting there thinking not so much about repair as about preventive maintenance.

As the NFL champions, we were given the last pick in the first round. Year in, year out, personnel directors have said, "We're going to take the best player available when we pick." In my opinion that is correct thinking. You really need to take the best player available, regardless of position. But since we've been in Dallas, we've augmented that philosophy, to make it more efficient. We try to trade so that our pick comes up when the player we want is the best player available. If you monitor what's going on in the rest of the league closely enough, you can "trade down"—barter your spot in the order to another team—and get yourself some additional draft picks, and still get the player you want. So in 1993, we traded ourselves right out of the first round.

Here's why: We were going to take Kevin Williams, a speedy wide receiver/kick returner whom I had recruited way back at the University of Miami, in the first round. In our minds, he was the best player available at the point of the last pick in the first round. Plus, he filled a definite need for us. We had lost our veteran kick returner, Kelvin Martin, to Seattle under the new free-agent rules. So to maintain the quality of our team in every phase of the game, we had to acquire a new kick returner.

But knowing what other teams' specific needs were, I took a calculated risk that no one would pick Kevin Williams before late in the second round. So why use our first-round pick, when we could trade it away for additional picks in lower rounds, and still get Kevin Williams? We gave our first- and fourth-round picks to Green Bay in exchange for two second-round picks they had, plus their fourth-round pick, which was higher than ours, and their eighth-round pick. What would have been our normal second-round pick had gone to San Francisco in the Charles Haley trade of 1992. Our normal fifth-round pick had gone to Pittsburgh in the Thomas Everett deal of 1992.

Here's what we got from the Green Bay trade: With our two new second-round picks, we not only got Kevin Williams, but we got a quick linebacker, Darrin Smith, also out of the University of Miami, to fill another need—Godfrey Myles was injured in the Super Bowl and had to have knee surgery in the off-season. With Green Bay's fourth-round pick, we got Derrick Lassic, the star tailback off Alabama's 1992 national championship team. With the eighth-round pick from Green Bay, we got Reggie Givens, a special-teams player from Penn State.

Also during draft week, we traded next year's seventh-round pick to Bill Parcells, now head coach of the New England Patriots, for veteran quarterback Hugh Millen. Bill had made quarterback Drew Bledsoe of Washington State the number-one pick in the draft, and no longer needed Millen, who in 1991 had started thirteen games and passed for more than 3,000 yards for the Patriots. We could use Millen as a backup to Troy, because we'd lost Steve Beuerlein to Phoenix by free-agency.

Whether the players we acquired in these two trades will work out remains to be seen. But here's what we were trying to do: 1) Replace the departed Kelvin Martin with Kevin Williams as a kick returner/ backup receiver; 2) replace the injured linebacker Godfrey Myles with Darrin Smith; 3) replace running back Curvin Richards, whom I'd cut for fumbling twice in the 1992 Chicago game, with Derrick Lassic, as a backup to Emmitt Smith; 4) bolster our special teams with Reggie Givens (if an eighth-round pick sounds like a longshot, remember that Leon Lett was a seventh-round pick, Kenny Gant was a ninth-round pick, and Larry Brown was a twelfth-round pick); 5) Replace a solid and experienced backup quarterback, Steve Beuerlein, with another solid and experienced backup, Hugh Millen.

Whether any of these players works out or not, the fact remains that we would have tried to take every one of them even if we had stood pat in the drafting order of 1993. But because we didn't stand pat, because we traded and replaced the choices we'd sent to San Francisco and Pittsburgh in 1992, here is a fact: As it turned out, we got Charles Haley and Thomas Everett, both of whom helped us win the NFC East division, the NFC championship game, and the Super Bowl, for *free*. They cost us absolutely nothing in personnel or draft-pick trades.

And so we continue to wheel, deal, evaluate, try to treat people right, and work our asses off. Jerry Jones has given me a responsibility and a freedom to work, to choose and coach people, that I probably couldn't have gotten from any other NFL owner. Yes, he gave me that trust because he knew me going in, and we liked and respected each other. But no, we were not buddy-buddy. He did not hire me because I was his friend, and I did not take the job because he was my friend. We both had our own motives outside of friendship.

People are still trying to figure out our relationship, and they're still misconceiving, going to one extreme or the other. The reality of our working relationship is that we communicate back and forth in a lot of different areas, but the responsibilities are clearly defined. When it's football and it's personnel and it's talent, I'll be making the decision. And, with Jerry being the owner, he is actively involved in making the financial decisions regarding those players. I hear, and we discuss, some of the other aspects of the club, but Jerry handles all those financial, operational, and aesthetic aspects, from player contracts, to stadium and complex operations, to the Cowboy Cheerleaders' costumes (he long ago abandoned his notion of bicycle shorts and kept the ladies in their traditional uniforms), all the way to the entire financial bottom line of the franchise (as he promised, right down to the socks and jocks).

Some people compared him unfavorably to Jed Clampett in 1989, but in 1993, *Fortune* rated the Dallas Cowboys the most valuable franchise in all of professional sports, worth $165 million ($25 million more than Jerry paid for the club), just ahead of the franchise which historically had been considered unshakable from the pinnacle, the New York Yankees baseball club, worth $160 million. Old Blackie Sherrod of the Dallas *Morning News* has been proved right in spotting something more than two rubes at the carnival when "the Jaybirds" flew into town. We have done what Jerry always said we would do, in one of his Arkansas colloquialisms: "Get in there and work back-to-back." Each handles his clearly defined role, and each trusts the other to handle the other role.

I truly believe, and I think Jerry believes, that we have the best working relationship of any in the NFL, or any in professional sports that I'm aware of. If it were anything less, we could not have turned this thing around nearly as fast, nor as thoroughly. (And he wouldn't have doubled my salary after we won the Super Bowl, redoing a contract that still has six years left on it.)

I know a good working relationship with a boss when I have one. I've had it the other way. Out of the stacks and stacks of congratulatory letters we received in the weeks following the Super Bowl, my secretary, Barbara Goodman, and I developed a system for which ones I would answer. She would take the ones she figured I would want to handle personally, draft a reply letter, and place it on my desk together with the congratulatory letter from the individual. I came in one day and found one opened envelope bearing the elaborate letterhead of the University of Miami, Office of the President, Edward Thaddeus Foote II. Barbara, being from Texas, had no idea of the protocol of Miami's administration, or how President Foote would prefer to be addressed. For the draft of the response, she took a guess, and began the letter, "Dear Eddie." I looked at it. I laughed out loud. I thought it might be fun to send it to him just that way. Then I said the hell with it, and threw it in the wastebasket.

Far more treasured, and the one I'll always keep, was the letter on Clemson University stationery from another old boss, Coach Frank Howard, who closed, "P.S. I also promise never to pee on your leg again."

Bill Parcells has told me he doesn't know how long anyone could go at our pace. So far, I'm fine. I do this job and put in the hours because I enjoy it, and when it gets to the point that I don't enjoy it, that's when I'll stop, and head on out to the beach for good. That may be ten years from now. Or it may be next year. It could happen when we're winning, if I get to the point where I don't enjoy putting in these hours. I don't have any burning desire to be the winningest coach, or to win so many titles, or accomplish so many things.

I just want to put myself in position personally where I can pick up and go on a day's notice. I will end up on the beach somewhere. The only question is which beach. Probably in Florida, because of the water. It's hard to scuba dive in the murky water outside my house at Crystal Beach, but who knows—it's the Gulf; it's home. Those offshore oil rigs on the horizon are, in a way, at the root of who I am, and what I am, and what I have become: still, all in all, Jimmy Johnson, a roustabout character, fairly smart and fairly savvy in matters of the human condition, who happened to love football most of all.

Back in 1988 just after we'd won the national championship at Miami, the Port Arthur Historical Society began a series of benefit dinners—roasts of Texans of note. I was the first one roasted, and they placed a bust of me in the public library. Bob West, sports editor of the Port Arthur *News*, who directs the celebrity roast program for the city, was up in Dallas in 1990, during our 7–9 season. He said, "Now Jimmy, if you win the Super Bowl, we'll roast you again." I corrected him. I said, *"When* we win the Super Bowl, we'll have another roast."

Dan Rather, the CBS News anchorman who is a native Texan, was scheduled to be the roastee in 1993. After we won the Super Bowl, they called Rather and postponed his ceremony for a year. On May 22 I went home again, and found—not far from the five-headed bust of Janis Joplin; not far from the busts of the Big Bopper and Buddy Holly, the Texas rock 'n' roll pioneers who died in that notorious 1957 plane crash in Iowa—that they had reinscribed the marble base beneath the bust of the guy with the neatest hairdo of the lot. It now read, "Jimmy Johnson . . . Thomas Jefferson High, '61 . . . Only coach ever to win both the national college football championship and the Super Bowl."

Somehow it all meant more to me at home than it had in front of a billion people. This story began on a boulevard in Port Arthur, with Baby Joe and I.E. And it ends in Port Arthur, on Jimmy Johnson Boulevard. When I went home on May 22 and saw it, I choked up.

INDEX

(Dates refer to year game was played.)